Foreword

Nematodes are worms and many a potential reader may ask himself what could possibly be so fascinating about worms? This the more so as the majority of species live in "shady" places like cow pads, intestines, decaying plants, mud and the like. However, these persons would be very wrong. Although anatomically rather uniform, nematodes are an excellent example to demonstrate how a group of organisms conquered nearly all available habitats on earth in the course of evolution due to their great versatility and adaptability. They can be found in hot springs and in glaciers, in the deep sea and on top of the Himalayas, in every kind of animal and plant.

Dr. David Richard Viglierchio has written a thrilling book about these inconspicouous but omnipresent worms. He had conceived the idea for this book early in his scientific career as a nematologist and this work represents a lifetime of collecting, digesting and arranging data, a tremendous task considering the rapid development and expansion of the science of nematology during the last decades. The book is a treasure of interesting information and unique in giving such a broad view on nematode biology. The main merit, as I see it, is that the scientific information is presented in a popular way and it is a great pleasure for me to introduce this book. Everybody interested in living organisms should read the book and enjoy its multifarious contents. The light reader can easily take what he wants leaving the more technical material to the professionally interested readers. Also expert nematologists will profit and derive considerable pleasure from the wealth of data and comments even if one or the other finds himself at variance here and there.

In short, this is a fascinating book on a fascinating subject and it is my hope that it will give pleasure to many, many readers!

Bernhard Weischer
Former Director & Professor
Federal Biological Research Center
Institute for Nematology &
Vertebrate Research
Münster, Germany

Preface

Nematodes constitute a diverse group of wormlike multicellular animals with truly remarkable characteristics and properties; moreover, they represent one of the major groups of the animal kingdom. Nematodes are present on the planet in enormous numbers and yet they remain generally unnoticed. Everywhere yet apparently nowhere, most are microscopic, dwelling at the bottom of freshwater ponds, lakes, rivers, and the sea; others are in the soil and within the tissues of plants and animals. Very large nematodes are hidden in the bodies of animals. It would seem that in creation they were designed to be obscure; nevertheless, in their absence, earth would be a very different place.

There are available numerous reference books about nematodes but invariably they are heavily biased in subject matter, dealing with plant parasitic or animal forms, free-living terrestrial forms, marine forms, ultrastructure, taxonomy, morphology or biology. All target the professional level and none can be considered light reading. This book is intended as an introductory overview of the fascinating world of nematodes for the non-nematologist. It aims to provide for the orientation and appreciation of nematodes by the naturalist, biologist, farmer, establishment regulator, gardener, student; in short for anyone who for some particular reason has occasion to wonder about nematodes. It is the earnest hope of the author that a reader may take portions according to his needs, ignoring the rest should he choose. There is sufficient technical information to provide a basic foundation for a sound perspective and to permit the dedicated reader to pursue his interest in depth elsewhere should this be desired. The reader who absorbs the essence of this book will unquestionably be more knowledgeable about nematodes than a random million of his planetary cohabitants.

No overview can pretend to be complete; exceptions and anomalies will persist as will contrary points of view. In any event, it is a beginning from which the reader can acquire the fundamental concepts and facts that will enable him to develop his own assessment and conclusions.

This work could not have come to fruition without the generous assistance and graciousness of many people, particularly my wife, Rena Sue, whose support, library research, typing, editing, and patience have been invaluable; Frances Fan-Wu for the preparation of illustrations; Bernhard Weischer, former Director & Professor at the Federal Biological Research Center, Institute for Nematology & Vertebrate Research, Münster, Germany; Benjamin F. Lownsbery, Professor Emeritus of Nematology, University of California, Davis, California; Ming Wong, Professor Emeritus of Parasitology, School of Veterinary Medicine, University of California, Davis, California; Thomas T. Yamashita, President of Sunburst Research & Development, Turloch, California and Nahúm Marbán-Mendoza, Regional Nematologist at the Center of Investigation & Teaching for Tropical Agronomy, Turrialba, Costa Rica, for reading the manuscript and offering corrections and suggestions; and the multitude of colleagues over the years whose research brought to light the wealth of information available to me. None of the above can be faulted for any errors and misunderstandings that are to be expected in this effort; the culpability is solely mine.

The striking cover illustration is a reproduction of an original painting by M. Talamé of Italy presented to the author by the Italian Society of Nematologists.

May the reader be awed and appreciative—as I have been for so many years—of the fascinating world of nematodes.

DRV

Table of Contents

Dedication

To my parents,
Davide & Mary Dorothy Viglierchio
whose unwaivering faith, encouragement & support
let so much be possible!

CHAPTER 1

Introduction

Human beings have an inclination to organize and systematize everything in the universe—including themselves—according to their perceptions, in an attempt to define the nature of things. Fortunately for us all nature continues to function without awaiting our conclusions. According to current wisdom, living things are organized into five kingdoms, depending on their complexity or cellular organization. Two kingdoms—prokaryotes and eukaryotes—comprise microscopic unicellular organisms. The remaining three kingdoms—fungi, plants, and animals—comprise the multicellular organisms. Each kingdom is further divided into different phyla where each phylum manifests a characteristic body plan with fundamental differences that distinguish it from all other phyla. One phylum in the animal kingdom consists of a group of micrometazoan (small multicellular invertebrate animals) organisms referred to as *Nemata* by one school of thought or *Nematoda* by another. A distinguished early nematologist, N. A. Cobb (often referred to as the father of American Nematology), proposed the term *Nema*. A century earlier, a European zoologist, C. A. Rudolphi, used the term *Nematoidea* (derived from the Greek nemato—meaning "thread-like"). Despite the ongoing polemics regarding a preferred name, representatives of this phylum are commonly referred to as nematodes or nemas, but also roundworms, and, in Northern Europe, eelworms.

Nematodes are unsegmented roundworms, often fusiform (long thin rods tapered at each end) or filiform (threadlike) but also spherical, pear-shaped or intermediate forms, with characteristic organ systems. Nematodes are as different from other "worms" with which they are often popularly confused, such as flatworms (Platyhelminthes—flukes and tapeworms), annelids (earthworm group) as they are from sponges, sea anemone, starfish or insects.

Nematodes may be found almost anywhere. According to Cobb:

> They occur in arid deserts and at the bottom of lakes and

rivers, in the waters of hot springs and in the polar seas where the temperature is constantly below the freezing point of fresh water. They were thawed out, alive from antarctic ice by members of the Shackleton Expedition. They occur at enormous depths in alpine lakes and in the ocean. As parasites of fishes, they transverse the seas; as parasites of birds, they float across continents and over high mountain ranges.

Under their own power, nematodes can move only several feet a year but they can be transported long distances in rushing streams and on the bodies of animals and birds. By violent dust storms they can cross oceans to reach other continents. Moreover, only within the last century have people recognized their own role in the dispersion of nematodes.

"Nematodes are found everywhere" is a truthful statement but it fails to convey an appreciation of its real impact, particularly in relation to other groups of animals. A crude estimate of the numbers of known species of the more common animal groups found in different habitats is indicated in Table 1.1 for comparative purposes. Only four groups of animals—nematodes, spiders, insects, and vertebrates—are found in all eight listed habitats. This information, therefore, supports the notion that nematodes can be found wherever nematologists choose to look.

The consensus among zoologists familiar with nematodes is that nematodes constitute the most abundant group of multicellular animals on earth in terms of numbers of individuals. Although nematodes were more numerous, for years it was believed that there was more diversity in insects, that is, a larger number of species. Revised estimates suggest that this perception may no longer be valid (Table 1.2). If nematodes, as has been long believed, are the most abundant of multicellular individuals and that now may rival insects in diversity and potential number of species, then how is it that the yearly research effort with nematodes, remains so low? Despite the significant proportion of animal life that nematodes represent, it is readily obvious that the number of research articles dealing with nematodes is on the order of 10% of the number of articles dealing with insects. Perhaps nematologists are not as industrious as they should be, but it should also be recognized that there are relatively fewer of them than professionals of other disciplines.

Table 1.1. Approximate number of known animal species according to habitat (k = 1,000, ecto = body surface type relation; endo = internal tissue relation; symbiotic = intimate relation necessary for survival of one or both partners). [Adopted from R.M. May, 1988.]

Phylum subphylum	Common representative	Habitat							
		Sea muds	Seas	Freshwater muds	Fresh-waters	Terrestrial moist	Terrestrial dry	Symbiotic Ecto	Symbiotic Endo
Porifera	sponges	1k–10k	—	1–100	—	—	—	1–100	—
Coelenterata	jellyfish, corals	1k–10k	100–1k	1–100	1–100	—	—	1–100	—
Platyhelminthes	flatworms, flukes, tapeworms	1k–10k	1–100	1k–10k	—	100–1k	—	1–100	10k–100k
Nemertea	proboscis worms	100–1k	1–100	1–100	—	1–100	—	1–100	—
Nematoda	roundworms	1k–10k	1–100	1k–10k	1–100	1k–10k	1–100	1k–10k	1k–10k
Rotifera	rotifers	1–100	1–100	100–1k	100–1k	1–100	—	1–100	1–100
Gastrotricha	gastrotrichs	100–1k	—	100–1k	—	—	—	—	—
Tardigrada	waterbears	1–110	—	100–1k	—	1–100	—	—	—
Mollusca	clams, snails	>100k	1–100	1k–10k	—	1k–10k	1–100	1–100	1–100
Annelida	earthworms	10k–100k	1–100	100–1k	—	1k–10k	—	100–1k	—
Arthropoda									
Crustacea	crabs, shrimp	10k–100k	1k–10k	1k–10k	100–1k	100–1k	—	100–1k	100–1k
Chelicerata	spiders	100–1k	1–100	100–1k	100–1k	10k–100k	1k–10k	100–1k	1–100
Uniramia	insects	1–100	1–100	1k–10k	100–1k	>100k	1k–10k	100–1k	100–1k
Chordata									
Vertebrata	backbone animals	1k–10k	1k–10k	100–1k	1k–10k	1k–10k	1k–10k	1–100	1–100

Table 1.2. A crude measure of research effort in different animal goups by number of published articles in relation to the estimated number of species. (Adapted from R.M. May, 1988.)

Phylum subphylum class	Common Representative	Manuscripts published (1978-87)	Estimated number of species
Protozoa	1-cell animals, amoebae, ciliates	3,900	260,000
Porifera	sponges	190	10,000
Coelenterata	jellyfish, corals	740	10,000
Echinodernata	starfish	710	6,000
Nematoda	roundworms	1,900	1,000,000?
Annelida	earthworm–like	840	15,000
Brachiopoda	fairy shrimp	220	350
Bryozoa		160	4,000
Entoprocta		7	150
Mollusca	clams, snails	1,000	100,000
Arthropods			
Crustacea	crabs, shrimps	3,300	39,000
Chelicerata			
Arachnida	spiders	2,000	63,000
Uniramia			
Insecta	insects	17,000	1,000,000?
Chordata			
Vertebrata			
Pisces	fish	7,000	19,000
Amphibia	amphibians	1,300	2,800
Reptilia	reptiles	2,400	6,000
Aves	birds	3,000	9,000
Mammalia	mammals	8,100	4,500

While it remains virtually impossible to determine the exact numbers of nematodes in a modest cube of natural habitat, three-quarters of a century ago Cobb estimated that in an acre foot of beach sand, the number of nematodes could be expressed in 10 figures, and in an acre foot of modestly fertile soil, in 11 figures. With our understanding of the abundance of nematodes, their great diversity, and their diffusion into all kinds of habitat, it is possible to truly appreciate another Cobb remark: "If all the matter in the universe except nematodes were swept away, our world would still be dimly recognizable—we would find its mountains, hills, valleys, rivers, lakes and oceans represented by a film of nematodes." After nearly a century of supplementary information, we could additionally identify kind of vegetation; kind of animal husbandry; polar, temperate or tropical zone, city size and location.

If there are so many nematodes and so many kinds, why are they so seldom seen by people? Most of them are small and invisible to the naked eye, but others are huge. The smallest known roundworm is a marine nematode approximately 80μm in length; a dozen of them laid end to end would traverse the thickness of a dime. One large species living in the kidneys of dogs and other animals can grow to a yard in length and have the diameter of a ballpoint pen (kidney worm). A huge nematode occurring in the placenta of sperm whales approximates the dimensions of a 25 foot garden hose. A few nematode species that can be found on the surface of leaves, blades of grass, or rooftops, are too small to be seen with the naked eye. All other nematodes, large or small, are "buried" in their habitat, whether ocean, freshwater, soil, or tissues of animals and plants.

In the course of daily living, the average person has little occasion to be aware of the nematodes walked upon, eaten in foodstuffs or comprising the parasite burden carried by pets. Awareness usually emerges when high nematode populations cause disease. If the known nematode species are grouped according to simple habitat categories, then of the total, 50% are marine nematodes, 25% are freeliving soil inhabiting nematodes (microbivorous and predators), 15% are animal-parasitic nematodes, and 10% are plant-parasitic nematodes. As a consequence of economic factors, research effort and support has been and continues to be concentrated on the plant and animal-parasitic nematodes. The collapse of the German sugar industry in the 1870's has been attributed to the sugar beet nematode. Today, even with the use of modern technology, 5 to 10% of agricultural production is lost to nematodes in developed countries; in lesser developed countries, the loss is even greater. Losses in livestock production are comparable. The untold human misery brought about by nematode parasitism, particularly in tropical regions, defies quantification.

The better known human parasitic nematode diseases include dracontiasis (guinea worm), filariasis, elephantiasis, onchocerciasis (river blindness), ascariasis, hookworm disease, trichinosis (raw pork) and the common pinworm. Dogs, cats, and pigs are susceptible to over 30 species of nematodes; cattle, sheep and horses are susceptible to well over 50 species. Of the over 30 nematode species parasitic to humans, at least 15 are able to infect both dogs and humans.

Nematodes occur in incredible numbers and diversity and manifest a high reproductive rate. If they were also longlived, earth could be rapidly overwhelmed by a writhing mass. This has not and will not happen because nature has feedback mechanisms which prevent such catastrophes. The life cycle of nematodes covers the period necessary for the natural timely development from the egg to the mature adult. For microbivorous nematodes, this period may involve several days, but an animal parasite may take a year or so. In the plant-parasitic cyst-forming nematodes, the female is genetically programmed to survive a matter of several weeks. The saccate female lays her eggs, most of which remain within her body, whereupon she dies and her body wall dries and hardens to become a simple egg container cyst. The males, on the other hand, are believed to survive longer, but exactly how long is unknown. Certain plant-parasitic gall-forming nematode females are similarly genetically programmed to survive only a short period. On the other hand, observations from clinical medicine suggest that some animal-parasitic nematodes are able to survive years. The longevity of adult nematodes remains virtually unstudied, despite the obvious importance to reproduction, survival, dispersion and therapeutic control measures. The survival of certain juvenile forms living in a habitat deprived of a food source or the key component necessary for continued development is similarly poorly understood.

What does this great number and variety of animals use for food? Some nematodes are herbivores, that is they feed upon plants; no plant has been found which cannot serve as a food source for one or more kinds of nematodes. Some of these herbivores, ectoparasites, feed from outside of the plant by inserting a slender stylet which serves as a hypodermic needle to withdraw plant cell contents. Others, endo-parasites, penetrate and move through the tissues, feeding en route and causing much damage. Another group is called sedentary because its representatives penetrate the plant partially or entirely, and set up a nurse-cell group from which the nematode withdraws its nourishment.

A large group of nematodes, mostly terrestrial, is carnivorous, that is the nematodes prey on whatever microscopic animals live in their environment, including their own kind; a number ingest their prey whole, while others suck only the body fluids and discard the carcass. Some predators possess a massive stoma that together with a toothlike structure and the application of tremendous suction rip and tear the victim for ease in digestion. These predaceous nematodes are opportunists and prey on whatever small animal they encounter, including any other kind of nematode; of course, when they misjudge, or are unlucky, they themselves are eaten.

For the nematode parasites of animals, a life cycle may require specialized steps and therefore be very complex. With few exceptions, animal-parasitic nematodes do not complete their life cycle and reproduce continuously within a definitive host. A definitive host is one in which the adults are found. They must at some point, commonly as eggs, exit the definitive host, continue their development in the soil or intermediate host until they again can become infective to a definitive host. An intermediate host is usually an invertebrate which serves as a temporary host for the nematode to develop to the infective stage. Some of these animal-parasitic forms have adapted to an alternate life cycle; in the absence of a definitive host or other adverse condition, they change to reproduce as microbial feeders until the adverse environment passes and they can be ingested by a host, whereupon a reversion to the parasitic cycle occurs. Some parasitic nematodes do not exit the definitive host as an egg, but as embryos (microfilariae) circulating within the definitive host's blood until that is withdrawn by bloodsucking insects.

The discussion so far has been concerned primarily with the 25% of the phylum that is parasitic. What can be said about the food source of the remaining 75%, the so-called free living nematodes which also include the predators? Some are known to feed on bacteria, while others prefer fungal mycelium; the overwhelming proportion have been referred to as saprophytic, which means that they feed on nonliving organic matter. But saprophytic feeding has never been proven. In fact, only several species of bacteria-feeding nematodes have been cultured on an abiotic medium; even then, they did much better on their normal bacterial food source. Several large marine nematodes have been shown to be indiscriminate feeders and able to ingest particles of colored plastic or wax in a medium. By so doing, they can easily ingest a wide range of microscopic organisms. At this point, it cannot be said whether all free living nematodes are microtrophic (that is, obtain their nutritional requirements by ingesting microscopic organisms) until the feeding habits of a great many more free-living nematodes have been determined.

Mammals, birds, fish, or insects become sick when infected by various pathogens and even bacteria become sick when they are infected with bacteriophage. Do nematodes become sick? It would be unusual if they didn't; however, to date no virus or microplasma-like particle has been shown to attack nematodes. Although certain nematodes are able to transmit virus particles from host to host, there exist only occasional observations that the longevity of such virus-containing nematodes may be somewhat shortened. By the latter 19th century it was found that certain bacteria and fungi were able to attack healthy nematodes by penetrating the cuticle and reproducing internally to overwhelm the animal. There is specificity involved in that certain nematodes can be attacked by certain bacteria or fungi and not others. Previously, predaceous fungi with special constricting loops and sticky knobs were believed to be indiscriminate in being able to attack any nematode. This appears to not be so. There is a kind of specificity involved, as with other bacteria and fungi.

The incidences of human-parasitic nematode infections in the world (an incidence means one nematode species, regardless of number, infecting one human) have been estimated to approximate the human population of the world. Obviously since not all humans are parasitized there must be a good many multiple infections. Similarly, the incidences of nematode infections of domestic farm animals and all wildlife are astronomical in number.

The loss in agricultural production due to plant-parasitic nematodes which ranges from 5 to 10% in industrialized nations together with the proportionally greater loss for the lesser developed nations, exceeds in value the national budgets of all but a few nations of the world. This reflects the impact of only 25% of the different kinds of nematodes known to exist. The remaining 75%, the "free living nematodes," which comprise the bulk of the nematode biomass on the planet, remains virtually ignored and unstudied. Does this incredible number of multicellular organisms exist solely as a caprice of nature with virtually no redeeming value as conventional wisdom appears to presume? Recycling of nutrients is an integral component of the balance of nature. It would be idiotic to consider the "free living nematodes" a blunder of nature. In all probability B. G. Chitwood, perhaps the only genius nematology can claim, was correct in having said, "Their interrelationships with other organisms, both dead and alive, might easily be so great that if they all disappear tomorrow, a few weeks hence the foul odor of death might pervade the whole earth as a balance might be destroyed." There is no mistake, nematodes are vital to nature as we know it.

CHAPTER 2

Origins and History

Attempts at resolution of the origin of nematodes in the remote past have been largely an exercise in futility. Soft-bodied animals which include nematodes are especially prone to decay and disintegration. When this is coupled with the generally small size and the special conditions necessary to generate a useful specimen, fossils become exceedingly rare incidences. In the geologically recent past, several nematode fossil specimens have been found in amber, an aged plant resin exudate. Regrettably, the morphological structures commonly used to characterize and distinguish nematodes have survived too poorly to be useful.

The resolution of the relationship of nematodes to other micrometazoan animal groups has been subject to zoological dispute for over a century. The micrometazoan animal groups— Platyhelminthes, Nemertea, Rotatoria, Gastrotricha, Kinorhyncha, Nematoda, Nematomorpha, Acanthocephala, and Entoprocta—have gone up and down the taxonomic scale according to their placement in different super groups, e.g., Acoelomata, Pseudocoelomata, Aschelminthes, Nemathelminthes, or other group. One is left with the view that the reorganizations were more a result of emotional conviction rather than incontrovertible evidence. The modern view is to treat these animal groups as separate Phyla. Although this attitude is in essence a procrastination, it does bypass the dispute until better evidence becomes available. Despite the absence of fossil specimens to fix reference points, a provisional evolutionary scheme can be formulated based upon nematode characteristics and properties. The major weakness of the scheme lies in the fact that the projections are based on surviving specimens. Nevertheless, Fig. 2.1 provides a crude nematode evolutionary scheme relative to geological and paleontological events occurring on earth within the last five hundred million years. Unfortunately, it is not possible to determine on what land masses different evolutionary lines originated and to what degree

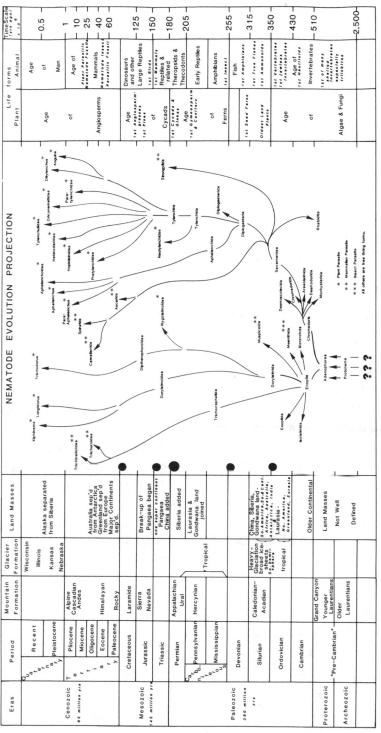

Figure 2.1. A schematic nematode evolutionary projection including a time scale of Eras and Periods in relation to selected geological events (mountain and glacier formation, land masses) and the development of plant and animal life forms. Filled circles (●) indicate 5 mass extinctions; the large filled circle at the end of the Permian Period indicates a mass extinction of 52% of the families of marine organisms while the other mass extinctions range from 11–14% of the families of marine organisms.

nematode dispersion or development was a consequence of land tectonics or transport by animals, wind and water.

It seems incredible to note that according to a recent World Health Organization report, the intestinal roundworm burden of the Chinese population produces enough *Ascaris* eggs per year to inoculate every man, woman and child in China with 18 milligrams of eggs, despite the fact that Chinese medicine recognized the disease-causing effect of *Ascaris*, 46 centuries ago (See Table 2.1 for a brief chronological history of Nematology). Whether this state of affairs can be attributed to the persistence and toughness of nematodes or the folly of humanity is open to question. For the first 43 centuries of development, Nematology appeared to be governed by primarily two considerations: a preoccupation of diseases of man and animals and the obvious size and ease of visibility of animal-parasitic nematodes, e.g., the intestinal Ascarid roundworms, the Guinea worm and the kidney worm. With the development of the microscope by Leeuwenhoek in the middle 17th century, the possibilities for exploration broadened considerably. Within a few years, Borellus' discovery of the vinegar eelworm was followed by Hooke's discovery of another microscopic eelworm in a paste concoction. However, another century was to pass before Needham described the first plant-parasitic nematode, *Anguina tritici* (still a plague in many parts of the world). A century later, Berkeley discovered the rootknot nematode and Schacht established the existence of the sugarbeet nematode. The sugarbeet nematode (later named *Heterodera schachtii*, in honor of its discoverer) established a milestone for Plant Nematology. About the middle of the 19th century, sugarbeets were found to contain a relatively high concentration of sugar that could be extracted for commercial use. A sugar refining industry based upon sugarbeet as a source was developed for domestic consumption and export. As a consequence, sugarbeet production expanded greatly and with the expansion came the dispersion of the sugarbeet nematode. Within a few short years, the effect of the nematode was devastating; the sugarbeet industry collapsed as did the economy of the German state. To this day, the sugarbeet nematode remains a formidable problem in central Europe as well as elsewhere in the world.

Table 2.1. Brief Chronological Development of Nematology

2700 B.C.	China Yellow Emperor's Classic of Internal Medicine (Huang T. Nei Ching) discussed symptoms of the intestinal worm, *Ascaris*.
1550 B.C.	Egyptian "Papyrus Ebers" referred to the intestinal worm, *Ascaris;* Guinea worm, *Dracunculus;* possibly hookworm, *Ancylostoma*.
1250 B.C.	Middle East Bible 21:6–9. Moses referred to the Guinea worm as the "Fiery serpent of the Israelites." The serpent of brass constructed by Moses may be the origin for the symbol of the physicians' caduceus.
430 B.C.	Hippocrates in "Aphorisms" discussed nematodes (probably pinworm, *Enterobius*).
384–322 B.C.	Aristotole in "Historia Animalium" discussed nematodes. (*Ascaris* & others).
181–146 B.C.	Agatharchides credited by Plutarch for describing the "Guinea worm" and so naming it.
53 B.C.–7 A.D.	A.C. Celsus distinguished between roundworms (nematodes) and flatworms (cestodes).
100 A.D.	Columella noted an ascarid (*Neoascaris vitulorum*) from a calf.
400 A.D.	Vegetius noted the horse ascarid (*Parascaris equorum*).
980–1037 A.D.	Avicenna referred to ascarids and dracunculids in a medical text.
1200–1280 A.D.	A. Magnus first recorded nematodes from birds in the falcon.
1519–1630 A.D.	Cæsalpinus discovered *Dioctophyma renale* (kidney worm) in the dog kidney.

1547 A.D.	Vinegia described a filarid and two intestinal nematodes from the falcon.
1650 A.D.	O. Leeuwenhoek constructed the microscope.
1656 A.D.	P. Borellus discovered the vinegar eelworm *(Turbatrix aceti)*.
1667	Robert Hooke reported an eelworm in paste *(Panagrellus redivivus)*.
1683	E. Tyson conducted early attempts at nemic anatomy by describing morphological structures.
1684	F. Redi compiled reports of worms in vertebrates and new hosts, e.g., lion, fish.
1707–1778	Linnæus established modern taxonomic nomenclature.
1745	F. Needham described the first plant-parasitic nematode *(Anguina tritici)*.
1780	A prize offered for the best essay on intestinal worms by the Copenhagen Academy of Sciences indicated the widening interest of biologists in nematodes and other worms. Incidentally, the winner's theory that the entire life history of these worms took place within the host tissue was in fact largely erroneous, whereas one loser's opposing view was not. "The triumph of form over substance apparently has been a confounding factor in science for some time."
1835	R. Owen discovered *Trichinella spiralis* in human muscle.
1859	M. J. Berkeley discovered the rootknot nematode and H. Schacht the sugarbeet nematode that effected the collapse of the German economy of the time.

1865	R. Leuckart and I.I. Metchnikoff established the alternation of generation in the life history of animal-parasitic nematodes and the obligate development of nematodes in an intermediate host. H.C. Bastian published the description of over 100 new species of free-living nematodes.
1878	P. Manson established the mosquito as the intermediate host in transmission of *Wuchereria bancrofti* (elephantiasis).
1907	N.A. Cobb began early American contributions
1914	N.A. Cobb proposed the name "Nematology" for the science in the USDA Yearbook, "Nematodes and their relationships."
1921	G. Steiner, Cobb's co-worker, began research on nematodes as did G. Thorne and others.
1931	I.N. Filipjev shocked an agricultural congress by saying there were about 4,500 nematode species.
1934	K.I. Skrjabin published a book "Veterinary parasitology and invasion diseases of domestic animals" and became the nematode authority in the U.S.S.R. A.A. Paramanov, a student of Skrjabin, advocated the evolutionary approach to nematological study.
1937	B.G. Chitwood published the first section "Introduction to Nematology."
1945	Up to this period, growth of nematology was gradual; thereafter growth became much more rapid from the contributions of greater numbers of researchers.
1985+	Traditional nematology is no longer in a balanced growth phase and is becoming increasingly fragmented.

During the last half of the 19th century, the study of nematodes broadened and diversified. Hundreds of new species of free living nematodes were described; the complex life cycles of animal-parasitic nematodes were explored revealing the alternation of generations in the life history the need of intermediate hosts in this cycle, and the first steps in searching for a means of plant-parasitic nematode control were taken.

Nematology matured as a science early in the 20th century with the work of Cobb, Steiner, Thorne and later Chitwood in the United States and Filipjev, Skrjabin and Paramanov in Russia, and Goodey and others in Europe. The growth of Nematology which was gradual before World War II became rapid after, and has continued until recent times.

What does the future portend for Nematology? The role of nematodes as causal agents of plant and animal parasitic diseases has long been of concern primarily to affected segments of society. However, their role as participatory agents in many disease complexes is slowly being recognized. Moreover, the role of free living nematodes in the balance of nature is essentially unknown with opinions varying on their significance from "of no consequence" to "vital."

The knowledge of nematodes currently available is overwhelmed by the body of ignorance remaining about them that is represented in part by: undiscovered species, poorly understood internal physiological functions, ecology, adaptability to unfavorable conditions, interactions with other organisms, and their function in nature. Rarely do parasitic nematodes effect spectacular events to capture attention and even in these incidences (e.g., gross human distortion by elephantiasis, guinea worm extraction from a leg, heartworm masses revealed in surgical exposures of dog heart or agricultural crops decimated by a nematode) produce only a transient shock value. In contrast, parasitic nematodes generally express debilitating ill-defined symptoms of unhealthiness that, in the absence of specific knowledge, could be attributed to any of a wide range of causes. Considering the enormous incidences of nematode infections of plants and animals, the suffering, deprivation and cost of reduced health remain impossible to quantify and certainly unappreciated. For example, how can the health-sapping effects of parasitic nematodes on human populations in Africa or Asia or Central America be assessed? Or how can the losses in food, fiber and lumber from nematode plant diseases be comprehensible. It is difficult to accept the fact that in U.S. rangeland biomes the plant-parasitic nematode populations accepted as normal by the growers, have been estimated to effect a forage energy loss equivalent to that due to pasturing livestock.

Unfortunately, the public is generally unaware of how much nematodes impact their lives, directly or indirectly, while the media finds nematodes neither spectacular nor newsworthy. In this climate, the growth of scholarly research of the progressive, productive but "unsensational" kind suffers. For many traditional, core disciplines, including Nematology, such apathy may precipitate a decline that some believe has already begun. For the welfare of society this research trend must not prevail; balance and common sense in direction and support of research is essential. The relevance of this argument for Nematology will be self-evident from the chapters of this book.

"A new scientific idea does not triumph by convincing its opponents but rather because its opponents eventually die."

Max Planck, 1928

CHAPTER 3

Form and Shape

Nematodes able to move about their environment usually have slender, cylindrical bodies whose lengths are some 25–50 times greater than their diameter. Exceptions do occur—some are shorter and stouter, while others are longer and more slender. Those nematodes whose body shape tapers from the mid-body cylindrical portion to the tip of the tail and head are called "fusiform" (spindle-shaped). Others, whose tail and head shapes are blunt, when short, and stout, are truly cylindrical. When the body shapes are very long and very slender they are called "filiform" (thread-like). Collectively, these nematode shapes are called "vermiform" (worm-like). Worm is a zoological convenience term applied to invertebrate animals with superficially similar form and behavior. While a nematode is a worm, a worm may be a flatworm (trematode), tapeworm (cestode), grub or caterpillar (insect), roundworm (nematode), or earthworm (annelid), all of which are in remotely related taxonomic groups.

Frequently, several terms are used when discussing nematodes. "Anterior" refers to the head-end of the nematode, "posterior," the tail-end, "dorsal," the top of the nematode, "ventral," the bottom portion of the nematode, and "lateral," the sides of the nematode. Nematodes exhibit bilateral symmetry: that is, if a nematode could be bisected through the dorso-ventral plane, the two halves would be symmetrical.

Nematodes live in an aquatic environment, whether at the bottom of the sea (benthos), in the inner-tidal zone, in lake and stream bottoms, in plant or animal tissue, or in soil. Some have stages that survive dry habitats but whatever their particular habitat, nematodes must be surrounded by water in order to move, feed, develop, and otherwise function normally. Despite the wide variety of habitats, vermiform nematodes are remarkably similar in basic form. Nevertheless, there are a number of nematodes which exhibit unusual and characteristic ornamentations (Fig. 3.1).

While an overwhelming majority of nematode species are vermiform throughout their lives, there are a small number which are

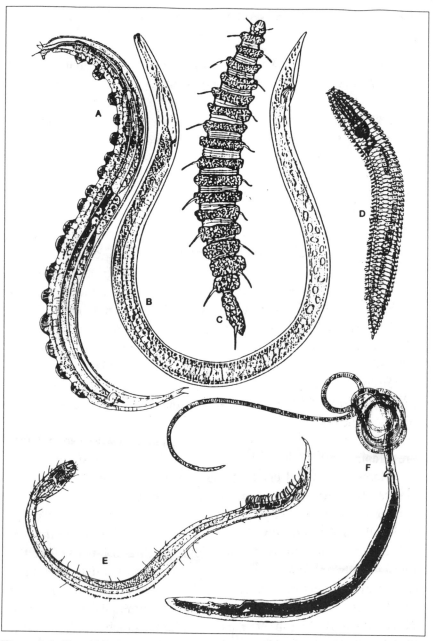

Figure 3.1. Vermiform body shapes of motile nematodes. A. *Bunonema inaequale,* soil and freshwater form, after Cobb, with permission of the U. S. Department of Agriculture. B. *Ditylenchus dipsaci,* male plant parasite, adapted after Thorne, with permission from Proc. Helm. Soc. Wash. C. *Desmoscolex americanus,* marine and freshwater form, after Chitwood, with permission from Proc. Helm. Soc. Wash. D. *Criconema octangulare,* plant-parasite, after Cobb, with permission from the U. S. Department of Agriculture. E. *Draconema cephalatum,* a marine form, after Cobb with permission from J. Wash. Acad. Sci. F. *Trichuris trichura,* animal parasite, after Georgi with permission from W. B. Saunders and Company.

vermiform only in the early stages. Some of these individuals destined to be female enlarge in later stages to become grossly swollen as adult females. Although these adult females can take on a variety of shapes (Fig. 3.2) many (mostly plant parasites) take on a characteristic pear-shape (pyriform). In swelling, these nematodes lose their locomotor activity and become sedentary.

Nematode size and shape appears to have been prescribed by nature in terms of the constrictions of the particular environmental niche. The fusiform, filiform body shape appears to have been chosen by nature for diverse animals, including nematodes, annelids, eels, snakes, and others. Soil-borne nematodes generally have very small body diameters, between 0.001–0.05mm (1 mm is approximately the thickness of a dime), and are able to move rather freely through the moist soil pore spaces while immersed in a thin water film surrounding each soil particle. Soil which consists of a variable proportion of colloidal clay (0.0002–0.00002mm), coarse clay (0.002–0.0002mm), silt (0.05–0.002mm), and sand (2–0.05mm) contains pore spaces of varying dimensions. This fact explains, in part, the field observations that plant-parasitic nematodes (phytonematodes) tend to cause less severe disease in heavy clay soils than in the more porous, light, silty, sandy soils. Nematodes can survive and function in heavy clay soils, which are seldom homogenous and contain particle aggregates of sand or clay with larger pores and cracks through which the nematode can gain access. The vermiform shape allows the nematode to hug the particle surface and wind its way through the intricate pathways that would inhibit the passage of a more bulky animal. These same vermiform shapes allow plant-parasitic nematodes to penetrate plant tissues either through cells or through the spaces between cells, much as animal-parasitic nematodes penetrate skin and migrate through animal tissues. Similarly, the long, elongated shape of the large animal parasites allows them to float and live in the intestine while the much smaller microfilariae float through the blood and lymph vascular systems. Moreover, the filiform shape of the tiny microfilariae allows them to take advantage of the physics of dynamic fluids. They align themselves axially with the blood vessel and move through the constricted openings of capillaries, a migration not possible with a bulkier shape of the same

Figure 3.2. Pyriform nematode body shapes. A. *Rotylenchus reniformis,* plant-parasitic form, after Linford with permission Proc. Helm. Soc. Wash. B. *Cacopauris pestis,* a plant-parasitic form, after Allen with permission from Proc. Helm. Soc. Wash. C. *Tylenchulus semipenetrans,* a plant-parasitic form, after Ayoub, with permission from the California Department of Food and Agriculture and C. S. Papp. D. *Meloidogyne* sp., plant-parasitic form, after Ayoub, with permission from the California Department of Food and Agrilculture and C. S. Papp. E. *Tetrameres* sp., a parasite in the crop of birds. Redrawn after Travassos. F. *Phlyctainophora lamnanae,* a parasite in the sharks head, redrawn after Steiner. G. *Bovienema tomici,* an insect parasite after Nickle with permission from Proc. Helm. Soc. Wash.

mass. The vermiform shape is therefore very well suited to the niches in which nematodes are found, whether they be soil, soil-like matrices, plant or animal tissue, or wherever motility of the nematode is essential. Inasmuch as most nematodes are aquatic, oxygen-requiring (aerobic) animals, the fusiform, filiform shape permits the direct uptake of oxygen, water, other gases, some ionic salts, and in certain cases other nutrients by diffusion rather than requiring a complex organ system to accomplish the same purpose.

The complex soil environment consists of (1) pore spaces containing water vapor, nitrogen, carbon dioxide, and sometimes methane as gases; (2) soil water solution containing dissolved gases, minerals, and organic solutes released by living or dead organisms; and (3) particulate matter consisting of plant, insect, and other animal components intermixed with the major component of mineral particles derived from decomposed rock. This non-living medium is shared by a wide array of living organisms, including bacteria, fungi, algae, protozoa, nematodes, mites, insects, annelids, mollusks, and plant roots, among others. These organisms are normally not evenly distributed throughout the soil, but tend to congregate around accumulations of dead plant or animal matter, and living growing plant roots which slough off tissue or release organic substances. The dead matter and living roots serve as food sources for some organisms which, in turn, serve as food sources for others. Nematodes spend part or all of their lives in this complex environment; some feed on bacteria, fungi, algae, protozoa, mites, and each other, others (plant parasites) feed on plant roots, and a few leave the soil to feed on the above ground plant parts. Nematodes can be viewed as intermediate links in the food chain, although some can serve as a food source (prey) for bacteria, fungi, and micrometazoans (small multicullular invertebrate animals).

In order for living processes to function normally, all organisms maintain an internal fluid pressure greater than that of the adjacent environment. Should the internal pressure of body fluids fall to match the external pressure, the organism would become flaccid, and its bodily functions would be disrupted to produce irreparable damage and death if the conditions persist. Therefore, a pressure difference characteristic of each organism must be maintained whether the organism lives on a mountain top or in a deep ocean trench with water pressures of a thousand times atmospheric (one standard atmosphere [Atm] = 760 mm Hg/cm^2). As aquatic animals, nematodes must also obey these general requirements. While most nematodes are too small for measurements of their internal pressures directly by current means, the internal pressure of some large animal parasitic nematodes has been determined to be in the range of 0.02–0.28 Atm above ambient pressure. As nematodes move, their internal pressure rises and falls, depending in part upon the body configuration. Indirect methods of estimating internal pressure have been tried on small nematodes, but the determinations are not very precise. Nematodes and other organisms maintain their higher internal pressure osmotically, i.e., by having more salts and organic molecules dissolved in the body fluids than are found in the environmental solution surrounding the animal. This can occur only if a semi-permeable membrane envelops the body, separating the outside environment from the internal contents. The semi-permeable property of the membrane maintains certain mineral and organic ions and solutes inside while allowing for free exchange of water, gases, and selected small ions with the external environment. Such properties are evident in diverse ways. Pressure differentials can be observed when the internal contents of a nematode (seen with a microscope) burst forth if the body wall is cut or punctured. Nematodes from deep sea samples retrieved quickly often show everted structures rather than the normally positioned ones. Osmotic effects can be seen under a microscope by observing a marine nematode immersed in tap water swell in size and even burst, or a soil inhabiting nematode immersed in sea water, shrink. In fact, if a nematode is immersed in a strongly osmotic solution of salts, the animal first shortens, then shrinks further in the fashion of a concertina bellows. If a strong sugar solution is used the animal becomes flat as a ribbon .

Gathering Nematodes

The difficulty in finding a nematode—a translucent particle approximately a millimeter in length and 1/50 of that in diameter—in soil or plant and animal tissue is akin to that of "finding a needle in a haystack." Nevertheless, extraction methods, albeit not very efficient and certainly not quantitative, have been developed to obtain nematodes free of debris. The major methods for separating nematodes from their environmental matrix take advantage of one or more of the nematode properties just discussed.

Sieving

The use of sieves of different aperture sizes was adapted from particulate, mainly soil, analysis. As a general rule, sieves with apertures approximately 1/10 the length of the nematode are effective. The principle involved in sieving for nematodes relies on the probability that a suspension of nematodes in water poured through a sieve will encounter the sieve surface with a sufficient component of the nematode body parallel to the plane of the sieve surface. Of course, a nematode whose body axis is vertical or near vertical when encountering the sieve surface will pass through the apertures. In the usual practice, the nematode-containing sample of soil or tissue macerate is suspended in an abundance of water, then poured through a sieve sufficiently coarse to allow the nematodes to pass through freely while retaining the larger debris which is discarded. The aqueous suspension containing the nematodes is passed through a second sieve of the appropriately-sized aperture to retain nematodes and associated like-size debris, while allowing clay and other smaller-sized particles to pass through. The collection on the sieve is then backwashed off the sieve into a cylinder, again suspended in water with vigorous stirring, allowed to settle for a short period, then decanted nearly completely, leaving only the sediment consisting essentially of the sand particles. The nematode suspension will still contain variable amounts of organic debris—very little if the sample was from a sandy soil and much more if from an organic soil or tissue macerate. The material can be used as it is, or purified to the degree needed by other methods.

Baermann Funnel

The Baermann funnel method has been adopted from a very old technique developed by helminthologists to separate parasites from fecal material. Normally it utilizes the 100 mm (4 inch) funnel coupled to a very short piece of rubber tubing whose terminus is closed by a pinching device. The funnel opening has an inset of a modestly coarse screen with a flat bottom upon which a suitable tissue paper is laid. Although a wide range of tissue papers may be used, they can vary greatly in their ability to permit the passage of nematodes without associated debris. The funnel is then filled with water and all bubbles removed. When the water level reaches the base of the screen and wets the overlying tissue paper, soil, tissue macerate, or sievings are added. More water is added to just cover the sample. The nematodes migrate through the sample, penetrating the tissue paper to the water underneath. Unable to swim or to return, they fall through the water to the bottom of the stem, free of soil and debris, other than the relatively small numbers of other organisms that follow them through the tissue. The process may require several hours to several days, depending on the nematode and the nature of the sample.

Misting is essentially a modification of the Baermann funnel technique, in which the funnel stem, instead of being closed with a pinch clamp is inserted into a small cylinder, and there is no standing water within the funnel. The remaining part of the assembly remains the same, but is inserted into a cabinet in which there is intermittent warm water misting. The misting provides well-oxygenated water in a very gentle flow to wash nematodes migrating through the paper into the collecting cylinder.

Density Flotation

While sieving takes advantage of the fusiform nematode shape in a passive manner, the Baermann funnel technique takes advantage of the fusiform shape together with the migrating capability of the animal. Density flotation, on the other hand, takes advantage of the semi-permeable properties of the nematode body wall. By selecting the appropriate salts or organic solutes it is possible to increase the density of a solution and correspondingly its osmotic potential. By suspending sievings, soil, or tissue macerate in water and centrifuging, particles more dense than water (including nematodes) can be sedimented into a pellet. The less dense material floats and can be discarded by decanting. Re-suspension of the pellet in an osmotic solution results in exosmosis of the nematodes (loss of water) which become somewhat more dense but less so than the solution. On centrifugation, the more dense soil particles and organic material saturated with osmotic solution sediment while the nematodes remain in suspension so that they can be collected by sieving. If the operation is done quickly, most nematodes can be recovered unharmed from the experience and returned to water. Some nematodes are more sensitive to this procedure than others, and if the process is prolonged, substantial injury can occur.

Certain of the basic techniques are more suitable than others for different nematodes. Usually several techniques used in combination are required to obtain a clean nematode sample. These methods are adequate for obtaining nematodes for identification and taxonomic purposes. Unfortunately, these methods, applied extensively for quantitative purposes, are subject to substantial error. Extraction efficiency, (the proportion of nematodes present in the sample that are recovered) with few exceptions, is 50% or less. Other factors being equal, extraction efficiency is a function of soil characteristics, tissue properties, nematode properties, extraction method, operator consistency, and counting method. For the present, rigorous quantitative methods for routine nematode population level determinations do not exist. Considering the complex media in which nematodes are found, the criteria upon which the extraction methods are based, and the summation of incremental losses at each step of the multi-step procedures, the poor results should not be surprising.

Diversity of Nematodes

Despite a certain constancy of general body shape and the arrangement and form of the internal organ systems, one should not lose sight of the fact that identification and taxonomic placement of the tens of thousands of known nematodes has been accomplished by noting diversity and differences in morphological features. Although most nematodes generally resemble the body shape depicted by the nematode in Fig. 3.1B, there is a substantial number of others, illustrated in Fig. 3.1 and 3.2, that even on a macro scale are different. What purpose, advantage, or survival value these features serve remains unknown, and as yet are a matter for speculation. Whatever the benefits, these features appear consistently in terms of size, number, shape, or location, and serve as identification markers for a particular kind of nematode.

The identification and taxonomic placement of nematode species suffers from inherent weaknesses which the astute nematologist must forever keep in mind. For example, uncertainty in taxonomic placement arises when a critical feature presumed to indicate a relationship may have arisen independently more than once during evolutionary development. Moreover, particular features in different nematodes may be similar in form and function, but of entirely different tissue origin. Such determinations are exceedingly difficult in the absence of other than currently available specimens. With no fossil record, the taxonomist can work only with currently available representatives, so the question of phylogeny is not amenable to rigorous objective resolution.

Perhaps the greatest uncertainty arises in deciding which features are fundamental, and therefore indicative of a true relationship, and which are incidental, and of little importance to evolutionary lineage. Such decisions can seldom be made objectively and are therefore arrived at in a subjective fashion. The quality of such decisions are dependent upon the experience, competency, judgement, and emotional satisfaction of the taxonomist. The end result is a continual polemic among the various schools of thought, which is evident in the literature, with respect to taxonomic placement, nomenclature, and phylogenetic relationships.

The preceding remarks relate largely to the intermediate and higher taxonomic groupings; a different set of difficulties emerge at the lowest taxon, i.e., species level. Unfortunately, there is no uniform set of criteria for the designation of species for all life forms. Consequently, the criteria designating a species in botanical life forms differ from those of zoological life forms, which differs from those of microbiological life forms. In Nematology, the species designation is essentially arrived at by default, i.e., the species designation results when the taxonomist examines two potentially different specimens and is convinced of the absence or presence of distinguishing differential morphological features. Despite the weak scientific principles employed, the process continues to provide useful, practical designations. Nonetheless, it is clear that in certain areas the process has reached its limits.

For example, in the plant-parasitic rootknot genus (*Meloidogyne*), the species designation is based heavily though not entirely upon the perineal pattern (characteristic cuticular striations about the vulva and anus of the female) with a certainty of perhaps 75% or better for some species. This means that three out of four specimens may have the characteristic pattern, whereas the fourth will not. In a pure population this poses no difficulty. However, in the event of a mixed population, or a population from a field sample, one can never be certain as to whether the one non-typical specimen is of the same species or another. This cannot be better illustrated than in a statement by B. G. Chitwood, who discovered the perineal differences, that given a large enough sample of *Meloidogyne incognita,* he could prepare sets of specimens with perineal patterns characteristic of several other species. This problem is not restricted to plant-parasitic nematodes but applies also to animal parasites, particularly the filarial forms. Explorations along different lines are currently in progress in an attempt to improve this species designation. Morphological characterization is being extended to suboptical levels by the use of scanning electron microscopy (SEM). In this way features not visible through the optical microscope can be used to form a species designation. Unfortunately, the procedure is rather lengthy and poorly amenable to routine identifications.

An alternate approach is biochemical and involves analyses of enzymes or other proteins characteristic of the species. This method is effective now for use with certain plant-parasitic Meloidogyne spp. And with modest improvement, a single large female can yield sufficient material to provide a characteristic electrophoretic pattern on a routine basis. The technique is relatively rapid, and with the incorporation of sufficient replicates of different females, the precision of the determination to upwards of 98% can be accomplished with little difficulty. Moreover, this method could be much more useful for determining species levels in mixed field populations. Other approaches are being studied, including that of characteristic deoxyribonucleic acid (DNA) segments, serological differentiations and monoclonal antibodies.

Perhaps the problem of categorizing nematodes is most distressing at the subspecies level, where categories are morphologically indistinguishable, and are referred to variously as races, biotypes, pathotypes, lines, or mutants. Different subspecies populations of particular importance to society are found in plant and animal-parasitic nematodes that have different host ranges. Subspecies populations appear to arise from long-term persistent stress, including temperature, therapeutic chemicals, or a poorly suitable food source. When subspecies differences have occurred in human species and the canine species, for example, morphological characteristics, e.g., size, shape, form, or color could be used to separate races or breeds. Since this is not the case with nematodes, there is an obvious need for not only better designation of such differing populations, but also a more rapid and reliable means of identification.

Despite its problems, differentiation by morphological characteristics has been of incalculable value for the identification and systematization of the thousands of known nematodes. The lay person can readily appreciate the diversity and character of animals in a large zoological park. But for some reason, nematodes, a taxonomic group several times larger than *Vertebrata,* take on a sameness. Perhaps this is in part due to the microscopic size of most nematodes, the generally invisible habitat in which they live, or that their differences are not boldly prominent in size, shape, appendage, or color. Nevertheless, nematodes manifest differences in size, shape, internal and external structure, niche, and role in nature.

Occasionally, under low magnification, nematodes can be identified by their body shape; however, this method is usually used to identify higher taxa, that is, genus or above. Usually the mid-body region of the nematode is a desert in terms of morphological characteristics useful in identification with the exception of the female vulva which in some species occurs in this region. In fact, most nematode descriptions utilize illustrations of the anterior and posterior portions of the nematodes and omit the central body. Therefore, examination is concentrated on the anterior and posterior segments of the nematodes which contain the greatest diversity of useful morphological structures.

Moderate magnification is sometimes sufficient to identify a nematode, but most often oil immersion lenses on the optical microscope must be used. In essence, a taxonomist must work at the optical limits of the best microscope capable of the most critical resolution. Even so, in some cases this is inadequate, and scanning electron microscopy capable of several orders of resolution greater than the optical microscope must be used. Descriptive illustrations reported at 3–4,000 magnifications are drawn with the aid of a camera lucida. This device consists of a prism mounted on the microscope eye piece, which reflects the specimen image in the eye of the microscopist, onto a drawing board. The image projection and magnification are faithful. However, the resolution (as measured by the capability of distinguishing two adjacent points) is limited by the microscope.

Scanning electron microscopy (SEM) requires that a specimen be dried in a special fashion and then coated with a thin layer of gold (by vapor deposition). The gold layer is opaque to the impinging electron beam under vacuum conditions, and that allows the operator to examine the specimen in surface relief. Although SEM can achieve higher magnification and resolution than the optical microscope, its usefulness is limited to discerning surface features of the specimen.

Transmission Electron Microscopy (TEM) is capable of high resolution and magnification. However, the depth of focus is so short relative to the thickness of the nematode that it is useless for whole mounts. For TEM to be useful, the specimen nematode tissues must be immobilized with minimum distortion (fixed) and perfused with an electron opaque agent, usually osmium tetroxide, followed by dehydration and impregnation with a resin which is allowed to cure and harden. The specimen is then sliced into a thin section (25nm = 0.000025mm) for examination under vacuum by TEM. By chemical bonding the osmium tetroxide reveals the location of unsaturated (double-bond containing) lipids in membranes, organelles, other cellular particles, as well as some carbohydrates. TEM is useful for the determination of three dimensional structures, both large and small within a nematode. Without attention to detail and particular care in the interpretation of observations the electron microscopist can commit gross blunders in his conclusions; it is much akin to an urbanite surrounded by trees attempting to describe the nature and topography of the forest.

The range in diversity of morphological features and structures observable in the anterior (head) region of nematodes is evident in Fig. 3.3.

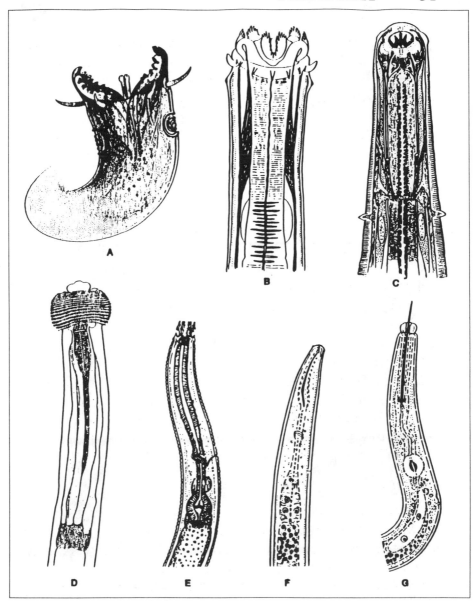

Figure 3.3. Illustrations showing the diversity of form and structure occuring in the anterior portions of different nematodes. A. *Selachinema ferox*, the predaceous so-called shark nematode, after Cobb, with permission of the U. S. Department of Agriculture. B. *Crossocephalus viviparus*, a parasite of zebra and rhinoceros, redrawn after T. Southwell. C. *Ancylostoma duodenale*, the animal-parasitic hookworm, modified from Chitwood with permission from M. Chitwood Buschong.. D. *Echinocephalus southwelli*, an intestinal parasite of elasmobranchs and rays, after Bayliss and Lane, with permission from Proc. Zool. Soc. London. E. *Acrobeles cervus*, a free-living form redrawn after Thorne, 1925. F. *Trichodorus obscurus*, the plant-parasitic stubby root nematode, redrawn after Allen. G. *Belonolaimus longicaudatus*, the plant-parasitic sting nematode, redrawn after Thorne.

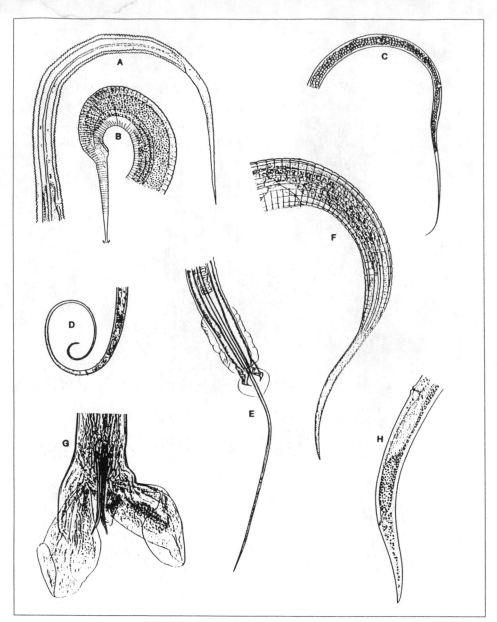

Figure 3.4. Illustrations showing the diversity in form and structure of the posterior end of different nematodes. A. *Atylenchus decalineatus*, a plant-parasite, after Chitwood and Tarjan, with permission from Proc. Helm. Soc. Wash. B. *Hystrignathus rigidus*, a free-living larval female, after Christie, with permission from Proc. Helm. Soc. Wash. C. *Onchocerca reticulata*, a microfilaria of the "river blindness" nematode, after Levine, with permission from Burgess Publishing Co. D. *Prismatolaimus stenurus*, a freshwater nematode, after Cobb, with permission from the U. S. Department of Agriculture. E. *Capillaria caudenflata*, intestinal parasite of birds, after Levine, with permission from Burgess Publishing Co. F. *Tylenchus cancellatus,* a plant-parasitic nematode, after Cobb, with permission from the U. S. Department of Agriculture. G. *Haemonchus contortus,* a male parasite of ruminants, after Georgii, with permission from the W. B. Saunders Co. H. *Ditylenchus dipsaci,* a female plant parasite, after Thorne with permission from Proc. Helm. Soc. Wash.

Not only the oral (buccal) cavity (stoma) but also the adjacent internal and external structures can differ greatly among nematodes. The great range and diversity of posterior regions of nematodes are illustrated in Fig. 3.4. Additional examples of different structures and shapes of anterior or posterior regions of nematodes are evident in Figs. 3.1, 3.2, 4.1, 5.2, 5.5, 5.6, 5.7, 5.8, 5.9.

Organization

In nematodes there is a certain constancy in the general form and arrangement of the internal organs regardless of the size of the worm. Nematodes are unsegmented roundworms, that is, the body is not divided into similar internal parts or segments arranged in a linear series along the body axis, as is the case for annelids and chordates, despite the more or less prominent annulations (see illustrations Fig. 3.1 to 3.4) evident on the cuticle. The strong, mostly transparent, elastic outer portion of the body wall serves as a primary barrier between the environment and the nematode interior.

The general arrangement of organ systems, and special features of the nematode (nematodes have some six basic organ systems which will be discussed in a later chapter) is illustrated by *Mononchus papillatus* (a predaceous nematode) in Fig. 4.1. The nematode is illustrated from the side (lateral view); a nematode resting on a flat surface while bathed with solution lies on its side and tends to curl ventrally. The illustrations of Fig. 4.2, including A., a face view; B., a cross-section through the esophageal region; C., a cross-section of the mid-body including intestine and gonad, help to provide a better understanding of the three-dimensional organization of the nematode. Although anterior structural features can differ in other nematodes (Fig. 3.3), as can posterior features (Fig. 3.4), the basic order is much the same. Beginning with the anterior end and moving posteriorly (Fig. 4.1) there are sensory organs called papillae and amphids; a face view (Fig. 4.2, A) shows the oral opening, a lip region, and farther back the cephalic setae, which are also sensory. The pharynx wall lines the stoma (buccal cavity) on whose dorsal wall is a cuticular structure called the dorsal tooth. While the tooth is not moveable, it protrudes into the stoma as a kind of hook to rip open larger organisms and nematodes pulled in by the tremendous suction of a feeding mononch. Between the base of the stoma and the intestine lies a heavily muscled structure called an esophagus. Exteriorly from the esophagus is a nerve cell, lying in the ventral cord, as

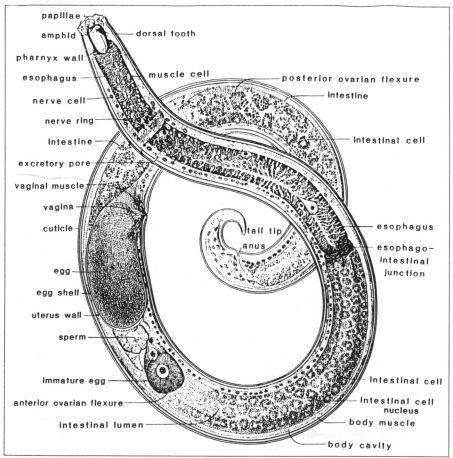

Figure 4.1. The general organization of most nematodes as illustrated by *Mononchus papillatus* in a lateral view. After Cobb with permission of the U.S. Department of Agriculture.

indicated in Fig. 4.2B. The lumen of the esophagus is triradiate (Fig. 4.2B); while the apices of the three-pointed star remain more or less fixed, the heavy esophageal musculature between the apices contract to open the lumen and create a tremendous suction force. The nerve ring, or, more precisely, the circumesophageal commissure, is the major coordinating nerve ganglion of the nematode. While subsidiary ganglia exist in the general nervous system, the nerve ring contains the most massive amount of nerve tissue. In this general region, the position varying with nematode species, a ventrally located excretory pore is found. At the base of the esophagus lies the esophageal intestinal

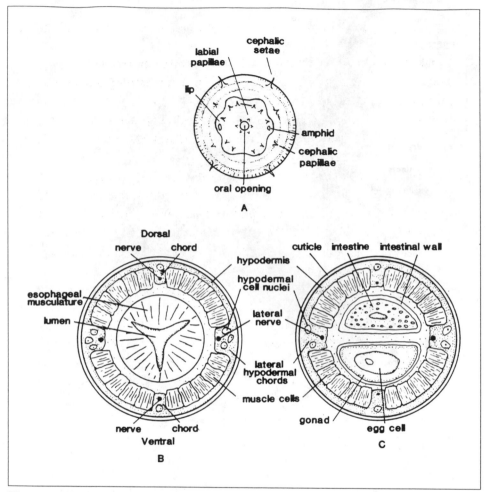

Figure 4.2. Radial sections of a generalized nematode illustrating common features, the cuticle of the anterior end, with a "face" view, (A); a cross-section through the esophageal region, illustrating the esophageal lumen and musculature, the body cavity, the somatic muscle cells, the hypodermal layer, and the chords embedding the hypodermal cell nuclei and the dorsal, ventral, and lateral nerves, (B); a cross-section through the mid-body region containing the intestine and gonad, (C).

junction, often (depending on the species) incorporating a uni-directional valve. Following the esophagus is the intestine, with the intestinal cells and their nuclei. The body muscles constitute a somatic musculature layer as indicated. Exaggerated drawings of Fig. 4.2B & C illustrate the muscle cells in each quadrant, the hypodermal layer exterior to the muscle cells, and the hypodermal cell nuclei which are usually imbedded in the dorsal, ventral, and lateral chords of the nematode.

The body cavity of the nematode lies inward of the hypodermis and the muscles, and constitutes the fluid-filled space bathing the internal organs. In most nematodes the body cavity volume is very small and consists of a small volume of fluid distributed in a thin layer that lubricates the surfaces of the different internal organs as they must slip past each other in an active animal.

The ovaries or testes of many nematodes reflex, or fold back on themselves, at least once, and sometimes many times; the anterior and posterior ovarian flexures indicate those points where the bend occurs. After a female is fertilized, the sperm are stored in a spermatheca and are used to fertilize the egg as it passes by. A mature egg ready to be laid is shown with its eggshell covering within the uterus of the nematode. The cuticle constitutes the outer non-living portion of the body wall. The vagina provides the opening through which the egg is expelled to the outside as the vaginal muscles enlarge the opening. The anus, located ventrally, is the body opening through which the intestinal waste is expelled.

The outward similarities of structure among nematodes, particularly among the smaller terrestrial forms exhibiting little change during their development to adulthood, led early zoologists to formulate a cell constancy hypothesis that has been an influence and encumbrance to the perception of general nematode structure and development. According to the initial cell constancy hypothesis, the fertile egg would reach the fully developed first stage larval form whose cell number, in the range of 500–1000 cells, was assumed to be characteristic of the species. Although the first-stage larva would molt four times before developing into the fully mature adult, the number of cells was alleged to remain constant and any growth that occurred was attributed to cell enlargement. It is true that there is a relatively small number of cells in the normal nematode; some 70-100 cells make up the esophagus, a like number the somatic musculature, and the rest are distributed among the intestine, the hypodermis, the reproductive system, the nervous system, and assorted glands.

It quickly became obvious that if nematodes were to reproduce, ovaries which produce eggs and testes which produce sperm must constitute exceptions to the cell constancy hypothesis. Despite the fuzziness of the hypothesis, it proved attractive and, apparently, emotionally satisfying to many professionals, as a cell constancy hypothesis rendered nematodes special and different from many other animals. Further considerations pointed out the fact that though a germinal primordium or stem cell was present in the mature first larval stage, the adults possessed fully developed reproductive systems. The female gonad consisted of ovaries, oviducts, associated structures, vagina, vaginal muscles, and vulva, while the male gonads consisted of testes, seminal vesicle, cloaca, spicules and spicular muscles. Gradually, as more systems were carefully examined, more and more exceptions were required. Recently, in a tour de force with *Caenorhabditis elegans*, a bacterial feeding nematode currently popular for genetic and biochemical studies, the embryology was followed cell by cell, from egg to fully developed first stage larvae : 550 cells were counted. The mature hermaphroditic adult consisted of 810 somatic cells, a 42% increase; the mature male consisted of 970 somatic cells, a 76% increase over the first stage larval component. So many exceptions to the rule have been invoked as to render the cell constancy hypothesis useless, even if only the normal sized nematodes, i.e., those on the order of a millimeter in length, are considered. As mentioned, certain animal parasitic nematodes grow to large sizes, and one, *Placentonema gigantissima*, grows to a huge size of 7 meters. To illustrate a *P. gigantissima* hypodermal cell, substantially smaller than a period on this page, in the normal sized first stage larval form, for the adult it would need to enlarge to the size of a golf ball. Cells of this size are unknown except in the extraterrestrial species of science fiction. Despite the ample discredit that has accumulated, the cell constancy hypothesis occasionally still appears in reports; hopefully it will soon disappear into oblivion. Nematodes clearly conform to the general rules applicable to all organisms of nature.

CHAPTER 5

Organ Systems

Although six organ systems are generally recognized in a nematode, these are not the only vital functions taking place in the body. There are a variety of glands, organelles, structures, and cells of relatively unknown function which may be critical factors in the life cycle of the nematode. Nevertheless, it is useful to review the various organ systems briefly to provide a better understanding of the diversity in each system that, integrated into the whole, renders one species of nematode different from another.

Organ Systems Present in Nematodes

Body Wall

The nematode body wall separates the internal portions of the nematode from the external environment and serves a variety of vital processes that allow the nematode to function in its peculiar way. Cross sections of the body (Fig. 4.2) reveal that the muscles of each quadrant are tight against the internal surface of the hypodermal layer (which constitutes the outermost layer of living cells of the nematode body; external to it lies a non-living multi-layered elastic cuticle) and appear to be part of the body wall. These muscle cells, however, derive from the mesodermal tissue of the embryo, whereas the hypodermis derives from ectodermal tissue; therefore the musculature tissue should not be considered part of the true body wall. The hypodermal layer is of one cell thickness with nuclei located in the hypodermal chords (Fig. 4.2). In some species the nuclei are all located in the thickened lateral chords. In others, usually larger nematodes, nuclei are also found in the dorsal and ventral chords; in very large nematodes, nuclei also occur in the layer between chords. The bulkier lateral chords extend the length of the body and exhibit "lateral lines" (more correctly: lateral incisures) which are grooves on the surface of the cuticle, while the thinner dorsal and ventral chords may also extend the length of the body but vanish posteriorly in a number of species.

The hypodermis is an extremely active tissue with many different functions. Current wisdom suggests that the hypodermal layer serves as a major energy depot by storing lipids and carbohydrates for use in time of need. Its membranes are probably responsible for the exchange of gases, water, select mineral ions and organic solutes with the external environment. Moreover, its membrane semipermeability permits the nematode to maintain an internal turgor pressure greater than that of the environmental bathing solution. Some nematodes are reported to possess hypodermal glands that duct to the outside while other glands may have an endocrine-like function.

Probably the best known function of the hypodermis is laying down the elastic cuticle outside the hypodermal layer. Remarkably, this occurs five times during the nematode's life cycle; it generates the cuticles (as thin as 1/100mm) of the first, second, third, fourth larval stages and the adult, which may all differ in structure. Each of the four molts that every nematode undergoes in developing into the adult is initiated by a stimulation of unknown nature or origin. Receiving this signal, the hypodermis secretes proteolytic enzymes, most likely, that loosen the adjacent cuticular layers, appearing to dissolve them according to microscopic observation. Why these enzymes are secreted only from the cuticular side of the cell and not inwards to the central body, and the question of whether the several hydrolyzed cuticle layer components are reabsorbed, are largely matters of speculation. Since only the few cuticular layers next to the hypodermis are dissolved, the remainder is shed; this includes the cuticle that lines the stoma, esophagus, vulva, cloaca, and other body openings. Concomitant with the early stages of this process, the new cuticle is being formed; this includes new setae, papillae, amphids (sensory structures), and other cuticular ornamentation.

The ultrastructure of the cuticle has been studied in a variety of nematodes via cross sections under the transmission electron microscope (TEM), since they are beyond the capability of the optical microscope. Astoundingly, variable numbers of discrete layers were found, depending upon the species. The nomenclature formerly used to describe and group layers precluded correlation of various layers between diverse species of nematodes. Recently a different nomenclature, derived from that used for arthropods (insects), appears to provide a better means of correlation (Fig. 5.1). In this system the cuticle is divided into four major components: the outer epicuticle; the exocuticle; the mesocuticle; and the innermost endocuticle; each component in turn consists of one or more distinguishable layers. It is

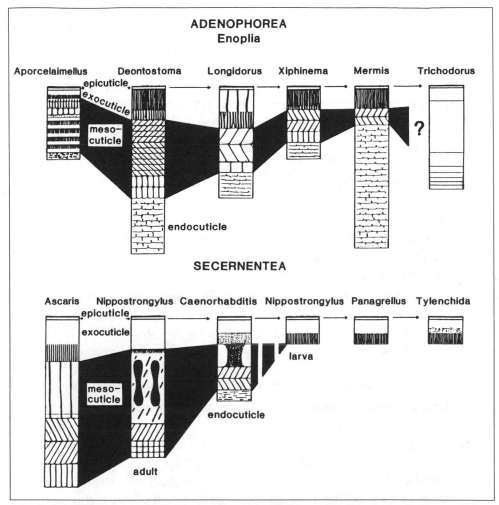

Figure 5.1. The ultrastructure of nematode cuticles indicates the various layers found in different nematodes. The cuticle is divided into four major parts: Epicuticle, Exocuticle, Mesocuticle, and Endocuticle. The postulated relations of the various zones among different nematodes are suggested. Adenophorea and Secernentea constitute the two major taxonomic classes of nematodes. Redrawn after Maggenti.

evident that in some nematode groups there is no endocuticle; for others, neither mesocuticles nor endocuticles. It is also clear that larval cuticles can differ substantially from adult cuticles in terms of ultra-structure.

The general composition of the cuticle is believed to be primarily of keratin-like and collagen-like proteins, but is also likely to include some of lipids, carbohydrates, and polymeric compounds like polyphe-nols. Whether the molting involves an initial cuticle loosening from the hypodermis or a dissolution of several layers before shedding, a new epicuticle must be in place immediately for the nematode to function. There is some belief that the outer surface of the epicuticle includes a fragile membrane, but this seems unlikely—especially for soilborne nematodes which migrate in a solid media of jagged edges.

Whether one believes that the individual layers are generated stratum by stratum or, as some have observed with certain nematodes, it slowly matures into the individual sublayers from a thick, amorphous stratum, the process remains a mystery. While certain layers appear amorphous, others have structure, e.g., granulations, striae, and fibers running in different directions, radial struts, or pillars. What means are in place to control the depth and structure of each layer? Can natural chemistry explain the development of a complex tissue? Is the complex final product generated from subsequent emanations of the hypo-dermis into the initial amorphous stratum? Are all layers preordained during the secretion of the amorphous layer but just invisible in the early stages? Moreover, what triggers the secretion of individual layers or subsequent catalytic emanations to migrate to the appropriate layer for the establishment of its structure? There are many unanswered questions in this process.

Should the complexity of nematode cuticles not be sufficiently striking, one can consider the wide range of surface cuticular ornamen-tations (Fig. 3.1, 3.2, 3.3, 3.4). Certain ornamentations (e.g., lips, probolae, setae, papillae) involve special hypodermal, muscle, and nerve cells. Other kinds of surface ornamentation occur, such as the perineal patterns about the vulval-anal region of the plant-parasitic females of *Meloidogyne* spp. (Fig. 5.2). These patterns are used to identify different species. The underlying hypodermal cells in some way transmit directions to the outer layers of the cuticle to generate the characteristic patterns. Under the prominent longitudinal and radial incisures (grooves) that often result in a waffle pattern or annulations (rings) around the body, the epicuticle and the outer layer of the exocuticle follow the surface indentations so that the surface variation is absorbed or smoothed out by the second layer of the exocuticle. In

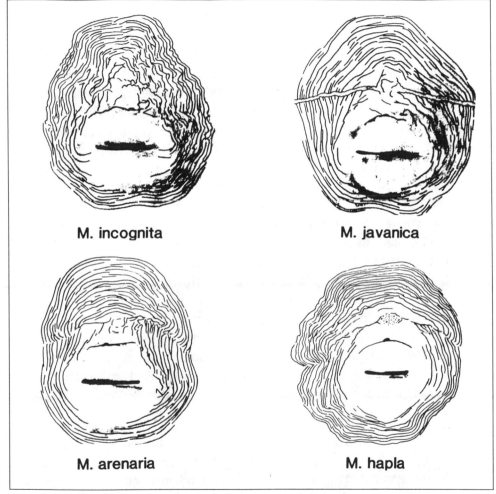

M. incognita

M. javanica

M. arenaria

M. hapla

Figure 5.2. Cuticular perineal patterns of four plant-parasitic rootknot species. *Meloidogyne incognita, Meloidogyne javanica, Meloidogyne arenaria,* and *Meloidogyne hapla.* The surface wrinkle distribution about the anus and vulva is sufficiently reproducible and characteristic to be useful for the identification of species. After Sasser, North Carolina State University, with his permission.

nematodes with unusual cuticular ornamentation, e.g., spines of various kinds, a tile-like character (*Criconemella octangulare*), lateral body alae (wing-like extensions), caudal alae (bursa), the cuticular ultrastructure is less clear. The thicker alae have a fluid-filled triangular tube at the base adjacent to the body. Some of the caudal alae tail structures are thickened but flat as is the body tail associated with it. What under-layers of cuticle occur and how these merge with those of the body proper are matters of speculation.

A different form of ornamentation, quite characteristic of the nematode, is illustrated by *Dirofilaria* species (heartworm) (Fig. 5.3). Short or long ridge patterns seem to be superimposed on a regular "corn ear" appearing cuticle. In *Gongylonema* (vertebrate parasite, Fig. 5.7B) rows of warts (cuticular bossae) of various shape and size occur along the body. The ultrastructure of the cuticle in the region of these ridges or warts has not been determined. A greater mystery involves the mechanism by which the hypodermis, from which the cuticle is generated, guides the formation of such bizarre ornamentation as ridges, warts, alae, and other cuticular extensions.

Why all nematodes molt is not clear. Arthropods and other organisms with rigid exoskeletons need to shed the hard cuticle in order to grow in size. Nematodes which enlarge many times as they develop to adulthood, have a similar problem. However, there are many nematodes which change little in size as they develop to adulthood. Nonetheless, there are other developments that require cuticular changes, particularly in the latter stages such as the development of the adult vulva or spicules, and changes in the stoma and adult ornamentation. It is evident that cause and function associated with cuticular molting are poorly understood.

Muscle System

The nematode body muscles consist of a variable number (depending on the species) of cellular bundles, pressed against the inner surface of the hypodermis and organized into quadrants separated by the hypodermal chords (Fig. 4.2). The mechanism by which the cell bundles are positioned against the hypodermis is uncertain. However, if the mechanism is similar to that occurring in flatworms, connective tissue strands between muscle and hypodermal cells keep them aligned. The spindle shaped muscle cell is approximately aligned with the longitudinal axis of the nematode and consists of two principle portions: a fibrillar belt consisting of contractile and noncontractile fibers which together generate the muscle pulling force, and a protoplasmic portion containing the nucleus (sarcoplasm). There are also other connecting elements to nerves and other tissues.

A century ago, the muscle cells were separated by researchers into essentially three types based upon the position of the fibers: those with few fibers present positioned flat against the muscle cell wall in contact with the hypodermis (platymyarian); those with an increased number of fibers extending up the cell wall perpendicular to the hypodermis (coelomyarian); and those cells with the fibers were positioned against the entire wall of the cell (circomyarian). Whereas in the first two types of cells the protoplasmic contents including the nucleus (sarcoplasm) fill the space away from the hypodermal wall, in the circomyarian cell the principle mass of sarcoplasm occupies the central portion of the cell. The first two cell types occur primarily in the somatic musculature whereas the circomyarian is found mostly in the specialized (vaginal, spicular, etc.) muscles of nematodes. As might be expected the detailed structure, position and form of the fibers vary among the different species.

Ultrastructure studies indicate that each fiber is made up of a series of contractile elements, each of which contains five bands; thick elements in a relatively wide band, flanked mixed bands of thick and thin filaments in turn flanked by bands of thin filaments. Each unit of the contractile element is separated from the next in the sequence by a composite zone reported to consist of vesicles, and fibrous materials, embedded in a sarcoplasmic reticulum. In higher organisms there are two basic muscle types: smooth and striated. Nematode muscle is like neither, but has mixed characteristics; in some nematodes muscle is reported to be very similar to that in crayfish.

Although muscle cells are aligned along the bundle in such a way that the long axis of the cell has a principle component parallel to the axis of the nematode, it is seldom completely parallel. When the cell axis is parallel to the body axis, the sequence of cells in the bundle is

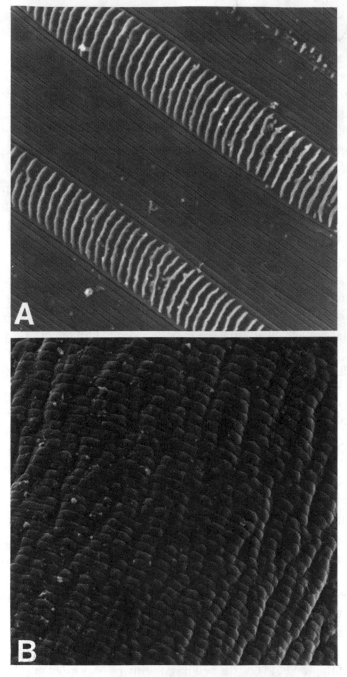

Figure 5.3. Mid-body cuticular surface patterns of filarid animal parasitic nematodes, are also used for identification purposes. A. *Dipetalonema* sp. (monkey). B. *Dirofilaria immitis* (dog). C. *Dirofilaria magnilarvatum* (macaques). D. *Dirofilaria repens* (raccoon). Micrographs reproduced with permission from M. M. Wong, Parasitologist, School of Veterinary Medicine, University of California, Davis.

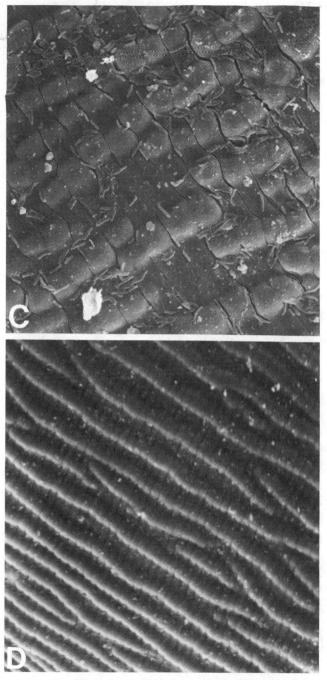

Figure 5.3

oblique to the body axis. The oblique nature of the cell sequence describes a spiral arrangement about the body. Superposing this macro arrangement over the micro arrangement of contractile elements in muscle fibers also manifesting dual opposing spiral characteristics (Fig. 5.4), confirms the premise that the resultant lines of force are oblique to the axis of the body and under neural control can provide the full range of bending, turning, and curling movements which nematodes accomplish in a smooth and fluid manner. There has yet to be noted a musculature manifestation which would explain the prefer-

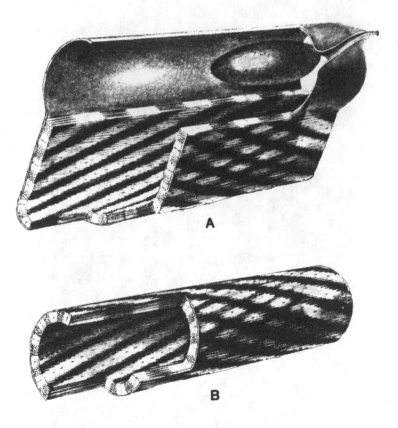

Figure 5.4. A schematic representation of nematode muscle cells, indicating the position and orientation of the fiber bundles. A. Coelomyarian. B. Circomyarian. Note the oblique orientation of the dense contractal elements and the opposing spirals generated. After Hope with permission from Proc. Helm. Soc. Wash.

ential ventral curling observed in nematodes.

There are exceptions to the musculature pattern described above. In *Criconemella,* e.g., (Fig. 3.1D), the muscle fibers are oblique, but the pattern is arranged differently, to allow movement and displacement in an earthworm fashion. Yet a different pattern occurs in *Draconema* (Fig. 3.1E), which together with its posterior positioned tubiform setae allow it to move forward in inchworm fashion. Undoubtedly other exceptions will eventually be found. It is painfully apparent that our knowledge of musculature structure is fuzzy at best, while the understanding of muscle function is non-existent. Perhaps additional studies at the ultrastructural level for a variety of nematodes, aided by electrophysiological studies of muscle resting and action potentials, will be more enlightening.

Alimentary System

The alimentary system in animals, including nematodes, commonly serves as a primary means by which the organism takes in food stuffs, processes the material to derive simpler components that can be absorbed to provide energy and the building blocks for growth, and to eliminate waste products. The alimentary canal of nematodes, by virtue of differences in morphology, function and tissue origin, consists of essentially three principal parts: the foregut (stomodeum) begins with the oral opening followed by the buccal cavity, the esophagus and ending with the esophageal-intestinal valve; the mid-gut or intestine (mesenteron), beginning at the esophageal-intestinal junction and ending at the intestinal-rectal valve; and the hindgut (proctodeum) beginning at the intestinal-rectal valve and ending with the anal, or cloacal, opening. Near the external openings both the foregut and the hindgut are lined with externally derived (ectodermal) cuticle. Near the intestine the lining is different, probably of mixed ectodermal-mesodermal origin. Ectoderm, mesoderm, and endoderm are types of embryological tissue. The stomodeum (foregut) is of mixed ectodermal and mesodermal origin, the mesenteron (intestine) derives from endodermal tissue, while the proctodeum (rectum) is mostly ectodermal in origin.

The oral opening is surrounded by structures called lips which are not part of the alimentary system, but of the outer integument (cuticle).

The normal form consists of six lobes (Fig. 4.2A) but have been modified in different species into unusual shapes, e.g., H-like pattern of *Meloidogyne* (rootknot) larvae (Fig. 5.5) or the probolae of *Acrobeles* (Fig. 3.3E) and like structures of *Crossocephalus* (Fig. 3.3B). The oral opening (mouth) serves as a food intake orifice for most species, but in the case of plant-parasitic nematodes and some fungal feeding nematodes, it serves as an exit opening for the stylet (an extendable feeding organ). The oral openings are of many shapes and sizes from small circles (Fig. 5.5; 5.6, A, D) to large circular forms (Fig. 5.6, B; 5.7, A), slit shaped (Fig. 5.7, B, C, D; 5.8) and the cavernous opening of *Selachinema* (Fig. 3.3A).

The buccal cavity (stoma) lies immediately behind the oral opening and takes on a variety of cylindrical or cup shapes depending upon the species. It may be essentially nonexistent in some forms, or large cavities in others. Stomas of similar size and shape may appear in widely diverse taxonomic groups, indicating that this structure arose independently during evolutionary development. This is supported by the observation that the stoma of one species may be largely of ectodermal origin and another of mesodermal origin. Furthermore it is common to find like stomas in unrelated nematode species and unlike stomas in related species. The size and shape of the stoma, together with the various modifications of the cuticular lining known as "stomatal armature," are associated with types of feeding. Whether modification resulted from an abrupt mutation, or whether it evolved slowly, is just another argument in the polemics regarding evolution.

The stomatic armature consists of modifications of the stomatal cuticular lining in the form of teeth. The stoma is called "dentate" if teeth are large, but "denticulate" if teeth are numerous and small. Large teeth that are moveable are called mandibles. Teeth function differently in different species. For example, in the predaceous nematode genus *Mononchus* (Fig. 4.1) the rigid tooth points forward and is allegedly used to rip open incoming prey. However, in the case of hookworm, *Ancylostoma* sp. (Fig. 5.7A), the teeth point inwards to help hold the intestinal mucous plug from which the parasite extracts blood. Some stomas have teeth on small plates, (e.g., animal parasites) as if they were used for grinding purposes (unproven). The stoma of most nematodes, however, is smooth and without armature.

A few species have mandibles, or moveable teeth, illustrated by *Selachinema* (Fig. 3.3A). A totally different moveable structure, believed to have derived from a tooth, moveable or otherwise, is found in all plant-parasitic nematodes and in some fungal feeders. These structures exist in two forms. The more common form is the stylet, a pointed tube whose base has knobs (usually three) of varying size, attached to muscles that extend or retract the stylet through the oral opening. Stylets vary in size and form, and function like medical syringes. The base of the stylet is connected to the esophagus by a tube to provide a conduit to the rest of the alimentary canal (Fig. 3.1B, D, Fig. 3.2B, Fig. 3.3G).

A second form, found in the Trichodorid group of plant-parasitic nematodes, is similar in outward appearance but is instead a pointed rod. It is not hollow, but has an axial groove to conduct incoming fluids to the tube connecting the feeding apparatus to the rest of the canal (Fig. 3.3F). This structure is usually called a "spear" because of its solid nature. Since the tapered point of the solid spear is used primarily to provide an opening in the cell wall, the nematode generates a small feeding tube by hardening saliva between its oral opening and the cell wall through which the spear can extend to unblock the tube if necessary, and to withdraw cytoplasmic contents. Although "spear" and "stylet" are often used interchangeably, "stylet" is preferred for the hollow device, and "spear" for the solid rod.

Next in the sequence of the alimentary system is the esophagus, heavily muscularized in part or in entirety. The nematode esophagus consists essentially of four tissues, viz., nervous, epidermal, glandular, and muscle tissue; the latter component usually makes up the bulk of the mass.

The form of the esophagus is an important characteristic for identification purposes, but has little value for indicating phylogenetic relationships. It is therefore convenient to distinguish types of esophagi: the one-part esophagus has a uniform diameter, whether thick or thin, throughout its length; the two-part esophagus has a change in diameter, namely one part is thinner, the second part is thicker; the three-part esophagus signifies two changes in diameter throughout its

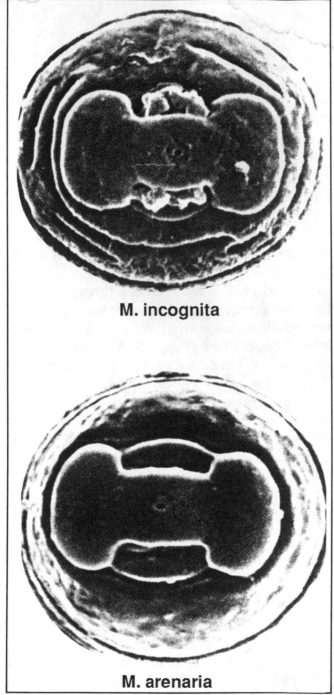

M. incognita

M. arenaria

Figure 5.5. Scanning electron microscope representations of face views of second-stage larvae (juveniles) of four plant-parasitic rootknot nematode species (*Meloidogyne* sp.) indicating modification of lips from the basic pattern and the small oral opening. After Sasser, North Carolina State University, with his permission.

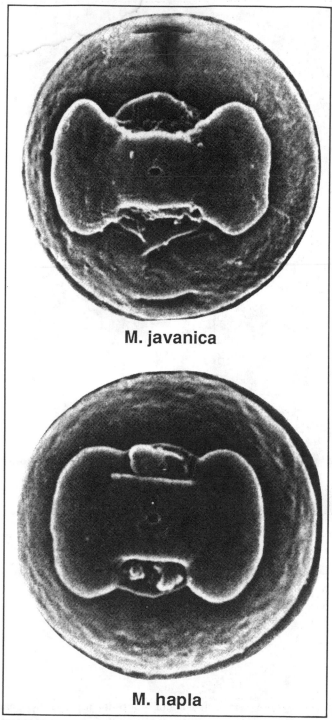

M. javanica

M. hapla

Figure 5.5

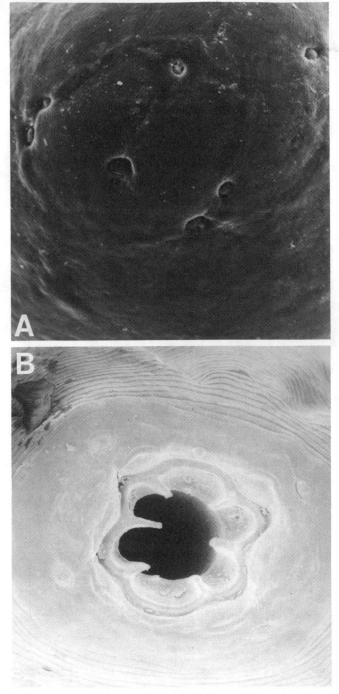

Figure 5.6. Face views of several different animal-parasitic nematodes exhibiting various sizes and forms of oral openings, cuticular patterns, and sensory structures. A. *Dirofilaria repens* (raccoon). B. *Streptopherigus* sp. (monkey). C. *Trichostrongylus* sp. D. *Dirofilaria corynodes* (monkey). Micrographs from M. M. Wong, Parasitologist, School of Veterinary Medicine, University of California, Davis, with her permission.

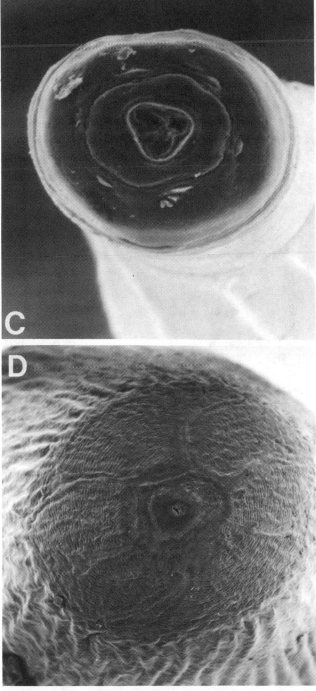

Figure 5.6

56

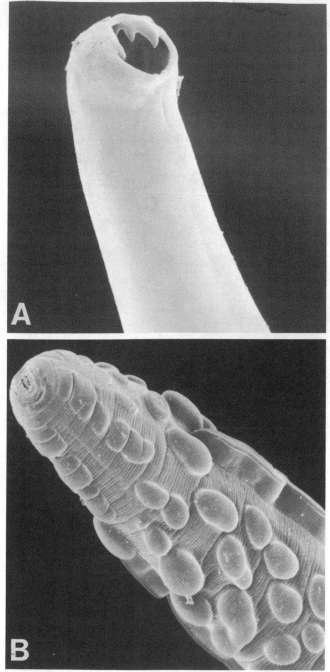

Figure 5.7. Scanning electron micrographs of the extreme anterior region of several animal-parasitic nematodes. A. *Ancylostoma caninum* (dog). B. *Gongylonema* sp. (monkey). C. *Rictuleria* sp. (monkey) D. *Lagochilascaris* sp. (humans). Micrographs courtesy of M. M. Wong, Parasitologist, School of Veterinary Medicine, University of California, Davis, with her permission.

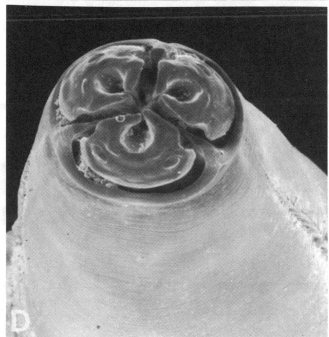

Figure 5.7

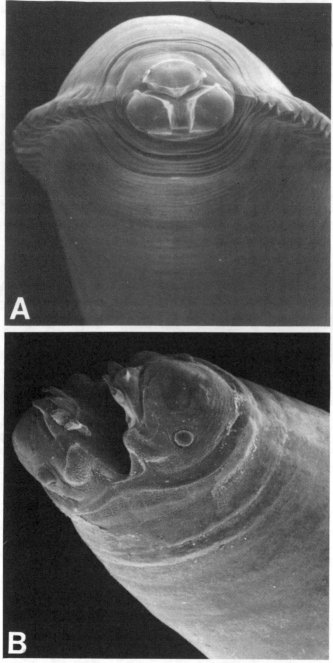

Figure 5.8. Scanning electron microscope views of the extreme anterior ends of several animal parasitic nematodes. A. *Toxocara canis* (dog). B. *Physaloptera* sp. (monkey). C. *Oesophagostomum* sp. (monkey, man). D. *Trypanoxyuris* sp. (monkey). Illustrations courtesy of M. M. Wong, Parasitologist, School of Veterinary Medicine, University of California, Davis, with her permission.

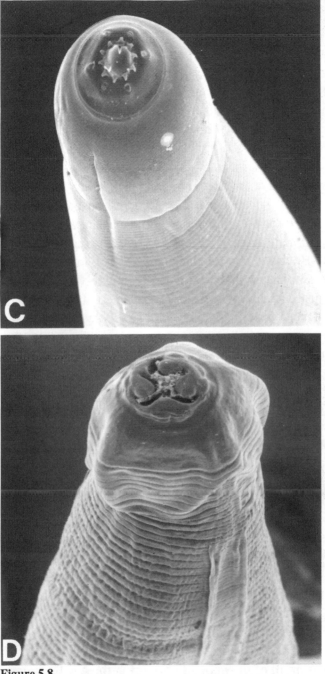

Figure 5.8

length, whether there are two thin parts and one thick, or two thick parts and one thin. In some nematodes the mid-esophagus thickening, as for example in stylet-bearing species takes the form of a bulb and is called the median bulb. Also, in stylet-bearing nematodes and some free-living forms, a thickening at the base of the esophagus near the intestine takes the form of a bulb and is called the posterior bulb (Fig. 5.9).

Cross-sectional diagrams of the esophagus musculature are often drawn to represent a radial fiber arrangement in which the muscles are attached to the lumen wall at one end and the esophageal outer surface at the other. Electron micrographs do show substantial tissue thickening that would be necessary for a strong muscle connection with the lumen wall. However, similar thickenings do not appear on the outer wall of the esophagus; therefore it seems unlikely the muscles are radial, i.e., perpendicular to the axis of the lumen. It would seem that obliquely directed muscles would be more likely to satisfy the laws of Newtonian physics regarding force and reaction.

There is little question that the esophagus or its bulbar portions serve as a pumping organ. It provides the motive force for taking in nutrients through the oral opening and moving them through the esophagus into the intestine and eventually causing the waste products to be eliminated through the anus. One-way valves in the median bulb or the esophageal-intestinal junction maintain the unidirectional flow and prevent regurgitation.

Various forms and shapes of esophagi are illustrated in Fig. 5.9 for animal parasites (top row), free-living forms (middle row), and plant-parasitic species (bottom row). Also illustrated are glands associated with the esophagi and the ducts through which they secrete their products at various points in the esophageal lumen. So-called digestive glands are situated posteriorly, either within the esophageal tissue or external to it. Usually there are three: one larger dorsal gland and two subventrals. In some nematode groups there are four subventral glands. In other nematodes, for example the animal parasite *Agamermis* (Fig. 5.9), there is a series of glands all along the esophagus.

The ducts of all of the normally occurring three cells may empty into the esophageal lumen close to each other. Often, though, the dorsal gland secretes forward of the other two and sometimes far forward into

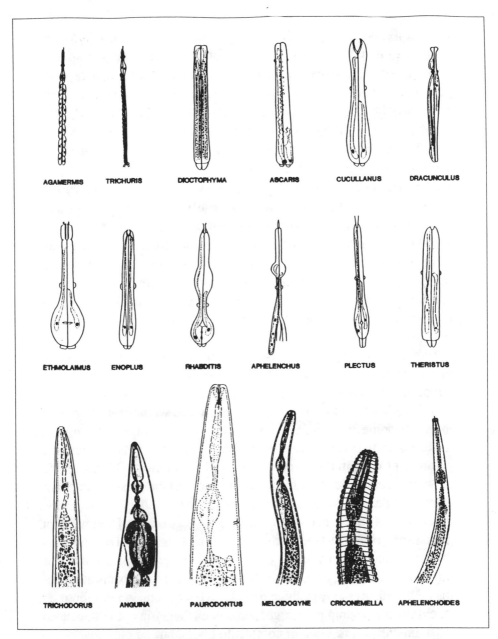

Figure 5.9. Schematic representations of diverse forms and shapes of esophagi occurring in nematodes. The top row illustrates diversity in esophagi of animal-parasitic nematodes; the middle row illustrates the diversity of esophagi in free-living forms; the bottom row illustrates the diversity of esophagi in plant-parasitic nematodes. Adapted and redrawn from Chitwood and various other sources.

the region of the stoma. This observation has lead to the belief that the dorsal gland has a somewhat different function than that of the subventral glands; its secretions can move forward, at least in the case of plant-parasitic nematodes, into the plant cell to initiate a kind of extra-intestinal digestion, making the contents more suitable for extraction via the stylet. The subventral glands, on the other hand, secreting into the esophageal lumen just ahead of the esophageal-intestinal junction, have their secretions swept into the intestine to aid digestion. This explanation of glandular function appears reasonable. Nevertheless, it should be emphasized that there is as yet no clear evidence that this is their function or what the nature of their secretions might be.

With the basic structural components of the esophagus having been discussed, there remains one additional component which activates and coordinates its function, namely the nervous system. Neuron fibers emerge from the major nervous system ganglion (circumesophageal-commissure, or nerve ring) and extend forward with the papillary nerve bundle, to eventually emerge and enter the esophagus. They form a network with three major trunks and a series of commissures interconnecting the various sectors. The network is believed to consist of motor, neurosecretory, sensory and connector neurons.

The intestine (midgut, mesenteron) is a tube whose wall is one cell thick. In some small nematodes the intestinal wall circumference is made up of two cells. However, larger nematodes have increased numbers of cells in the intestinal wall circumference. Of course, the longer the nematode, the longer the intestine, and the greater number of cells to make up the whole tube. The lumen wall of the intestine exhibits a layer of microvilli (minute finger-like projections) that provide additional surface for the absorption of nutritional components from the intestinal chyme. Casual examination suggests that the intestine is the same throughout; however, cytological examination of the cells indicates at least three regions. This conclusion is supported by cytological staining. In larger nematodes there may be collagenous amendments or a network of contractile fibers, but no muscles.

It has been said that the anterior portions of the intestine are secretory of digestive juices and the posterior portion absorbative. While this may be true in higher animals, there is no evidence for this process in nematodes. Digestion and absorption obviously occur in the intestine. However, the mechanisms by which proteins, polysaccharides, and lipids are degraded into soluble absorbable components, and the sources and the nature of the various digestive ferments, have not been established. The situation may not be the same for all nematodes. Those nematodes which live in a medium rich in amino acids, sugars, and other metabolic substrates (for example intestinal animal-parasitic nematodes) may absorb these components directly without any need for degradative digestion.

The hindgut (proctodeum) begins at the junction of the rectum and the intestine, at which there is a sphincter muscle and a one-way valve. As previously mentioned, the rectum is lined with cuticle, which in the female is simply a tube leading to the anus. In the male, the rectum is usually replaced by a cloaca, into which not only the intestinal contents pass, but also the contents of the reproductive system. The cloaca has also a dorsal wall pouch which houses the spicules (secondary male sex organs) in the retracted position. The anus is a slit like structure under muscular control which serves as the external opening of the rectum. By contraction of the anal muscles and relaxing the intestinal rectal sphincter, fecal material is expelled by the higher internal intestinal pressure pushing the waste contents out.

In some nematodes there are rectal glands, usually three, which duct into the rectum. Their function is unknown. In the female rootknot nematode (*Meloidogyne* spp.) rectal glands produce a gel matrix into which eggs are laid and expelled to the outside to form a so-called egg mass. Interestingly these females no longer have a functional anus; the connection to the intestine is atrophied. Inasmuch as the female is pyriform, a student once asked: "… is this the reason she is so swollen?" A good question, however, that effect is negligible; the swelling is more likely to be the result of maturation, particularly the massive enlargement of ovaries and the prolific production of eggs.

This is not the only case of proctodeum modification. The insect parasitic *Mermithidae* have no rectum, and the intestine terminates in a large sack which is reported allegedly to be a food storage organ. Apparently in nematodes the alimentary system may be nonfunctional at either end depending upon the stage of the nematode (for example, the proctodeum as described above for *Meloidogyne* or citrus nematode females, and the stomodeum for the intermediate larval stages of the same *Meloidogyne* sp., which molt quickly without feeding.

Nervous System

The living nematode must perceive the environment with its sensory organs (Chapter 3), and make the appropriate response by activating the systems already described and others to be discussed. Moreover it must not only activate, but coordinate a sequence of events, for example, in somatic musculature—so that the animal can move forward or backward, rotate its head region, or execute whatever action sensory information suggests is desirable.

In alimentation, it must detect a suitable food item, then activate and coordinate the muscles and valves of the stomodeum to take in the food and propel it through the intestine, and eventually activate the rectal sphincter and anal muscles to eliminate the waste. A similar kind of protocol must exist to control the reproductive system and the excretory system. As sensory receptors sample the external environment, and internal proprioceptors monitor internal conditions, information is conveyed via electrical impulses through the nerve fibers.

A nervous system network is schematically illustrated in a simplified form (Fig. 5.10). The greatest center of complexity is probably in the anterior region, with lesser centers located in the vulval, spicular and anal regions. The many minor ganglia distributed throughout the body are usually associated with nerve junctions (for example, a longitudinal nerve is joined by a nerve linking commissure, a sensory structure or other organ). Small ganglia consist of a small number of neural cells. The largest neural cell concentration involves the nematode's major ganglia complex immediately anterior and posterior to the circumesophageal commissure (nerve ring). This appears to serve as a primary communication link between the major ganglia, and the cephalic (towards the head) and main body trunk nerves. It is evident that the nomenclature derives from nerve tissue position and connection, rather than function.

Although the central nervous system connects via specialized nerve bundles to a major set of sensory receptors (e.g., cephalic

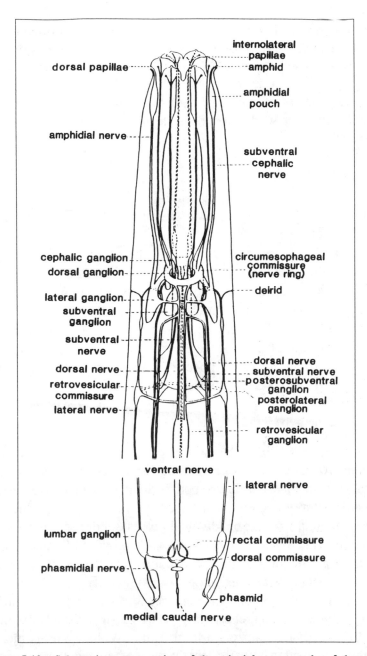

Figure 5.10. Schematic representation of the principle nerve paths of the central nervous system, typical of nematodes; top—diagram of the anterior portion of the nematode in the region of the circumesophageal commissure (nerve ring); bottom—diagram of the tail region. Redrawn and adapted from Chitwood.

papillae, amphids, genital papillae, and several other structures) there is, in some nematodes, an additional peripheral net that connects to the remaining setae and papillae of the body (Fig. 5.11). The net reticulations are more dense in the cephalic region (Fig. 5.11A) and in the genital region to accommodate the greater number of papillae in these regions. But the network is less dense at mid-body (Fig. 5.11B) where fewer papillae and setae are found. While the longitudinal nerve trunks of the central nervous system run in the hypodermal chords (Fig. 4.2B, C), information collected from the setae and papillae by the peripheral nerve net are conveyed to the central nervous system via neural connections. The peripheral nerve net appears to be exterior to the central nervous system network.

To stain the peripheral nerve net, it is necessary to ex-osmose the nematode before placing it in a dilute silver solution; the live nematode with functioning membranes takes up the silver solution carrying the silver ions deeper into the cuticle than is possible otherwise. If a nematode so stained is opened longitudinally by surgical incision, laid flat on a surface and the nematode internal contents (muscles, hypodermal chords, and most of the hypodermis) scraped away, the reticulated network of the peripheral system is very clear. It appears, therefore, that in marine *Deontostoma* species, the peripheral nerve net is situated external to the hypodermal layer, perhaps in the endocuticle.

Female Reproductive System

The greatest majority of nematode species exhibit sexual dimorphism; they are dioecious in that both male and female individuals are required. However, there are a lesser number of species which are hermaphroditic, where one individual produces both eggs and sperm, either at the same time, or else the sperm is produced first and stored while the gonad shifts to egg production. Other species reproduce parthenogenetically, an asexual process not involving fertilization by sperm. While in some vermiform species the male tends to be smaller than the female (in one species a tiny male lives in the female's uterus), size differences are not necessarily the rule. While the proportion of males in a population is usually less than that of females, there are many exceptions. It is not uncommon to find abnormal individuals (usually

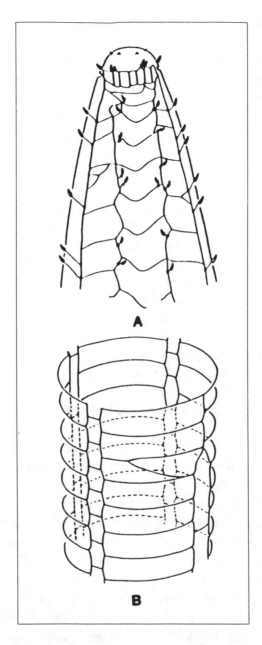

Figure 5.11. Schematic representation of the peripheral nerve net of some nematodes. A. Diagram of the extreme anterior region showing connections to setae; B. The network pattern somewhat posterior to A. Redrawn and adapted from Croll and Maggenti.

females) which are intersexes, exhibiting both female and male characteristics. In such individuals the female reproductive system is functional, despite the presence of male spicules in the tail region. It
remains a mystery why hermaphroditic species, for example
Caenorhabditis elegans (used widely for basic studies in embryology,
genetics, and development) maintain a low proportion of functional
males, as do some parthenogenetic species, such as the plant-parasitic
rootknot nematode *Meloidogyne* spp. It is difficult to accept the notion
that the males in these species serve no useful purpose, and are present
only as a caprice of nature.

The basic morphological sequence of the female gonad in dioecious species is thus: ovary, oviduct, spermatheca (the receptacle
storing spermatozoa), uterus and vagina (Fig. 5.12). In this illustration
the ovarial tip is reflexed (folded back upon itself). The cap cell, the
primordial germ cell, retains its tip position but divides continuously,
sending daughter cells backward to continue development and growth.
Eventually the mature ovum proceeds down the oviduct past the
spermatheca and in the process is fertilized by sperm, then on to the
uterus for further development and additional covering of the egg
membrane before being expelled through the vagina and out the vulva.

In several species the typical ovary is modified so that there are
several germinal centers along one or both sides; the developing ova
somewhat resemble berries on a stem. While the basic arrangement of
features in gonads remains the same, the form and shape can vary
greatly in different species. Although eight characteristic forms are
illustrated (Fig. 5.13 top row), there are many species in which the
female gonad takes on a form that appears to be a blend of two or more
of the types illustrated. In some species there is one ovary (Fig. 5.13F)
but generally there are two, which may be extended and straight (Fig.
5.13B, C), or reflexed (Fig. 5.13A), or spiral shaped (Fig. 5.13D). The
ovaries may extend in two directions, forward and backward, (Fig.
5.13B, C) or in the same direction (Fig. 5.13G, H).

Multiple ovaries exist in certain species (Fig. 5.13E). In fact the
largest nematode known, *Placentonema gigantissima* from the
placenta of the sperm whale, has 32 ovaries, each of which can produce several million eggs.

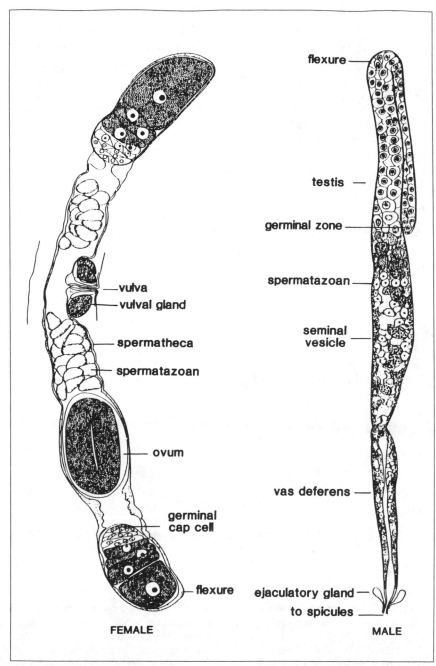

Figure 5.12. Schematic illustration of simple female and male reproductive systems of nematodes indicating the principle component parts. The female reproductive system is that of *Halichoanolaimus robustus*; the male reproductive system is that of *Rhabditis lambdiensis*. Illustrations are adapted and redrawn from Chitwood.

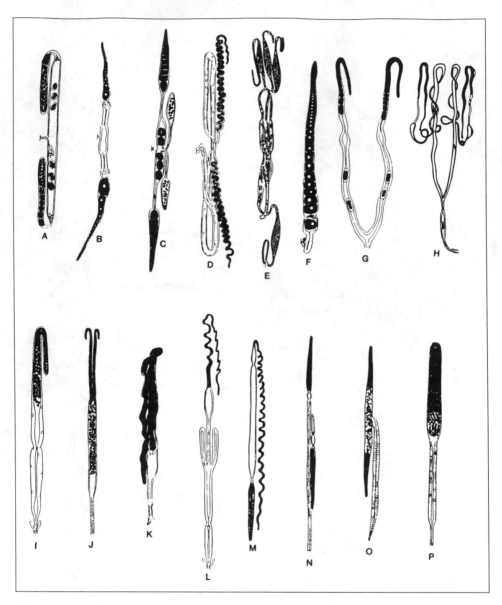

Figure 5.13. Schematic representation illustrating the diversity of female reproductive systems in nematodes. A. *Rhabditis strongyloides;* B. *Tylenchorhynchus dubius;* C. *Sabatieria hilarula;* D. *Chromadora* species; E. *Tanqua tiara;* F. *Theristus sentiens;* G. *Meloidogyne hapla;* H. *Hedruris armata.* The diversity in male reproductive systems is illustrated in the bottom row. I. *Rhabditis lambdiensis;* J. *Meloidogyne hapla;* K. *Cucullanus heterochorus;* L. *Heterakis gallinarum;* M. *Trichuris suis;* N. *Agamermis decaudata;* O. *Desmolaimus zeelandicus;* P. *Chromadora quatri-linea.* Adapted and redrawn from Chitwood.

The oviduct may be a simple tube, or in some cases may be lined with special cells to secrete an additional covering for the egg membrane, or be covered externally with a thin muscle layer. In some species, the oviduct may form a seminal receptacle near the junction with the uterus to store spermatozoa.

The next structure encountered by the egg on its journey to the outside is the uterus. It is more heavily muscularized and innervated as a means of controlling peristaltic movements to move the egg along. In most species the egg membrane is covered by additional layers secreted by cells lining the uterus. Also, in most species, the uterus forms pouches of varying sizes and forms, which serve as seminal receptacles (spermatheca, as indicated in Fig. 5.13A, B, C). The vagina is a short, heavily muscularized tube connecting the uterus to the vulval opening and, being derived from ectodermal tissue, is cuticularly lined. The vulva has a special set of muscles to open and close the vulval slit allowing the egg access to the outside.

Male Reproductive System

The function of the female gonad is to produce ova, which may or may not require fertilization to become eggs that subsequently embryonate and develop to become new adults. The function of the male gonad is to produce spermatozoa, and store them in the seminal vesicle for subsequent delivery into the female vagina, then be stored in the female spermatheca. From there sperm are released as needed to fertilize the passing ova. The male gonad is simplistically illustrated in Fig. 5.12.

The testis tip does not have a germinal cap cell, but rather a germinal zone of several cells, which divide to produce daughter cells. The daughter cells move backward into the gonad for eventual storage in the seminal vesicle as spermatozoa. In times of need, the spermatozoa move down the vas deferens to join the contents of the ejaculatory gland in the cloaca and eventually to the outside of the male body. The male gonads can assume various sizes, forms, and shapes (as do female gonads). Illustrations indicate some of the typical characteristic arrangements (Fig. 5.13 I–P). The testis may be straight (Fig. 5.13 P), single and reflexed (Fig. 5.13 I), single, long, reflexed, thick and twisted (Fig. 5.13 K), thin, reflexed, short, and spiral (Fig. 5.13 L), or reflexed, long and spiral (5.13 M). Some males (usually Adenophorean) have two testes, one extended straight forward (anteriorly) and the other straight backwards (posteriorly) (Fig. 5.13 O); and similarly but connected differently to the vas deferens (Fig. 5.13 N). Some species' males have two testes forwardly directed, but reflexed near the tip (Fig. 5.13 J).

What drives the spermatozoa out of the seminal vesicle down the vas deferens at times of copulation is a mystery; what contribution is made by the internal pressure or muscles, if any, is a matter of speculation. The ejaculatory duct of males of some species is heavily muscularized, but in most others it is thinly muscularized.

As already mentioned the males have a cloaca, an elaborate pouch which can receive products from the intestine or the gonad, depending upon which controlling sphincter muscles are open. The cloaca also has a specialized dorsal pouch which houses the male copulatory organs, the spicules, in the retracted position. Structurally, the spicule is essentially a curved, pointed rod with a cytoplasmic core in which there is a nerve process. The spicules are believed to function as a means for clasping the female tightly while maintaining an open pathway from the male cloaca to the female vagina for sperm transport. A recent morphological study, however, of males of a nematode parasite of birds reports spicules containing a duct connecting the vas deferens to the outside, consequently bypassing the usual cloacal pathway.

Normally spicules are paired and of equal length (Fig. 3.4G). In some animal-parasitic males, however, they have varied shapes and lengths, as in some bird parasites in which one spicule is conventional and short, and the other one spiral and very long. There is great diversity in the male copulatory structures across the spectrum of the phylum. In some species males have no spicules, while in others they have one, but generally there are two. In some species, the male spicules are connected by a band of tissue so they resemble blades, while others have extendable sheathes (Fig. 5.14). Spicules can vary from thick and short to long and slender, but all invariably exhibit curvature that can vary from a mild crescent to a near fishhook form, depending upon the species.

Excretory System

The alleged excretory system in nematodes, as currently perceived, is poorly understood. An organized excretory system is not of universal occurrence in nematodes, but when it exists the venting pore is usually situated ventrally forward from mid-body, sometimes approaching the head region. It is termed an excretory system largely because of its structural similarity to systems of known excretory function in higher animals; there is no convincing evidence of a release of excretory products to the outside. Nevertheless, the excretory system, as a structural feature, exists in a diversity of nematodes, but not in all nematodes. The organized excretory system, when it occurs, exists in a wide range of forms (Fig. 5.15).

Although a number of nematodes exhibit no evidence of a system, others have a one cell system with a body and a duct to the exit pore located in the cervical region of the nematode (renette cell, Fig. 5.15H); some nematodes have two such cells, sharing a common duct. The structural complexity increases from the single cell to incorporate a single posteriorly directed tube (Fig. 5.15G). In other nematodes, a longer tube extends posteriorly while a shorter tube extends anteriorly (Fig. 5.15C). In the more complex structures there are two tubes, that is there are two cunnicular regions connected to a common duct in the cell body region thereby resembling a backward pointing tuning fork "in which the duct represents the handle" (Fig. 5.15F). In more complex systems, the cunnicular regions assume a modified H form (Fig. 5.15A, B, D, E). The cunnicular extensions are joined in the cell body region where the duct to the outside initiates.

The different forms are distinguished primarily by the position of the cell bodies and the duct entrance. Conventional wisdom believes that these structures are generated by one, two, or three cells, although several reports indicate that in some instances the tubes may be polycellular. The bi-cunnicular regions are arranged symmetrically in the lateral regions of the nematode, whereas the single tube type is asymmetric and situated along one lateral region. Furthermore, the tube lumens are believed to be cuticularly lined. There remains much mystery surrounding these systems. For example, how do one or two cells generate one or two tubes that extend most of the length of the

74

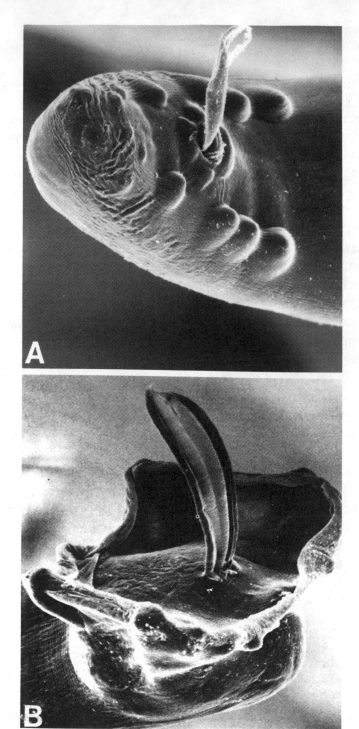

Figure 5.14. Scanning electron microscope views of spicules, copulatory bursa, and other ornamentation of the tail of several animal parasitic nematodes. A. *Dirofilaria immitis* (dog); B. *Angiostrongylus costaricensis* (rat). C. *Oesophagostomum* sp. D. *Trichuris trichiura*. Micrographs from M. M. Wong, Parasitologist, School of Veterinary Medicine, University of California, Davis, with her permission.

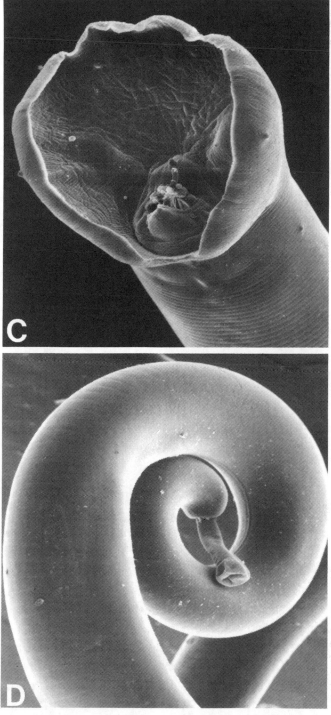

Figure 5.14

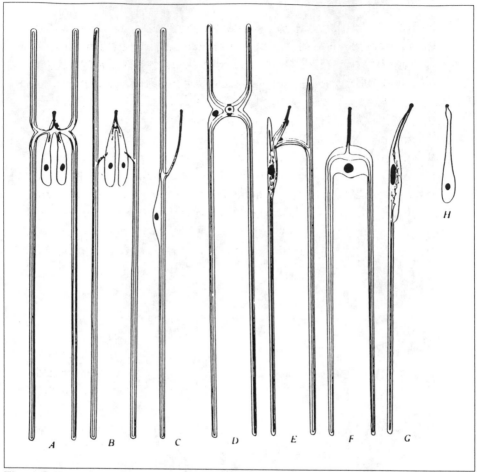

Figure 5.15. Schematic representations illustrating the diversity in excretory systems of nematodes. A. *Rhabditis* sp.; B. *Oesophagostomum* sp.; C. *Tylenchus* sp.; D. *Oxyuris* sp.; E. *Ascaris* sp.; F. *Cephalobus* sp.; G. *Aniskis* sp.' H. *Chromadorid* and *Enoplid* sp. Adapted and redrawn from Chitwood.

body, and then line the tube lumens with cuticle? The elimination of excretory products and waste is not in question, for carbon dioxide, ammonia, amines, amino acids, organic acids, peptides, and other wastes, have been identified in bathing solutions; it is the release route which is uncertain. Other important questions need clarification: how do nematodes without an organized excretory system release their excretory products? How efficient can a single cell in the neck region be in eliminating excretory products originating at long distances from the cell? Or for that matter, by what mechanisms does a cunnicular region along one side of the body preferentially separate metabolic substrates from waste products to be collected and eliminated? And is the excretory system involved in the molting process, as some reports suggest, or does it serve as a means of osmotic regulation, as others propose?

Even more nebulous is the role of glands with exit pores to the external environment. Caudal, rectal, and genital glands, as well as hypodermal glands, and even amphids, which are assumed to be primarily sensory in nature, have been observed to exude some substances. Does this exudation of substances serve a part in excretory function, as some reports suggest, or is it simply an incidental aspect of some other function? Clearly our understanding of excretion and the excretory system has need of much improvement.

Organ Systems Absent in Nematodes

Circulatory system

An organized circulatory system does not exist in nematodes. Heart, blood vessels, and blood fluid are absent. Gases, organic and inorganic solutes, and water move through tissues principally by diffusion . This is aided by some mixing action of the fluids in the body cavity and the chyme in the intestine as a consequence of body movements and other muscular activity. Although the body cavity extends nearly the length of the animal, it docs not constitute a cavernous space, but a very limited volume filled with viscous fluid that bathes the tissues and lubricates the movement of internal structures. As such, any mixing action is unlikely to be efficient in terms of taking up a solute at one point and transferring it elsewhere, especially to remote body regions.

Respiratory system

The respiratory system in the traditional sense, consists primarily of an organ with the express property of creating an enormous surface area to facilitate the transfer of oxygen in air to the body fluids on the other side of the surface, while at the same time allowing the reverse process to operate for carbon dioxide. Nematodes have no such respiratory system, although the majority of nematodes are aerobic (requiring molecular oxygen from air). There are reports in the literature of "oxygen gulping nematodes" that swallow small bubbles of air for passage through the gut; however, this is usually not the case in nematodes.

Any nematologist beginning to work with plant parasitic, free-living, soilborne, or animal-parasitic forms of nematodes quickly learns to provide adequate aeration for the maintenance of a highly active population. Although aerobic nematodes require oxygen for normal activity, they are able to survive relatively short periods in the absence of oxygen; some expire within a day, others can survive for weeks. Without a special apparatus, the oxygen-requiring tissues of the nematode must receive their oxygen from the environmental atmosphere by a process of diffusion, driven by the higher partial pressure of oxygen in the environment to the lower partial pressure within the nematode. Diffusion can therefore be described by an equation:

$$V = -AD \frac{dp}{ds}$$

Where V = volume of gas diffusing in cm^3/hr, A = the area of surface through which the diffusion takes place, D = the diffusion constant, dp = the pressure difference between two regions separated by a short distance (ds). If the vermiform nematode, in the first approximation, is assumed to be a cylinder, and a small m equals the oxygen consumption in cm^3/cm^3 of tissue per hour, and P_0 is equal to the partial pressure of oxygen at the outer surface, then it is possible to derive an equation for the maximum radius of the cylinder.

$$r_{max} \leq \frac{2\sqrt{P_0 D}}{m}$$

By a similar process one can derive an equation for the maximum radius of a pyriform nematode using the approximation that it is spherical, as is the case with some plant parasitic forms. In such a case:

$$r_{max} \leq \frac{\sqrt{6 D P_0}}{m}$$

Now, if one assumes that m equals 0.1 cm^3 of O_2/cm^3 tissue hour, as is the case with many animals including nematodes and tapeworms and $P_0 = 0.2$ atmospheres as is the case in a medium in equilibrium with air, and $D = 8 \times 10^{-4}$ cm^2/atm. h, using the approximation of the value from frog muscle as being equal to nematode tissue, then the maximum radius of a vermiform nematode is about 800 micrometers and that for a spherical shape female is about 1,000 micrometers (1 millimeter).

Despite the crude assumptions made to derive the formulas and to approximate the variables, in most vermiform nematodes the radius of the body falls well within one to two percent of the maximum allowable predicted radius. Similarly with pyriform nematodes, the radius is usually less than half of the maximum allowable calculated radius. The diffusion process, therefore, appears to provide an adequate supply of oxygen to meet the nematode requirements.

In nature there are habitats in which nematodes abound, but where oxygen is virtually non-existent and so constitute anaerobic environments. Aerobic nematodes can derive their energy requirements efficiently by metabolic processes that degrade carbohydrates to carbon dioxide and water, and nitrogen-containing substrates to carbon dioxide and ammonia by utilizing oxygen. However, anaerobic nematodes must derive their energy from anaerobic processes without employing oxygen. The anaerobic process produces less energy for the animal, and an assortment of organic end products which are mostly organic acids and amines. Anaerobic nematodes can therefore be found in bodies of water or waterlogged soil with extraordinarily high burdens of organic matter that deplete the available oxygen, or in deep ocean trenches where the residual water rarely mixes with the aerated surface water miles above, or in a variety of animal tissues. Though oxygen may be toxic to some anaerobic nematodes, there are a greater number which are facultative; that is, they can either utilize oxygen for the more efficient energy-producing aerobic process, or they can derive energy from the less efficient anaerobic processes if oxygen is unavailable. Animal-parasitic nematodes seem to consist of all types: aerobic forms that can derive oxygen from body fluids, including some of the larger intestinal worms which have special haemoglobins in the body fluid to scrub the oxygen released by the host's blood, and facultative forms which can utilize oxygen only in certain stages as they pass through well-aerated body fluid, but can't when situated elsewhere. Large animal-parasitic forms apparently must use an haemoglobin assist or anaerobic processes, because, even in complete equilibrium with air, diffusion processes are unable to satisfy their oxygen requirements.

Nematodes have been found in mid-ocean ridges and other zones where magma uprising from the interior adds to crustal formation. Of particular interest are those whose habitat is in the immediate vicinity of the so-called "black smokers" which are rising plumes of iron sulfide. The question arises as to whether these nematodes metabolize anaerobically in the normal fashion, or whether they utilize the sulfur compounds from the smokers.

Immune System

There is no known immune system or function in nematodes. Although cell bodies (coelomocytes) can be observed distributed in the body cavity, they appear to have no immune function, as similar bodies found in the insect haemocoel do. No nematode invaded by a microorganism or virus has been shown to recover.

Skeletal System

The rigid skeletal system, as traditionally understood, which occurs internally in vertebrates or externally as in crabs and insects, does not exist in living nematodes (the brittle cysts of cyst-forming nematodes are simply the old body walls of the dead females which have dried and whose body wall phenolic content has polymerized). For movement, animals with skeletons require articulation (body and appendage joints) accomplished by different opposing muscles anchored to the skeleton to move the jointed parts. Animals without rigid skeletons must use different mechanisms. They move by utilizing only tensile forces, the kind that a rope transmits. Since a muscle can only be stimulated to contract, there is need for an opposing muscle or some other mechanism for it to return it to its original resting length or to stretch it longer. The muscle volume remains constant, i.e., a contracted muscle is short and thick, but equal in volume to its long and thin extended form. The muscle is therefore incompressible. This feat is accomplished, since it is in essence a fluid filled organ, by taking advantage of the property of fluid incompressibility at physiological pressures.

In soft-bodied animals with large fluid-filled cavities the incompressibility property is utilized to transmit externally directed forces created by the increased fluid pressure produced by regional contraction of body muscles, but contained and restrained by an elastic body covering. When the muscle stimulation ends, the internally directed force of the stretched body covering restores the muscles and the body to the normal resting position. Movement generated by this type of mechanism has been termed to employ a "hydrostatic skeleton" to substitute for the opposing muscle in rigid skeletal systems. While such a system operates in soft-bodied animals, e.g., polyps, and an assortment of worm-like invertebrate animals, appendages and organs of larger animals utilize a modified system, the "muscular hydrostat."

These structures have no fluid-filled cavities, but are entirely composed of muscle tissues. However, inasmuch as muscle tissues are bathed by cellular fluids the incompressiblity property remains an important component of function. The muscular hydrostat is unique in enabling structures such as elephant trunks, snake and cat tongues, squid tentacles, and octopus arms (cephalopods) among others, to move, twist, bend, rotate, extend and contract smoothly and elegantly. Whereas a "hydrostatic skeleton" utilizes a tough elastic outer covering to maintain a constant volume, the "muscular hydrostat" employs layers of circular, radial and oblique muscle bundles to maintain the constant volume of the organ as it performs its functions.

Nematodes have been long alleged to utilize a hydrostatic skeleton principle to facilitate their movements. It may be, however, that what exists is an intermediate mix involving elements of the "hydrostatic skeleton" and the "muscular hydrostat." Nematodes have a tough elastic cuticle of which the mesocuticle consists of different fiber layers in spiral and counterspiral orientation for radial strength in maintaining a constant volume. The longitudinal muscle bundles are arranged peripherally adjacent to the hypodermal layer in quadrants, separated by the hypodermal chords. Although the muscle bundles are longitudinal the muscle cell arrangement and the muscle fiber striations are oblique, similar to the cephalopod arrangement. In the absence of radial or circular muscles this kind of somatic musculature, peripherally located for maximum leverage, enables the nematode to perform smoothly and elegantly its wide range of body motions, while simultaneously aiding the cuticle in maintaining constant body volume. The internally positioned alimentary and reproductive systems serve a similar function to that of internally positioned muscles of the "muscular hydrostat" as an incompressible medium for force translation throughout the body.

Endocrine System

An organized endocrine system, as traditionally understood for animals with circulatory systems, appears not to occur in nematodes. However, a form of rudimentary endocrine function must exist. There is an assortment of cells, cell bodies, and glands distributed in the nematode whose function is uncertain; some of these may have endocrine function. In many animals, the reproductive system, the gastrointestinal system, and the nerve system are known to exhibit endocrine function. These three systems exist in nematodes, in addition to the hypodermis, which may also have endocrine properties.

Of the reproductive system, one may ask, how does a nematode realize when its gonad (male or female) is ready for reproduction, or receptive to fertilization, and communicate this message to the other sex? How does the female realize its spermatheca is empty and in need of re-filling? In times of stress, when nutrition is reduced, what triggers the response that favors male over female progeny? And, what sex hormones are produced?

Of the gastrointestinal system, one can ask: What triggers feeding, secretion of digestive enzymes, gastric motility, chyme emulsification or replacement of mucosal lining? Are hormones produced that participate in the modification of neuro responses and control growth? Do gut cells in some way produce any insulin-like substances? And, does a gravid female promote greater lipid availability for depot storage by the developing ovum?

Of the nervous system, one may ask, does neuro secretion enhance or retard digestion and reproduction processes? Do nematodes have rest periods (sleep-like episodes), and if so, what triggers them?

Of the hypodermal system, one may ask: what triggers molting? And, what triggers the orderly laying down of different cuticular layers?

It is unlikely that any one system will have exclusive control, but instead will involve the participation of other systems to a greater or less extent. The conservatism of nature would imply that processes widely used in other animals, with modification perhaps, would also occur in nematodes.

Wound Repair Systems

Injury repair mechanisms are unknown in nematodes. Although several reports in the literature have suggested wound repair mechanisms, they are based on one-time observations of events such as a peculiarly stubbed or bent tail conformation, or a thickened body wall structure that conceivably could have arisen as a result of injury repair. In most nematodes excising a tail, for example, or making a modest incision in the body wall, releases a large volume of body contents into the surrounding medium. However, there are marine nematodes in which the body contents, upon removal of the tail, form a plug, so that turgor pressure is retained in the remaining portion of the nematode and enables it to move. How small a puncture a nematode can sustain in a septic environment is unknown. While a number of higher invertebrates and some fish and reptiles are able to shed an injured body part and to regenerate a new one, no nematode is known to have this capability.

*"The goal of Life is living
in agreement with Nature."*

Zeno, 335–263 B.C.

CHAPTER 6

Life Cycles

Molting, in its broad general connotation, is not an unusual event in the animal kingdom; however, its forms can vary greatly. The adult bird "molts" or replaces its feathers yearly, and the reptiles "molt" or shed their skins regularly. Crustaceans, e.g., the crab, molt or shed the hard external body covering to immediately develop a new one. While some insects also molt to shed their exoskeleton, others have modified the process in a major way, whereby there is a general reorganization of internal and external body tissues, a process called metamorphosis. It is through this process that wriggling caterpillars become moths or butterflies.

In general, nematodes, whether free-living forms from marine, freshwater, soil or plant habitats, follow a typical life cycle of six discrete stages: the egg, four juvenile stages, and the adult. Traditionally, the stages between the egg and the adult have been called larval stages and designated as first, second, third, and fourth larval stages. Currently the favored term is "juvenile," inasmuch as this term conforms to entomological nomenclature for organisms which molt but do not undergo metamorphosis.

The basic nematode life cycle (Fig. 6.1) is usually continuous so long as environmental conditions are favorable; on the advent of adversity (lack of moisture, low temperatures) nematode activity slows or stops, but resumes as favorable conditions return. Should adverse conditions persist long enough, the animals would eventually die. In amphimictic species where males and females are required for reproduction, the ovum moving down the oviduct past a spermatheca becomes fertilized. With the fusion of the ovum and the sperm the resulting egg is ready for embryonation. The egg then embryonates into the fully formed first stage larva (juvenile) but remains encased in the original egg shell. The first stage juvenile then molts and develops into the fully formed second stage, also remaining in the original intact egg shell. The fully formed second-stage nematode then perforates the egg shell (hatches), feeds and continues its development, eventually molting into the third stage form. The third stage nematode may or may not feed, but continues its development, eventually molting into the fourth stage. The fourth stage nematode may or may not feed, but continues its development finally molting a fourth time into the fully formed adult. The time required from passage from one life form to the next varies, and life cycle studies determine the time spans required for each step under prescribed environmental conditions. The complete life cycle may be accomplished in as little as several days, or as long as several months or years.

Although all nematodes progress through each of the six stages of the basic life cycle, it is in the animal-parasitic nematodes that unusual modifications, specializations, and optional deviations occur. These perturbations appear to take place between the embryonation step and the completion of the fully formed third-stage juvenile. For pedagogical purposes it is useful to describe distinct and characteristic cycles; however, it should be kept in mind that variation in cycles may

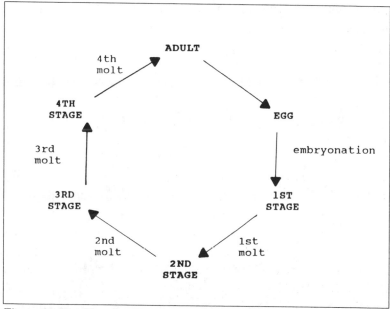

Figure 6.1. The life cycle of any nematode involves six life forms and four molts. This life cycle applies to microbivorous nematodes in a soil, freshwater, or marine environment, and with minor changes to plant parasitic forms.

occur in different nematodes. Perhaps the best way to illustrate the complexities and differences in animal-parasitic nematode cycles is through the description of the events for different systems.

A common life cycle occurs in *Ascaris,* the intestinal roundworm of pig or man (Fig, 6.2), and is basically the same as that discussed for free-living and plant-parasitic nematodes (Fig. 6.1), except that the egg arrives unembryonated into the soil with the host fecal discharge, whereupon it embryonates into the first stage larva, molts and develops into the full second-stage form but remains within the intact egg shell. The entire process, from the egg arriving in the soil to the fully developed but unhatched second-stage juvenile, takes place in the soil and requires several weeks. The fully developed but unhatched second-stage nematode must await ingestion to complete its life cycle within the host. The infective eggs containing second-stage juveniles hatch in the gut of the host. The emerging larvae penetrate the mucosa of the gut and migrate via the blood circulation to the lungs, leaving the blood for the lung tissue, then up the trachea to the throat and back down through the esophagus and stomach to the intestine, arriving as fourth stage

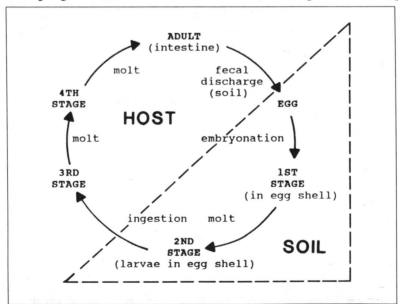

Figure 6.2. A common life cycle of animal-parasitic nematodes is illustrated by *Ascaris suum* from the pig. Adapted from Georgi. A similar cycle occurs in Trichostrongyles.

juveniles or pre-adults. Having undergone their second and third molt after leaving the gut as hatched larvae, they undergo their fourth molt, to become full adults and ready to resume the cycle.

In the ascarid intestinal roundworm of dogs (related to the intestinal ascarid roundworm of pig and man) the basic cycle of Fig. 6.2 remains; however, there are additional alternate loops by which infection can take place (Fig. 6.3). In the direct route, fully developed second-stage larvae within the egg shell are ingested by the dog, hatch in the gut, and migrate as described before, to reside eventually as adults in the small intestine. If the dog is a female with pups, the pups become infected via tracheal migration of the nematodes into the pups. In an alternative pathway the eggs in soil are ingested by a paratenic host. In the paratenic host, a rodent or earthworm in this case, a parasite may hatch, penetrate the tissue, and become encysted, unable to complete its life cycle until ingested by its definitive host, in this case the dog. As before, if the paratenic host is ingested by the female dog with pups, the pups become infected as well.

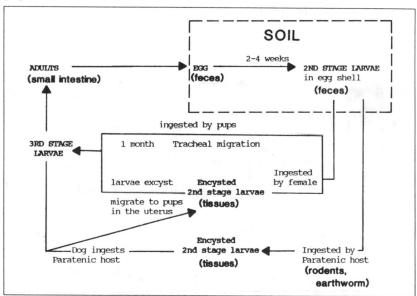

Figure 6.3. Alternate life pathways for *Toxocara canis,* an Ascarid nematode parasite of canines. The infection may be direct if the host ingests the egg containing second stage larvae from the soil or somewhat indirect if the host ingests a paratenic host, which had previously ingested the parasitic egg from soil. A paratenic host serves to maintain a parasitic stage without further development. Adapted from Georgi.

In the dog hookworm, a conventional pathway modification occurs, and an alternate infective pathway appears as well. As with the
Ascarids previously discussed, hookworm adults mate in the intestine
and eggs are laid and excreted with the feces by the host. In the feces
the eggs embryonate to first stage larvae, then hatch to continue
development into second stage, then into infective ensheathed third
stage larvae. The development pattern is modified at this point, in that
the first and second stage larval forms have a rhabditid type esophagus,
and therefore feed upon microorganisms. This adaptation enables them
to prolong their viability and increase the probability of infecting a
suitable passing host. The infective third stage migrates out of the feces
ready to infect the host. Ingested, the infective larvae pass through the
intestinal wall into the circulatory system which carries them into the
lungs. Then they leave the lungs to rise up to the trachea, cross over to
the esophagus, and down into the stomach and small intestine (Fig. 6.4)
to recommence the cycle.

In an alternative pathway, perhaps more common than the basic
one just described, infective third stage larvae are attracted by the body

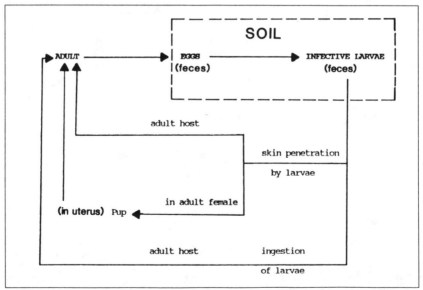

Figure 6.4. Alternate life pathways of the hookworm (*Ancylostoma caninum*) of dogs.
Nematodes employing this life cycle have added a skin penetration to ingestion as a
means of infection. Adapted from Georgi.

heat of a bare foot for example, penetrate the skin, and enter the circulatory system to complete the cycle. These soil-inhabiting stages are mildly tolerant of environmental changes, but are unable to withstand desiccation or freezing temperatures, and therefore are more prevalent in the warmer climates of tropical and subtropical regions.

A large wide-ranging group of nematodes, parasites of birds, fish and mammals, appears to have evolved a more complex cycle. These nematodes are no longer able to complete their life cycle with just one host; they must use an intermediate host for part of their life cycle (Fig. 6.5). In this group of parasites, the eggs deposited with the host feces must be ingested by an intermediate host, usually a crustacean or an insect, for embryonation into the first stage larvae to take place. Subsequently, there follows a molt, development of the second stage, a second molt and development to the infective third stage larvae. Nematode development stops at this point until the intermediate host is ingested by the definitive host. The cycle then resumes, to be completed in the definitive host.

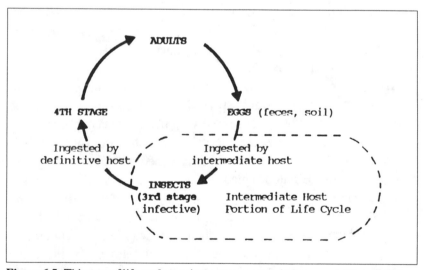

Figure 6.5. This type of life cycle requires a crustacean or insect as an intermediate host for the egg to develop to the infective third stage before being eaten by the definitive host to enable completion of the life cycle. This pattern is common in spirurid nematodes. Furthermore, this type cycle, frequently found in avian, fish, or pet host systems, reduces the free-living or soil portion of the cycle segment to a transfer function between definitive hosts and intermediate hosts. Adapted from various sources.

The diagram illustrates the cycle in which nematode eggs are released in the host feces, but other release mechanisms are known. In the guinea worm (*Dracunculus medinensis*) cycle the intermediate crustacean host, *Cyclops*, ingests the first stage nematode juveniles previously released in the water. The juveniles pass through the gut into the haemocoel of *Cyclops* to develop into third stage infective larvae. Humans in less developed countries often live in communities with poor sanitary practices, and are likely to drink water containing infected copepods. The nematode juveniles from the ingested copepod pass through the intestinal wall of the host into connective tissues to mature. After about a year, the mature female, about 2 feet in length, migrates to the legs and feet. All that nematode in the thin subcutaneous layer forms a bulge which ulcerates. Since the ulceration usually itches and burns, the host is likely to wash it. Upon contact with water, the nematode uterus prolapses out of the nematode through the ulceration to discharge copious numbers of first stage juveniles into the water where they can reinfect the copepods. This type of cycle utilizing a host, a free-living segment and an intermediate host segment, in which the passage from segment to segment may involve different kinds of mechanics, is of wide-spread occurrence not only in diverse mammals, but also in birds and fish.

If one reviews the life cycles so far discussed in terms of changes in basic features, a trend towards specialization and complexity can be noted. Initially, microbivorous free-living nematodes completed their entire life cycle in the soil. The first step toward specialization occurred, according to current evolutionary theory, when a small group of fungal feeding nematodes incorporated a plant-parasitic segment in their life cycle. Meanwhile a similar small group of bacterial feeding nematodes evolved to incorporate an animal-parasitic segment of their life cycle. Many animal parasitic nematodes, despite the adaptation of alternate pathways, retain the free-living soil segment of the cycle which usually involves the steps between egg development and the completion of the infective third stage. Further specialization led to the incorporation of a required intermediate host segment in the cycle, thereby reducing the soil or free-living segment to a brief role as a transfer site between host and intermediate host (Fig. 6.5). The trend towards increased specialization has continued with the development of life cycles excluding the free-living soil segment entirely. This step is accomplished in at least two different ways by utilizing a basic axiom, the feeding characteristics of special groups of animal hosts.

In one special group of animal parasites, the filariid nematodes, a change in the normal embryonation step takes place. Eggs embryonate partially and then become arrested (mechanism unknown). These arrested, partially developed embryos, no longer eggs and not yet first stage larvae, are commonly referred to as microfilariae. Microfilariae, sometimes called motile embryos, are small fusiform entities comparable in size to the smallest known nematodes, but they appear to have no internal structure. While some microfilariae develop in the blood from the females dwelling in the circulatory system, others must migrate into the blood system or other body fluid vessels and sacs from females residing in subcutaneous tissue. Whether some or all of the different species of microfilariae have muscles or contractile fibers to aid their movements in migration has not been resolved. It may be that the propulsive forces of the motile embryo are generated by microtubules as they are for amobae and other cells. In addition to other concerns about microfilariae, one salient question revolves around the diurnal behavior in some populations. In certain host populations, the micro-filariae concentration in the peripheral blood rises tremendously at night and may decrease to barely detectable concentrations during the day. A common explanation postulates that the diurnal increase arises to accommodate the feeding habits of mosquitoes, which vector the parasite. The problem with this simple explanation is that in a different area with similar hosts, the same nematode species and the same mosquito species, diurnal fluctuations do not occur. With the availability of blood or other body fluid containing microfilariae, a fluid or blood-sucking insect withdraws microfilariae with the food supply into its gut. There embryonation resumes and development continues as in the normal intermediate host cycle segment, to the infective third stage larvae. Development of the nematode stops until the insect feeds again, at which time the infective stages migrate to the insect feeding organ to be injected directly into the wound, or to migrate down the proboscis into the wound, and therein complete the host segment of the cycle.

This tissue-to-tissue transfer of nematode parasites by body fluid sucking insect is perhaps best known with filarial nematodes; but similar systems also occur with non-filarial nematodes in which eggs embryonate into first stage larvae, which migrate to lachrymatory ducts and glands, there to be taken up by an intermediate host feeding on the lachrymatory fluid.   This life cycle (Fig. 6.6) utilizes the feeding characteristics of body fluid sucking insects as an integral component.

A totally different tissue-to-tissue transfer life cycle, far simpler, is based upon an even more primitive feeding characteristic of a large group of animals, namely, the need of carnivores and carrion feeders to eat flesh. The best known parasitic nematode using this type of cycle is *Trichinella spiralis*.   In a typical host, pig for example, the male and female embed themselves in the intestinal mucosa to feed and copulate. The female does not produce eggs, but live first stage larvae which are

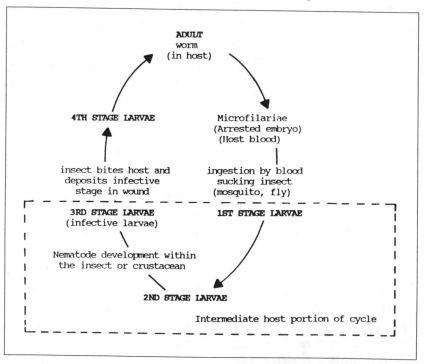

Figure 6.6. This diagram illustrates a generalized life pathway of filarial parasitic nematodes. Part of the development takes place within an intermediate host, the rest in the definitive host with no exposure of the parasite to the external environment. Nematode transfers tissue to tissue. Adapted from various sources.

released into the mucosa from which they migrate preferentially to voluntary muscles. The host muscle tissue responds to invasion by walling off the foreign body and encysting the larvae to prevent any further development. Although eventually the adults die and end the active infection, the viable inactive encysted larvae remain. If, upon the death of the host, the raw flesh is used as a food source for any carnivorous animal (rat, dog, cat, lion, man, etc.) the cycle resumes. Upon ingestion of the muscle containing encysted larvae, the cyst dissolves releasing the larvae to continue their development into adults buried in the intestinal mucosa, and thus recommence the cycle.

The host range of this parasitic nematode is extremely broad, and is common among carnivores and carrion-eating mammals. Moreover, it is known to infect herbivores, for example, horses. The incidence of parasitism in herbivores is rare inasmuch as a preferred vegetative food source precludes any but an accidental uptake of flesh contaminated with *Trichinella* .

An unusual survival strategy is utilized by a large group of animal-parasitic nematodes (*Strongyloides*), which involves two alternate reproductive cycles (Fig. 6.7). One cycle is entirely free-living, incorporating microbivorous feeding and sexual reproduction by copulating adults. The alternate cycle is similar to other animal parasites in that it incorporates a free-living soil segment and a parasitic segment, in which the adult female in the intestine produces eggs parthenogenetically. The first stage hatches in the intestine and is eliminated with the feces into the soil. It then molts to form the second stage, which molts again to form a special infective third stage, that with the arrival of a host, either penetrates the skin or becomes ingested to continue the parasitic portion of the life cycle.

Interestingly, at the third stage a key decision is made. Under the influence of uncertain factors the developing second stage molts into an infective third stage, in part influenced by the presence of a suitable host and favorable environmental conditions to penetrate the skin or become ingested or else to molt into a third stage microbivorous form to continue the free-living cycle.

Anthropomorphic reasoning would suggest the nematode can use the parasitic cycle to disperse, and the free-living cycle to ensure survival. According to one school of thought the presence of alternative pathways constitutes a first step toward obligate parasitism, and could be inserted in the trend towards specializations (between Fig. 6.1 and 6.2). An alternative view (not in current favor) would suggest that an obligate parasitic predecessor with a hookworm-like cycle (Fig. 6.4) including infection by skin penetration or ingestion, under persistent

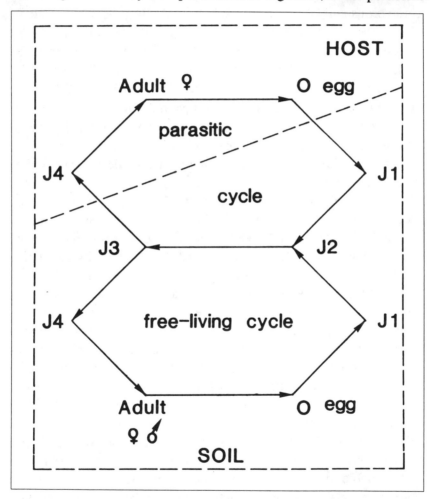

Figure 6.7. Schematic representation of alternate life cycles utilized by *Strongyloides*. In response to unknown factors, the second stage form molts into either an infective third stage parasitic form or a third stage microbivorous form. In the microbivorous or free-living cycle, males and females copulate to produce eggs, while in the parasitic cycle, the adult female produces eggs parthenogenetically. Redrawn after Croll and Matthews.

adverse conditions had readapted to an optional microbivorous free-living cycle for added survival value. The fact that one group of animal-parasitic nematodes has adopted a set of alternative pathways in mammals, while a different group has adopted a similar set of alternative pathways in amphibians, provides additional obfuscation to a unified scheme for the evolutionary development of parasitism.

The life cycles discussed are well-known and useful to illustrate diversity and perhaps trends of possible evolutionary pathways. Moreover, life cycles impacting humans, pets, livestock or agricultural and ornamental plants are more likely to attract attention and hold an interest. Heightened interest notwithstanding, myriad variations and complexities occur in the life cycles of nematodes. Many nematode life cycles are not understood, particularly when wildlife is involved. Ocean-dwelling fish, crustaceans and mammals are known to be parasitized. But some life cycles, for example that of the 25-foot nematode found in the placenta of the sperm whale, remain a mystery. So do life cycles in birds, reptiles, amphibians and a range of invertebrates other than insects. Current knowledge recognizes two, three, and four-component systems: two-component systems may involve the nematode and a host or other food source, be it plant, bacterium, fungus, mammal, mollusk, annelid or insect arthropods. There is variation in that the parasitic form may involve the later stages, together with the adult, as indicated in the cycle illustrations. With a different nematode parasite, the adult may be free-living in the soil and the larval stages parasitic (mermithids).

Three-component systems exhibit additional life cycle complexity: nematode-plant-insect, where the nematode has parasitic cycle segments in the plant and the insect (oats and fruit fly) or has alternate generations, one in the plant followed by the second in the insect (Eucalyptus and the Eucalyptus gall fly), or else cycles repeatedly in either host depending upon environmental conditions (*Deladenus siricidicola*); nematode-insect-mammal-bird or -fish (e.g., filarid cycles); nematode-crustacean-mammal (guinea worm) -bird or -fish; nematode-microorganism-plant, as found in certain facultative plant parasites (potato rot nematode) or nematodes feeding on the mycorrhizal symbionts of plants, as well as nematodes-microorganisms-animals as indicated in the cycle illustrations. A somewhat different three-component system is found among entomogenous nematodes, where the nematodes feed on a special bacterial associate, but carry the bacteria into the insect by cuticle penetration. Once within the insect the bacteria reproduce at the expense of the insect, providing food for the nematode.

Four-component systems are known: nematode-insect-microorganism- plant, in which the nematodes feed upon fungus in the beetle galleries or the plant, depending upon cycle stage, and infect new plants by being carried on the body of the migrating beetle (Pinewood nematode - *Bursaphelenchus xylophilus*).

A comprehensive review of nematode life cycles is beyond the scope of this tome. The intent is to illustrate the substantial plasticity apparent in life cycle patterns as well as the range of life cycles, from the simple to the more bizarre, that nematodes have developed for the exploitation of niches in nature.

"Nothing Endures but change."

Heraclitus of Ephesus,
580-540 B.C.

CHAPTER 7

Motion and Displacement

Nematodes need to move and change their locations as do most other animals and for essentially the same reasons: to find a food source, to escape a threat, to locate a mate, to disperse or to establish themselves in a preferred site. Most nematodes displace by means of an undulatory or serpentine-type propulsion, common in nature. This kind of propulsion is found in snakes, eels, arthropod larvae, nematodes, and filaments of spermatozoa, zoospores, and protozoa. Although nematodes are capable of exquisitely controlled three-dimensional movements, in very thin water layers the undulation is primarily dorsoventral. Why the preferential motion is dorso-ventral rather than lateral has not been explained. In fact, how a nematode moves around soil particles in motoring from place to place is largely a matter of speculation based on simple case assumptions.

Locomotion

Undulatory or serpentine-type propulsion is referred to as "crawling," if the nematode is in a soil matrix, "gliding" if the nematode is in a very thin water layer, or "swimming" if the nematode is in deep water. The basic forces involved are essentially the same. Typically, undulatory progression through a rigid environment depends upon three fundamental factors:

i) Internal muscular forces (bending couples) that alter the curvature of each body segment to that previously characteristic of the adjacent anterior segment;

ii) the phase of the bending body segment which varies as the wave progresses along the length of the animal body;

iii) the presence of external restraints preventing segments of the body from moving in any direction other than along the line of propagation.

Undulatory movement in nematodes takes advantage of the fact that:

i)   there is no rigid skeletal structure either internally as in vertebrates or externally as in arthropods;

ii) the nematode cuticle is flexible and elastic, but the body is resistant to sheer stress;

iii) the body is under turgor pressure;

iv) the somatic musculature runs longitudinally along the body under the hypodermis in each of the four quadrants (Fig. 4.2).

The physics describing the propulsion of a nematode in a natural habitat is very complex and therefore poorly defined and understood; however, a highly simplified and idealized illustration may convey some appreciation of mechanisms effecting nematode propulsion. Arbitrarily divide a portion of a nematode body into three segments (as in Fig. 7.1A). While the longitudinal muscles of the segments of either end of the central segment remain unactivated, those on one side of the central segment contract. The contraction shortens that side of the body, but, since the segment contents are incompressible, in order to maintain constant volume the outer portion of the body segment must stretch. In this process, the body bends and generates torque. The torque so generated in a body segment is equal to the product of the axial force and the radius of curvature of the body segment (Fig. 7.1B). R_1 and R_2 are fixed restraints transmitting resistive forces N_1, N_2 equal to the respective forces that the nematode exerts against them. Without the restraints the center of curvature, 0, would displace under a force, F_0, equal in magnitude but opposite in direction to F_p. With restraints, F_0 equals zero, and point 0 does not displace, so torque is generated resulting in a component of F_p along the axis of propagation. The consequence of these events is summarized (Fig. 7.1 C), where L_1, L_2, L_3 represent forces, friction, etc., resisting axial movement forward and θ is the angle between the body axis and the direction of propagation.

$$\text{Propulsive forces} = \Sigma N \sin \theta$$
$$\text{and}$$
$$\text{Drag forces} = \Sigma L \cos \theta$$

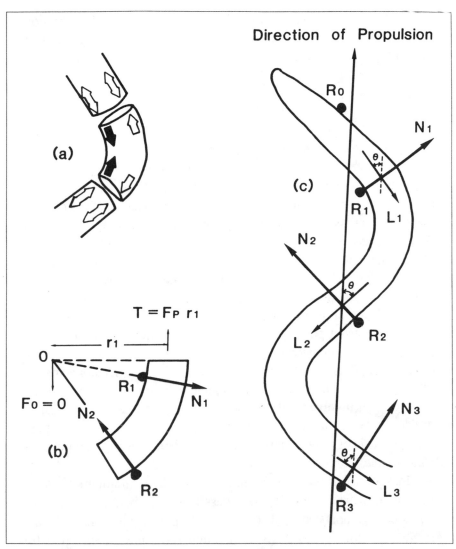

Figure 7.1. Idealized scheme illustrating the mechanism of locomotion utilizing highly simplified physical concepts. a) Internal forces effecting bending of a nematode segment. Longitudinal muscular contraction is indicated by the dark heavy arrows; open arrows indicate passive forces. b) The torque (T) or moment of force generated by the nematode as a function of radius of body curvature (r_1), and positioning of restraints (R). N represents a resistive force of restraint against the nematode body. F_p represents a propulsive force. F_o represents a potential backward force, but in the presence of restraints equals zero. c) Illustrates the propulsive component of force as a function of θ, representing the angle between the nematode body axis and the direction of nematode translation. N represents the resistive force exerted by the restraint (R). L represents the axial backward force effected by drag. Adapted from various sources.

When $\Sigma N \sin\theta > \Sigma L \cos\theta$, the nematode moves in the direction of translation. The counteracting restrains (R_0, R_1...R_n) prevent a lateral movement, that is

$$N \cos\theta + L \sin\theta = 0.$$

When the waves generated by the nematode move from head to tail (posteriorly) the propulsion is in the forward direction; when they move from tail to head (anteriorly) the propulsion is in the backward direction. The resulting propulsive force generated along the axis of displacement is a function of the wavelength, λ (decreasing with λ), the amplitude of the wave (increasing with amplitude) and the frequency of the wave (increasing with cycle frequency). The foregoing explanation was based on a highly simplified and idealized system with frictionless restraints, ample open space, a sine wave form for the nematode and a smooth cuticle. But the cuticle of a nematode is not smooth; it possesses annulations or longitudinal striations that may be shallow, deep, or different in shape with protuberances of various kinds.

The idealized physics of undulatory movement as described applies to a two-dimensional system, with essentially a smooth surface and few restraints. Most nematodes inhabit a three-dimensional matrix like soil with orders of magnitude of greater complexity. A resolution of the physics involved in the propulsion of a nematode in such a matrix has not yet been attempted. Furthermore, in some nematodes, the path along the axis of progression may take on a helical form, as it does for *Haemonchus contortus*.

In few nematodes do the undulatory waves maintain constant amplitude or wavelength as they pass along the body. The rate of propagation is not necessarily constant. The transverse velocity and the angle of inclination to the axis of progression may be different for different elements along the body. The previous explanation assumes that the water is in contact with each element of the body and is at rest relative to the ground, and not affected by the activity of neighboring elements. In reality, some variation in the water motion occurs. The explanation also neglects a special condition which existed at the apices of the nematode, especially involving events occurring in soil.

Nematode locomotion in thin films of water is usually called gliding; and though the mechanics of undulatory motion are the same as has been described, the nature of the restraints is different. In thick films or deep water, nematodes must locomote by swimming or gliding on the bottom surface, aided only by gravity to increase the frictional forces resisting slip. To swim, a nematode must generate its propulsive force from the surrounding water. In the water, the waves move back relative to the ground, unlike a rigid environment where they are stationery. Each element of the wave must provide a component of motion at right angles to its longitudinal axis in order to develop thrust. The speed of the nematode is therefore equal to the speed of propagation of the waves back along the body minus the speed of the wave relative to the ground. Plant-parasitic nematodes, for example, can't swim in deep water; they all just sink. They are unable to generate the required wave frequency for sufficient speed of waves, relative to the ground, to develop the necessary propulsive thrust. Some free-living nematodes like *Turbatrix aceti* are able to support themselves suspended in vinegar solutions, but there is little directional displacement. Cinographic exposures of such "swimming" nematodes have shown that a series of circulating vortices are formed, and that each successive vortex circulates in the opposite direction to its neighbors. Individual vortices travel backward at the same speed that the crests of the waves travel backward relative to the ground. Inasmuch as the water immediately behind the posterior end of the small nematode shows no trace of movement, the vigorous nematode activity provides some measure of lift and the nematode is essentially "treading water."

In thin films of water, less than the diameter of the nematode, surface tension forces supplement the gravitational force pressing the nematode to the surface, thereby increasing the frictional forces resisting slip. In such a thin film with a stationary nematode, surface tension forces on one side are equal to those on the other side to provide a vertical downward force on the nematode; as the nematode initiates undulatory movement, the film surface is distorted, increasing the tensing force on the side in the direction of motion. Therefore, if the thrust (P) of the nematode against the film is equal to the frictional force plus the product of the resultant surface tension force and cos α, where α is the angle between force R and force P (Fig. 7.2), there is no

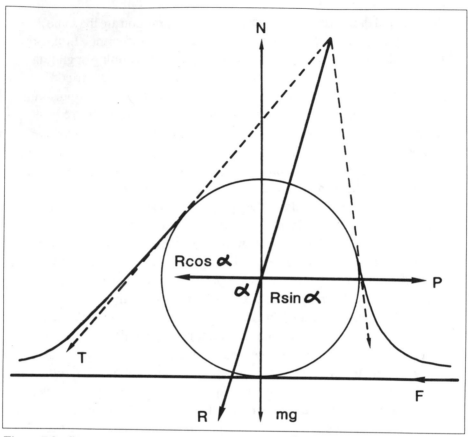

Figure 7.2. Cross-sectional representation of surface tension forces affecting a nematode as it moves in the thin film of water. N represents the reactive force to surface tension of the nematode at rest. T represents the surface tension on either side of the nematode in motion, P represents the force of lateral movement exerted by the nematode, R represents the resultant force by the unequal surface tension forces on either side of the nematode, mg represents the gravitational force of the nematode, F equals a frictional force and α equals the angle between the propulsive force (P) and the resultant surface tension force (R). Redrawn from Croll.

slip and the nematode leaves a sinusoidal track of the same thickness as the body.

With the appropriate film thickness, foliar nematodes like *Aphelenchoides* are able to overcome gravitational forces and climb chrysanthemum plants to attack stems, leaves and meristem, while the animal-parasitic hookworm can climb a blade of grass to improve the probability of infecting a host. As the film thickness increases, the resultant surface tension forces pressing the nematode to the substratum diminish allowing slip and the nematode track widens. With sufficient water thickness, of course, there is no surface tension effect and the nematode responds as if in deep water.

While most nematodes migrate by utilizing the serpentine motion described, some nematodes utilize a different mode of locomotion, which in varying degrees supplements or replaces undulatory motion as a propulsive force. *Criconemella* species are shorter and fatter than most nematodes, and exhibit a very sluggish undulatory motion. They appear to translocate in a fashion similar to that of annelids, in that an axial contractile wave motion initiates posteriorly and moves anteriorly. The body length changes and the accentuated annulation, assisted by the retrorse edges, resists backward slip. In this case the somatic musculature in all four quadrants contracts in unison, forcing the anterior portion of the body forward as a contractile pulse moves anteriorly. While most nematodes do not use this mode of muscle control as a means of locomotion, they probably have the capacity to employ this kind of muscular activity, for several nematodes that locomote primarily by undulatory motion are known to pass through apertures somewhat smaller than their body diameters.

Several groups of free-living nematodes possess unusually long tubiform setae connected to internal glands. The nematodes appear to be able to activate the glands to secrete a sticky substance which reduces the tendency of the setae's tip to slip on the surface. In *Desmoscolex* species (Fig. 3.1 C) these tubiform setae are distributed along the body and the nematode moves on these micro-stilts. It is questionable whether these tubiform setae are under individual muscular control; it appears more likely that the animal progresses annelid style, as do criconematids, by simultaneous muscular contractions in all four quadrants with the contraction wave initiating posteriorly and progressing anteriorly, pushing the nematode body forward. In other nematodes, illustrated by *Draconema* species (Fig. 3.1 E), the tubiform setae are arranged anteriorly and posteriorly so that the nematode can locomote inchworm style. The marine nematode *Chaetosoma* also locomotes in this fashion. In this process the posterior region of the nematode is fixed to the surface by the sticky posterior tubiform setae, while the forward part of the body is extended to attach the anterior tubiform setae to the surface. After which the posterior tubiform setae release and the body loops outwardly as the posterior region of the nematode is brought forward for reattachment of the posterior setae near the anterior ones, and so on. How the nematodes are able to unstick the tubiform setae at will has yet to be resolved.

Some nematodes utilize a kind of leaping ability to serve special purposes. For example, *Steinernema carpocapsae* (insect parasite) uses this method to gain access to the surface of an insect in close proximity. In a drying atmosphere the nematode forms an upward loop with the anterior and posterior ends held tightly together by the surface tension of a small drop of water. Endeavoring to release itself, the longitudinal muscles on the outside of the loop are contracted, but the separation of the adjacent posterior and anterior termini is resisted by the surface tension (Fig. 7.3). The droplet gradually evaporates or drains away, eventually breaking the surface tension, and the nematode ends snap away from each other. The action is sufficiently violent that the momentum of the anterior end hurls the nematode into the air to reach the insect surface. In a similar fashion a marine nematode (*Theristus* sp.) has been reported to hop by use of caudal gland secretions.

There are a range of body movements which are part of other kinds of behavior than locomotion, such as nictating and swarming. Some animal parasites glide up a thin water film to the extreme tip of a grass blade, attach their tails to the blade tip with a caudal secretion, then wave the entire body above the grass blade tip in a fashion that circumscribes a cone. In swarming, nematodes gather together, locomoting in the normal fashion, often becoming entangled with the aid of caudal secretions. This swarming is distinct from the aggregation on glass surfaces which often is seen in mass cultures of nematodes and is effected by surface tension of very thin films of water.

The foregoing discussion on locomotion purports to be reasonably correct and consistent with superficial observations. In reality the conclusions are subject to some severe limitations; foremost perhaps are the abilities to explain how a nematode can generate the tensile forces with contractile fibrils located in some two dozen muscle cells in

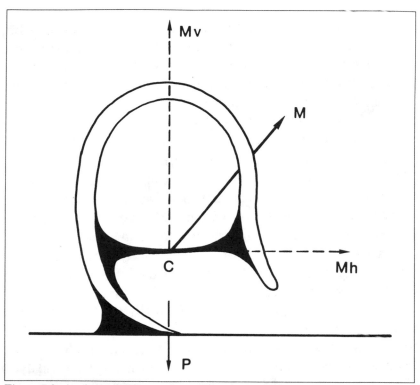

Figure 7.3. A schematic presentation to illustrate the mechanism of nematode leaping. The shaded area indicates the surface tension forces from a small water droplet. Nematode somatic musculature contraction eventually breaks the surface tension generating a resultant body momentum (M), M_v indicates a vertical component of momentum, M_h indicates a horizontal component of momentum, and P the downward force of gravity plus the restraining force of surface tension at the tail tip. $M_v > P$ launches the nematode in the direction of M.   Redrawn after Croll.

each of four quadrants along the length of the body, or how these fibrils are attached to give the required wavelengths, amplitudes, and frequencies—all of which may change as the waves move along the body, and how the various wave forms that may be generated in various body segments are controlled.   Whatever our anthropogenic explanatory failures, nematodes are admirably adapted to motoring around in their environment to suit their needs.

Dispersion

From the preceding discussion of nematode locomotion one can conclude that if ancient forms moved in similar ways, it would not be reasonable to expect them to disperse widely by means of their own muscular propulsion. For example, a typical nematode could migrate on the average of a yard per year, conditions being favorable. It would mean a displacement of some 570 miles per million years, or about the distance from Sacramento, California, to the Mexican border, or from Zurich to Rome. The last ice age ending about 14,000 years before the present brought a sheet of ice hundreds of feet thick ,lasting many centuries, over the temperate zones of the northern hemisphere; conditions were sufficiently adverse to eliminate higher life forms including nematodes. Since this event nematodes would have been able to migrate under their own propulsive power some 15 km (~10 miles) from the ice face. In fact they are now found in excess of 1,600 km (1,000 miles) northward of the terminal moraine. Plant forms disperse naturally at a more rapid rate as do nematodes, according to research evidence from recent years. Clearly, nematodes must take advantage of other mechanisms to disperse as widely and as rapidly as they have been observed to do.

The obvious option is for a nematode to hitch a ride on something that moves faster—water, wind, or animals, including birds and flying insects. Nature has used all these methods; the strategy has worked well. With the advent of man and the development of his modern intricate society, the pace of dispersion has increased and within the last few millenniums has accelerated to the present rate. Man's activity is probably the most important current means of dispersion. Perhaps a good way to convey the range of dispersal strategies implemented by nature and reinforced by man's activities is by means of specific examples. In some cases, several mechanisms come into play, for which there are undoubtedly many variations. Moreover there are probably dispersal mechanisms which we have yet to recognize.

Animal Parasites

As might be surmised by the variation in life cycles of animal parasitic nematodes, their dispersal mechanisms are equally wide-ranging. Dog heartworm is a nematode parasite of canines that is growing in seriousness in California. *Dirofilaria immitis* originated elsewhere since it was not in the wild canine species in the Western

U.S.; however, it has been a problem of long standing in southeastern United States, from which it appears to have spread throughout the country. To illustrate, the veterinarians in a county of West Virginia took blood samples from dogs housed in several shelters in different areas and examined them for microfilaremiae. The incidence was generally low, approximately 5%, except for one area of the county with a preponderance of stray dogs. Autopsies showed local dogs had low numbers of adult heartworms—but one dog, having lived in Georgia, had high numbers, leading the veterinarians to believe that the local infection was introduced by this dog from Georgia.

A half century ago, dog heartworm was unheard of in the Sacramento Valley of California. While the current incidence in some areas is on the order of 5–15%, in others it is two to four times greater. Furthermore, microfilaremiae exists in the coyote populations which serve as wild reservoir hosts. It is likely that this nematode was introduced from the southeast United States, probably with infected dogs as pets of a migrating human population. The vector for many filarids is the mosquito, and dog heartworm is believed to be exclusively a mosquito-borne disease. Some 60 mosquito species around the world have been implicated in this transmission; California has at least a dozen of these. A tree hole mosquito (*Aedes siriensis*) found commonly along the foothill area of the Sierras is a particularly suitable vector. It feeds readily on canines, and has a long lifetime.

In Massachusetts, a mosquito survey indicated that 23 species collected in the field, of which three were those of *Aedes,* harbored natural infections of filarids. Of nineteen species allowed to feed on an infected dog, ten were found to support the development to the infective stage. In the mosquito survey the heartworm incidence was 10%. There are many other filarids borne and vectored by mosquitos to amphibia, rodents, rabbits, horses, raccoons, and felids.

Hookworms are common in humans, dogs, cats, and other species, particularly in the warmer regions of southern U.S. and the Caribbean. As the animals move about, eggs deposited with the feces develop to the infective stage and penetrate the skin (usually the feet of the host). Transport of these animals transports the nematodes. There is a different nematode also present in the Caribbean region that is found in the rogue domestic cat, gapeworm (*Mammomonogamus ierei*), that lives in the nasal pharynx causing respiratory distress, i.e., mucoid nasal discharge, sneezing, and breathing noises. Eggs appear in the feces; but they do not infect when given orally. How they transmit is not known, nor is their ability to infest man. This nematode feeds like a hookworm, but in the nasal pharynx. This observation simply illustrates that there is much to be learned about nematode dispersion, distribution, and infection by way of pets.

The stray dog has been shown to be a good distributor of helminths in many areas around the world. This can be illustrated by the following examination of fecal deposits of stray dogs in a Nigerian city. Of 166 fecal samples, incidence of parasitism was determined as follows:

22%—*Spirocerca lupi*
25%—*Trichuris vulpis* (nematode)
38%—*Toxocara canis* (nematode)
43%—*Taenia* and *Echinoccus s*pecies
68%—*Dipylidium caninum*
71%—hookworm (nematode)

Trichinella spiralis, the nematode parasite long associated with pork, is common in flesh-eating predators. Herbivores are also susceptible; however, feeding on herbage precludes infection, except if the herbage is contaminated with infested animal tissue and ingested. Parasitized animals normally roam their territories, some for hundreds of miles. Upon their demise, the tissue may be consumed by local predators to serve as the new hosts. Even the raccoon which is sought for meat or pelt or that dies naturally is a source for infection. Rodents, particularly the rat which roams considerable distances, are an infective source for predators including the domestic dog, cat, or even carrion feeders. A graduate student responsible for lab preparations used to frequent the city dump to shoot rats which served as a source of *T. spiralis* for a parasitology lab. Bears are notorious for being infected with this nematode, not only in arctic regions (polar bears) but also in the wilds of the continent (brown, black bears).

Other wild animals may have different nematode infections which cause problems. For example, some years ago a Frenchman appeared at a hospital in Somalia with "creeping eruption" on the back of a hand, a common disease in the southern part of Africa. Biopsy revealed nematode larvae in the eruption; the patient was treated with an anthelmintic and within a week was clear. Six months later he was back—the same thing but the other hand and wrist region. Again, larvae were found. Where did they come from? It turned out the Frenchman had a mated pair of pet cheetahs, and examination of the cheetah fecal material showed that they were heavily infected with dog hookworm and cat hookworm. An interesting story, perhaps, but also illustrative of unusual ways of dispersion.

Some years ago, the University of California, Davis, Primate Center imported from Northern India 100 *Rhesus* monkeys that were placed in quarantine for examination and treatment with anthelmintics. Stool examination indicated eight genera of nematode parasites with incidence of 40–70%. This is typical of findings that serve to justify the prohibition of indiscriminate importation of animals, and the quarantine of imported wildlife.

In Russia, *Onchocerca* microfilarae were found in cow's milk. Examination revealed microfilariaee localized at the base of the teats and in the immediate surrounding area. One wonders how did they get into the cow, vectored perhaps by midges or culicordes, and who drank raw milk?

Avian nematode parasites are also very troublesome, particularly to chicken, turkey, duck and goose husbandry. Entire chicken flocks have been decimated with inadvertent introduction of infected stock. Wild birds are also infected, e.g., a wild turkey survey in Florida showed a wide range of nematode parasites. Fortunately, these birds seldom moved out of the wildlife management area. But what about other migratory water fowl or songbirds? We know little about the epidemiology of nematode parasites of birds which are mostly spiruroids with an intermediate host, probably a dung beetle.

The situation is similar for fish parasites. Marine animals have a wide array of nematode parasites—herring, salmonids, cod, rockfish, crustaceans, etc.; some of these swim very long distances. Even sea mammals, seals and whales have their burdens. Some nematodes appear to be highly specialized, like *Placentonema* from the sperm whale. Whales migrate between polar regions and wide expanses of ocean; we know little about the life cycles of these nematodes or their modes of transmission.

Sewage wastewater is an excellent mechanism for dispersion of nematode parasites, especially the resistant forms. German researchers have observed that even though parasites in sewage sludge could be destroyed by anaerobic pasteurization (30 minutes at 65–70°C) or aerobic compostation, the tremendous volumes of unpasteurizable raw waste fluids contained an abundance of parasites, which, when discharged into the environment, would be available for reinfection. An interesting option for dispersion of certain animal parasitic nematodes involves earthworms and related annelids. Earthworms ingest infested cow dung and become infected; should they be subsequently eaten by birds or moles, the nematodes (oxyurids) can be transported long distances to infest new sites.

Human Parasites

Community sanitation levels are very important in the dispersion of animal parasites. A World Health Organization study in India of two schools of similar level, but different social class, found the general population burden of 42% in one area and 68% in the second, while the student burden was 63% in the first area and 97% in the second. The more common nematodes were pinworm, hookworm, and *Ascaris*. Epidemiological analysis revealed several interesting factors: i) students defecating in fields carried much higher burdens than those using latrines; ii) Students not using footwear carried much higher burdens than those with footwear; iii) Those students with dirty fingernails had higher burdens than those with clean fingernails; and iv) Students tended to have higher parasite burdens than the general population.

River blindness of the tropics (Onchocerciasis) is caused by a filarial nematode that is transmitted by a small black *Simulium* fly. The fly picks up microfilariae during a blood meal, supports the nematode internal development to the infective stage, then injects the infective stage into the source of a second blood meal. Although one fly species predominates in areas of high infestation, other species can also transmit over ranges which overlap that of the primary vector.

Onchocerca was not normally believed to be transmissible by mosquito; however, recent findings have indicated that a strain of *Aedes aegypti* mosquito can transmit *Onchocerca volvulus* to humans and other *Onchocerca* species to animals. The point is that there is no absolute relationship in dispersion; while there may be a primary vector, this mechanism can merge with others which may be less important, but overall the dispersion is broadened by vectors with different characteristics and habitats.

In a different example, *Loa loa,* the nematode eyeworm of man, is transmitted by biting flies (*Chrysops*) of warm-blooded animals. The same flies, which also transmit *Loa loa* to other primate species, occur in the forest canopy of tropical rainforests, serving as vectors to different primates including man. They are also found in temperate zones in special situations, like stable flies. The point is that flies not only transmit microfilarids in indigenous zones, but if either infected flies or infected hosts including man are transported elsewhere, the flies' relatives at the new site can transmit the nematode from there.

Can human transport be considered a serious problem? Consider the results of these studies. Stools of Peace Corps volunteers to Nepal were examined, and of those individuals showing no symptoms, 700 of 1700 contained eyeworm, hookworm, roundworm, or a combination of these parasites. Of those showing gastrointestinal symptoms, 1600 of 1900 showed nematode parasites. In a different study, Russian specialist workers returning from the tropics were examined for filarial infections; 100 of 300 were infected with *Onchocerca* sp, *Loa loa, Dipetalonema*, and *Wuchereria*.

An unusual case involving a long-time Northeastern U.S. resident blood donor surfaced in a pre-donative blood smear test when microfilariae were found. The resident exhibited no symptoms other than an occasional stiffness of load-bearing joints; the invasive agent was the nematode parasite *Mansonella ozzardi* which as an adult resides in serous cavities of the body (lymph pools) and is of uncertain pathogenicity. Infection was believed to have been acquired during four yachting trips in the Caribbean of two weeks each during a seven-year period. This case illustrates several facts involved in dispersion: 1) Parasites are easily acquired in very subtle fashions, in this case by a yachtsman living mostly on board. 2) Once acquired, the infection can be transported to a nonendemic region, in this case another environmental zone and cultural area. 3) Upon arrival in the new area, the parasitic agents are subject to dispersion by other means.

These factors are particularly relevant as a consequence of a recent Canadian report discussing health problems of Southeast Asian refugees. In Southeast Asia, 75% of rural Vietnamese and 56% of the urban residents harbored one or more parasites. Of the refugees in North America:

Parasite	Canada	U.S.
Ascaris	10%	31%
Trichuris	1	1
Hookworm	1	4
Strongyloides	0.2	1.2
Pinworm	0.7	—

These results have prompted some researchers to suggest that under Canadian conditions—high standards of sanitation, different eating habits, lack of appropriate vectors, and low winter temperatures—dispersion and transmission may be less important factors. In the U.S., however, depending upon region, temperatures are warmer, concentrations of refugees higher, and living habits and customs may be closer to the native ones, and a wide array of vectors may be present for those parasites requiring them. Any lessening of high sanitation standards would aggravate the situation. Keep in mind that hookworm was indigenous to the South and part of California, as was elephantiasis at one time. Mosquitoes, snails, and other paratenic and intermediate hosts are plentiful and available to serve as potential avenues for dispersion when needed. In fact, the dispersion of animal and human nematodes diseases from indigenous areas appears to be on the rise.

Plant Parasites

While an animal-parasitic nematode may find itself in a new habitat many miles from its origin, having been transported and left there by the host after a brief intimate relationship, the plant-parasitic nematode does not have this option. Nevertheless, there have developed alternate mechanisms for such nematodes to disperse by taking advantage of other natural processes.

Water Transport

The nematode, as an aquatic animal, can take advantage of the properties of fast moving water to be transported downstream. After a heavy storm, a placid meandering stream can become a raging torrent. When the water collecting from its drainage basin exceeds the capacity of the stream to move water away, the water overflows to inundate the surrounding land. Inasmuch as the carrying capacity (particulate matter) of a flowing stream increases as the eighth power of its velocity, water overflowing the banks quickly loses its velocity, and the carrying capacity quickly diminishes, the heavier particles settling first, the lighter ones settling last as the flow ebbs. Nematodes, being just slightly more dense than water, can disperse essentially to the limits of the flood flow. All the stream and river drainage basins of the world are subject to this phenomenon. As a consequence the flood plain is infested with all nematodes acquired by the flood waters upstream. For example, most California flood plains are well infested with rootknot nematode; in mid-western United States different groups of nematodes are dispersed on the flood plains of the Platte, Missouri, and Mississippi Rivers.

Furthermore, man has introduced a new dispersal technique called irrigation, which can use not only pristine water, but drainage water from infested fields. While this practice can be observed in any local river delta, it has taken place on an immense scale with the Egyptian Aswan Dam Irrigation Project. One of the principal goals of the Aswan Dam was to provide water to open up entirely new agricultural areas for production. Although the dam's waters were essentially free of plant-parasitic nematodes, infested transplants from the lower Nile were brought up to establish the new fields of Phase I, all of which became well-infested. According to plan, the salvaged water from the drainage of Phase I fields was to be used for irrigation of Phase II fields. At this point the fields of Phase I, as well as those of Phase II, became fully-infested with plant-parasitic nematodes and the process was repeated for Phase III of the project.

Wind Transport

Although no nematode is known to have wings of its own, many nematodes are able to survive desiccation, provided the process is sufficiently slow to allow for adaptation, and therefore can be wind-blown. There are many windblown areas of the world where soil is raised and moved with frequent, intense dust storms in which the soil deposited downwind can be measured in feet. Dry nematodes are light. When something like a dust devil or whirlwind occurs, or a farm implement is drawn across a field, light soil particles rise in the air, and from heights of 10 meters (30 ft.) a mild wind current of 3 meters per second (7 miles per hr.) can carry the dust plume 40 kilometers. Furthermore, if the phenomenon of saltation (particles bouncing along the soil surface) is added, the distance particles can be transported may become much greater.

There are enormous notorious windblown areas in the semi-arid regions of the world: the Middle East, North Africa which gives rise to desert winds blowing northward towards Southern Europe (the so-called Scirroco) that can result in muddy rains on Rome and other European cities, Southcentral United States which gave rise to the dust bowl of the 1930s, and on a more local basis dust storms in West Texas, New Mexico, and Arizona. In Australia the cereal cyst nematode is alleged to have been dispersed largely by wind.

When mankind changed from a hunter/gatherer to an agriculturalist society, the dispersion process accelerated greatly. As civilizations developed, so did interaction in commerce amongst the various constituencies. For millenniums exchanges of plants, soil and animals (including infected soil, animals and plants) was unrestricted. Restrictions and quarantines have essentially been a creation of the twentieth century. A region like the Mediterranean basin has had ample opportunity to redistribute all disease agents acquired during the growth of the Babylonian, Greek, Egyptian, Roman and later eras up through the nineteenth century. Transport of infested soil is an important dispersal means and, despite restrictions, continues to this day, even though it tends to be accidental or inadvertent. Transplanting of seedlings, whether agricultural or ornamental, occurs widely in all countries—

and unless special precautions are taken, plant-parasitic nematodes can be transported as well. Animals and birds with muddy feet can transport infested soil to new areas. Furthermore, infested plant material may be ingested in one area, then transported for deposit elsewhere in a viable condition. Farm vehicles and implements transported to different fields without cleaning and pasteurizing with steam or detergent or other chemical wash can release contaminated soil. This idea seems trifling or inconsequential, however it is not. For example, dust settling on farm implements a meter or more above the soil surface was found to contain a wide array of free living and plant-parasitic nematodes in a dried state that, upon moistening, revived. In fact, nematodes recovered from a tractor air filter could be revived by moistening.

A clear-cut case of field contamination by unclean farm implements took place in the Imperial Valley of California. About a quarter of a century ago, growers in the Imperial Valley were in need of an additional field crop for production purposes, and turned to sugar beets. The sugar beet nematode did not exist in the valley and so the crop seemed ideal. The difficulties arose when large sugar beet growers operating in infested areas elsewhere moved into the Imperial Valley with their equipment. Within a few years the sugar beet nematode appeared, and now the valley is as infested as all other beet growing areas.

Insects are involved in the dispersal not only of animal parasitic nematodes but also plant parasitic forms, sometimes as intermediate hosts, but more often as phoretic carriers with the nematode merely being transported on their body surface to another host site.

Distribution

It is a given fact that nematode distribution is intrinsically dependent upon a nutritional source. Therefore the distribution of animal-parasitic nematodes is assessed via autopsy or biopsy of host tissues, usually as incidence, i.e., presence or absence of a nematode stage, for the purpose of counseling appropriate prophylactic treatment. Fecal samples, though not normally considered biopsies, are similarly analyzed as to egg and larval content. Occasionally, whether the burden is light, moderate, or heavy may factor into the treatment protocol. Similar practices apply to intermediate host carriers for more esoteric studies. Geographic regions are similarly characterized according to whether incidences are slight, moderate, or heavy. High incidence levels usually correlate with increased individual burdens.

Free living nematodes (microbial feeders) are generally of reduced economic interest, so their distribution, other than in general terms, is of minor concern. The exception occurs with esoteric studies involving population dynamics in which the methodology widely used with plant-parasitic nematodes is adopted. Indubitably, the greatest need to assess distribution with precision occurs with plant-parasitic nematodes. Even though plant-parasitic nematodes usually require a host to reproduce, they may survive several years in the absence of susceptible plants. Modern agricultural practices normally require crop rotations over a period of several years to reduce pest, nutrition and soil structure problems. Moreover, rotational crop cultivars can differ in susceptibility to different nematode species. Rarely is it practical to utilize alternative crops completely immune to the prevalent parasitic nematode species, and it is equally rare to find all alternative crops in a sequence to be equally profitable. Economic considerations therefore dictate that the farmers must grow the more profitable crop (often the most susceptible) as frequently as possible.

A precise assessment of population levels and their distribution in a target field would be of immense value to a farmer in deciding pest management strategy, whether it be chemical, biological, cultivational, or none at all if the population is sufficiently low. Theoretically, the distribution determination is straightforward; it is only necessary to take samples, extract the nematodes, and count the numbers of each parasitic species. Practically, the population estimates are crude approximations at best; the problems associated with sampling and extraction have already been discussed elsewhere. The current cost for processing each sample through to the determination of numbers of each species ranges from $30–$100 (U.S.), depending upon which analytical laboratory is used, the difficulty in determining species, and neglecting the exceedingly poor agreement of analytical results between different laboratories. The processing of one sample is costly,

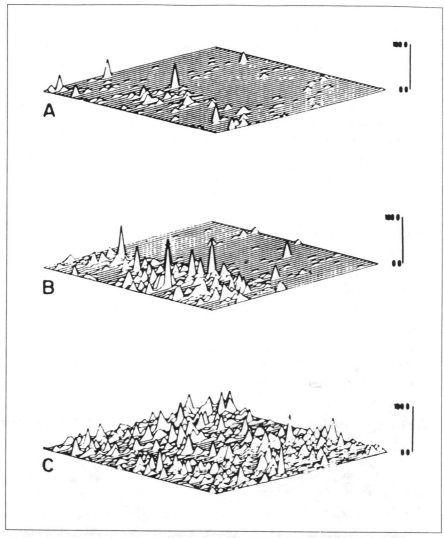

Figure 7.4. Detailed distribution of nematodes in a small microplot square, six yards on edge. A, B, and C indicate the distribution in numbers of nematodes for each of three species. After Goodel and Ferris with permission.

and also time consuming, requiring perhaps on the order of one man-hour. Inasmuch as the distribution of nematodes in a field has seldom been observed to be uniform, a great number of samples must be taken for a trustworthy assessment. The costs involved in such a venture on a field scale are generally prohibitive.

The distribution of nematodes in a field can be illustrated by a detailed distribution analysis of a small square microplot six yards on edge (Fig. 7.4). A, B, and C represent the distribution of three different nematode species in the same plot. The distribution of individual nematode species is not only dependent upon crop history in terms of susceptibility of each crop, but also upon other factors such as soil type, irrigation, and cultural practices. Although the illustrations (Fig. 7.4) represent distributions in a very small plot, fields reflect similar ranges in nematode distributions. Inasmuch as detailed distribution analyses of fields is impractical, appropriate sampling design utilizing reduced numbers of samples can provide a crude approximation of the level of field infestation. In any event, it should be borne in mind that as a tool for nematode management, field population levels determined by soil analyses, particularly for fallow fields, is a measure of last resort in terms of effectiveness, cost and reliability.

Chapter 8

Reproductive Biology

Nematodes are aquatic animals but, this obvious ecological limita-tion notwithstanding, have diffused into most ecological niches in a truly remarkable manner. They function well under the restrictive environmental conditions that exist in plant or animal tissues or in thin films of water. Moreover, many representatives have ventured out of a water environment by developing different mechanisms to withstand desiccation or other adverse conditions. This ecological success has been facilitated, in part, by the range of reproductive strategies which nematodes employ. All the principal types of reproductive phenomena exhibited in the animal kingdom have been utilized, in essence, by nematodes. While no mechanism is unique to nematodes, as a group they have appeared to employ whatever reproductive strategy was most suitable and expeditious to their environmental niche needs.

Modes of Reproduction

Parthenogenesis

Parthenogenesis is probably the second most common mode of reproduction among nematodes. This mechanism may be either meiotic or mitotic. In meiotic parthenogenesis meiosis proceeds normally from the primary oocyte (Fig. 8.1) to yield the haploid egg and the polar bodies. In some parthenogenetic species (e.g., *Meloidogyne* sp.) the haploid egg reabsorbs the second polar body to restore the normal somatic chromosome complement for embryology to proceed. In an alternate mechanism utilized by different nematodes (*Heterodera* spp.) there is an endomitotic division which takes place at a faster rate than the cell cleavage division, therefore doubling the chromosome number before the cleavage division is complete. Somatic chromosome number in the egg is therefore achieved for embryology to proceed.

In mitotic parthenogenesis (Fig. 8.1) the mature oocyte undergoes a single mitotic division, forming a polar body and a diploid egg. The somatic chromosome number is conserved and embryogenesis can

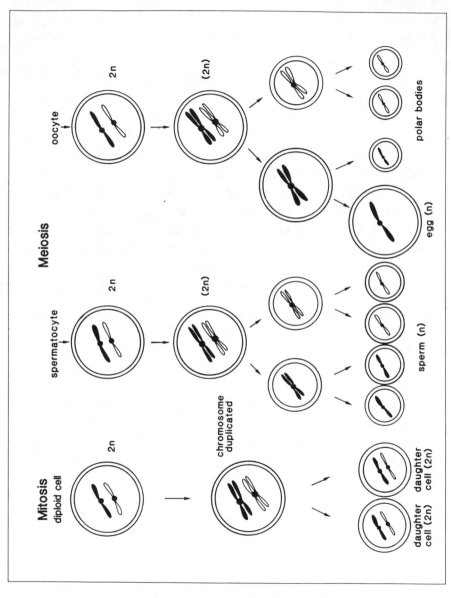

Figure 8.1 The fate of chromosomes during mitosis of somatic cells (chromosome duplicates once and cell divides once) or meiosis of gamete cells (chromosome duplicates once and cell divides twice). For simplicity and clarity only one chromosome pair is illustrated; in nature the entire complement of chromosome pairs follow the same sequence. Redrawn and adapted from various sources.

proceed. According to some authorities, meiotic parthenogenesis and a low number of males appears to prevail in *Meloidogyne* species when environmental conditions favor rapid reproduction. Mitotic parthenogenesis is most frequent in the family *Heteroderidae*. In the interest of perspective one must recognize the foregoing as a description of a sequence of events occurring in different processes. There is little insight as to how certain steps are initiated or controlled and how different options are triggered. There is no doubt that parthenogenesis occurs in certain populations of nematodes as a mode of reproduction, for entire populations have been reared in a laboratory beginning with one second-stage juvenile. Uncertainties arise, however, in any attempt to assess the importance or the proportion of a natural population that arises parthenogenetically or syngamously (female fertilization by a male). In any survey of a nominal species purported to be parthenogenetic it is not uncommon to find literature reports indicating the presence of a male as absent, rare, or few, with low or high numbers depending on the particular source of each population. In those populations reported to have few or no males the thoroughness of the search and the inefficiency of extraction technology render the results suspect. These issues may appear to be trivial at first glance, but are in fact of substantial significance. While parthenogenesis uses a restricted gene pool to simply increase the number of individuals, cross fertilization by males not only increases the number of individuals but broadens the gene pool in terms of quality and diversity. The relative worth of each mode of reproduction to the propagation of the species can bias the population for short or long term survival benefit as well as adaptability, selection and vigor.

Hermaphroditism

The hermaphroditic mode of reproduction is well entrenched in the nematological literature. The first report of this kind of reproductive activity appeared well over a century ago. In the last quarter century or so frequent reports have alleged that this mode of reproduction occurs in diverse groups of nematodes. Hermaphrodites occur in either of two arrangements. In one the female is normal and the hermaphrodite is a male which produces both eggs and sperm. The normal females are fertilized by the hermaphroditic male which can also fertilize its own eggs (*Heterogonema ovomascularis*, a mermithid insect parasite). The gonad of the developing hermaphrodite separates into an anterior lobe to become a functional testis, and a posterior lobe, which becomes a functional ovary. In this species there are two parasitic generations; one that consists only of females without a vulva which reproduce parthenogenetically, and release larvae when the female bursts.

In the other arrangement, the hermaphrodite is a female that also produces sperm and the male is normal. The female hermaphrodite may self-fertilize or be cross-fertilized by the male (*Caenorhabditis elegans*, for example). Recent findings suggest that the sperm of the cross-fertilizing male are used preferentially until the supply is exhausted; then the self-produced sperm are employed. The frequently reported incidences of hermaphroditism are usually based upon two factors—the presence of a spermatheca and the absence of males. As previously discussed, the apparent absence of males may be deceiving; inasmuch as promiscuity is common among nematodes, fewer males may suffice. Moreover, in a number of cases, careful examination has indicated that the spermatheca contained neither sperm nor the darkly staining elements in their walls that are usually associated with sperm production. Other animal-parasitic species, initially considered hermaphroditic, were later shown to reproduce by parthenogenesis. While hermaphroditism as a mode of reproduction exists in nematodes the reported frequency of incidence is suspect; too often a rigorous verification has not been available.

Pseudogamy

Pseudogamy should perhaps be viewed as less a mode of reproduction than a special event which triggers further development. In this situation a mature egg pauses in its development until a sperm penetrates. Penetration serves to activate the egg to trigger embryonation. No fusion of the pronuclei takes place; instead the sperm pronucleus degenerates. This event is viewed by some as a step in the development of parthenogenesis and by others as a step in the development of amphimixis. This triggering event has been reported for both hermaphroditic and an amphimictic *Rhabditis* species as well as a plant-parasitic *Meloidogyne* species.

Syngamy (*Amphimixis, Gonochorism, Cross-fertilization*)

Other than the few exceptions already noted, where reproduction occurs exclusively by parthenogenesis or hermaphroditically by self-fertilization, by far the most common mode of reproduction in nematodes is the fertilization of females by males and the resultant fusion of the male and female pronuclei. The oocyte and the spermatocyte are haploid (or the polychromosomal equivalent) and upon fusion result in the normal somatic chromosomal complement. Notwithstanding the great egg production of some nematodes species or the enormous number of offspring generated by nematodes as a whole, surprisingly little is known concerning the particulars of the process of union of gametes.

Eggs

Though the female gonad can be viewed as a tubular structure between ovary and vulva, different reactions occur along its length as the maturing egg migrates towards its exit. Perhaps the most complex region is the uterus, which provides secretions for different egg layers, sperm storage, and probably other as yet unknown functions. Recently, inwardly directed spines of an unknown function have been observed in several *Xiphinema* species. With perhaps two exceptions, the entire gonad in all nematodes is retained within the nematode body. In these exceptions the uterus grows prodigiously to evert partially or entirely out of the vulva (*Sphaerularia bombi*, a parasite in the haemolymph of the bumblebee, Fig. 8.2). This phenomenon has also been observed in *Simondsia paradoxa*, a parasite of pigs. Most probably, in cases of everted uteri nutrients are absorbed directly from the bathing fluids, as is the case for the uterus of *S. bombi*. Unfortunately, there appears to be little known about the development trail from germinal cell to the infective third stage larvae found in the bumblebee haemocoel. Nematode eggs, with one known exception, range in size from 0.02 to 0.05 mm in width and 0.05 to 0.1 mm in length (whether the egg comes from a 7-8 meter long *Placentonema* of the sperm whale or the 0.3 mm long plant parasitic *Paratylenchus*). The known exception is the egg of the 3-4 cm long *Deontostoma timmerchioi*, a marine nematode from the

Antarctic, which produces eggs 0.24 - 0.35 mm wide by 0.87 - 1.1 mm long. While most eggs are ellipsoidal, others are not (Fig. 8.3). The surface of most eggs is smooth but many have filaments, usually originating from the polar ends of the eggs, that can differ in number, length (Fig. 8.3 A-G), or branching pattern (Fig. 8.3 H). Others may have spines (Fig. 8.3 K) or different forms of "dimple" patterns (Fig. 8.3 M, Q, R). The "dimple" pattern is illustrated by the micrograph of eggs within the uterus of the hair-lip *Ascaris* nematode (Fig. 8.4).

There is much scientific uncertainty regarding the structure and composition of the nematode eggshell. The multi-layered shell generated by the egg appears to consist of an innermost membrane originating as a cell wall, followed by a lipid layer referred to variously as a vitelline

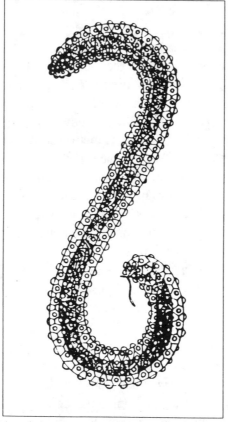

Figure 8.2 A representation of the swollen prolapsed uterus of *Sphaerularia bombi* (bumblebee parasite). The body of the nematode female is the small worm at the lower end of the uterus. Reproduced from Chitwood with permission.

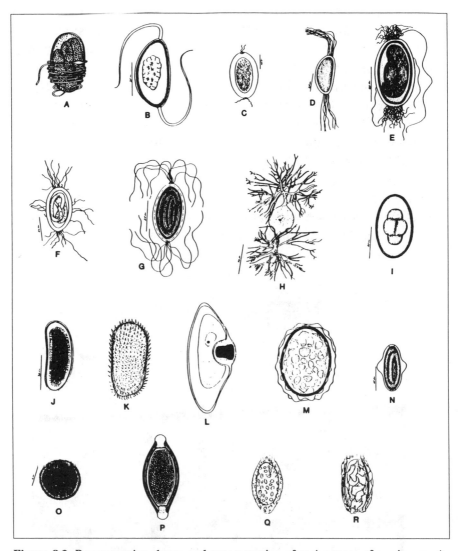

Figure 8.3. Representative shapes and ornamentation of major types of nemic ova. A. *Pseudonymus* sp. B. *Citellina marmotae*. C. *Metabronema magnum*. D. *Tetrameres nouveli* (bird parasite). E. *Tetrameres* sp. (from American woodcock). F. *Rhabdochona ovifilamenta*. G. *Cystidicola stigmatura*. H. *Mermis subnigrescens* (insect parasite). I. *Necator americanus* (American hookworm). J. *Meloidogyne* sp. (plant parasite). K. *Anaplectus granulosus*. L. *Protrellus aureus*. M. *Ascaris lumbricoides* (intestinal round-worm of man). N. *Hedruris siredonis*. O. *Dracunculus medinensis* (guinea worm). P. *Trichuris leporis* (whipworm). Q. *Dioctophyma renale* (kidney worm). R. *Hystrichis acanthocephalicus* (bird parasite). Adapted from Chitwood with permission.

membrane or an ascaroside layer, in turn, covered by a lipoprotein layer, containing chitin in the eggs of some nematodes species, which is covered by an outer lipoprotein layer. This basic structure, essentially common to all nematode eggs, is generated by the egg. Subsequently, an additional layer is contributed by the female uterus. It is this layer that can provide distinctive egg characteristics such as filaments, spines, or dimples. The physical and chemical characteristics of the nematode eggshell endow the egg with the near biological ultimate in a developmental form; a self-contained, self-maintaining, and resistant environmental unit. The egg must contain all of the nutritional substrates and precursor elements accessible to the developing embryo. In general, nematode eggs contain large amounts of glycogen (carbohydrate), lipids, proteins and lesser amounts of assorted minerals, as well as chitin and polyphenols in some species. Phospholipids and proteins have been identified in the various eggshell layers. The protein

Figure 8.4. Scanning electron microscope photograph of eggs within the uterus of *Lagochilascaris minor* (harelip *Ascaris*). Reproduced with permission from M. M. Wong, parasitologist, School of Veterinary Medicine, University of California, Davis, California.

complement usually consists of some 15–18 amino acids in varying proportions. In some species proline and hydroxyproline have been found in high concentrations, which together with other colorimetric tests suggest the presence of a collagen-like protein; in other species proline and hydroxyproline and tryptophane may be absent.

In general, the nematode eggshell's unusual properties, remarkable in the animal kingdom, inhibit passage of a variety of substances through the shell in either direction. While gases like oxygen and carbon dioxide appear to pass freely, most other substances do not. For example, fat solvents are unable to penetrate the eggshell of a human pinworm (*Enterobius vermicularis*); nor can vital basic dyes which stain the shell but do not penetrate into the egg of the intestinal round worm of humans (*Ascaris lumbricoides*). In the latter case, it is the innermost ascaroside layer which is impermeable; de-coated eggs with this layer intact will embryonate into active motile larvae even though the egg is bathed in 2 N HCl, 2 N HNO_3, 2 N NaOH, 0.5 N NH_4OH, 3.3 N formaldehyde or 4 N NaCl. The larvae die quickly if the covering membrane is ruptured. While water can pass readily through the nematode cuticle, it does not pass through the nematode eggshell. The eggs of a number of nematode species have been shown to develop normally in either hypotonic or hypertonic solutions; plasmolysis of eggs has never been observed, if the internal egg layer remains intact.

Sperm

Spermatazoa arise from the maturation and morphogenesis of spermatids. Spermatozoa of different nematode species exhibit different forms and shapes (Fig. 8.5). Though the sperm of some species have long tails (Fig. 8.5 A, G), similar to the flagellated sperm of higher animals, they are considered pseudo-flagellate because of the different structure. Other shapes include forms that are spheroidal or ellipsoidal (Fig. 8.5 B, C), trapezoidal (Fig. 8.5 F), stubby tailed (Fig. 8.5 D), or amoeboid (Fig. 8.5 E, H). Attempts have been made to categorize sperm into type groups depending upon shape, tail form, and the presence and location of internal structures including organelles, mitochondria, microtubules and chromatin material but with very limited success. Diagramatic sperm evolutionary schemes have been devised; however these are generally inconsistent with the accepted phylogenetic taxonomic schemes.

The primary energy source for nematode sperm appears to be endogenous glycogen, which it contains in considerable quantities. Sperm generally need to move to reach the egg and most are believed to accomplish this movement by swimming or pseudopodal activity, sometimes involving temporary sticking to and releasing from the uterine wall. It has also been suggested that sperm migration may be assisted by local uterine contraction induced by hormone-like substances released by the male and accompanying the sperm.

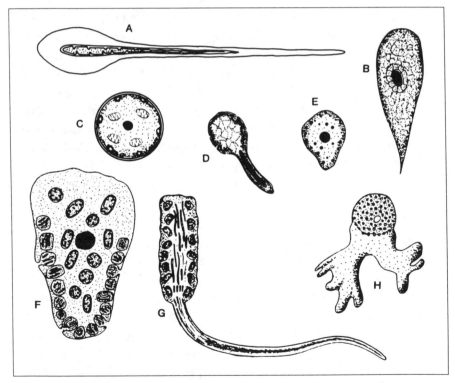

Figure 8.5. Schematic representation of sperm types observed in Nemata. A. *Aspiculuris tetraptera*. B. *Enoplus communis*. C. *Globodera rostochiensis*. D. *Ancylclostoma* sp. E. *Axonolaimus spinosus*. F. *Ascaris* sp. G. *Nippostrongylus brasiliensis*. H. *Rhabditis strongyloides*. Redrawn and adapted from various sources.

Genetic Aspects

Chromosomes

Nematode chromosomes are exceedingly small relative to those of many higher organisms. Their size and shape depend upon the stage of nuclear division and therefore the degree of condensation of the chromatin material. For example, the prophase chromosomes of *Meloidogyne incognita* (rootknot nematode) are distinct, rod-shaped and 0.5–2.5 micro meters in length and 0.4–0.5 micro meters in diameter, at metaphase when they are further condensed they appear to be spherical or ellipsoidal. Moreover, at this stage they are very close to each other and sometimes touching, therefore rendering counting and morphological observation difficult, particularly so since the observation must take place at the limits of the resolution of the optical microscope. Electron microscopy, capable of higher resolution, has rarely been used for chromosome observations in whole nuclear mounts because of the extreme difficulty in specimen preparation. The observational problems notwithstanding, these chromosomes are not identical in size and shape; while the chromosomal complement may consist largely of spherical and ellipsoidal shapes, others assume the form of straight, bent or curved rods or, in some species, crosses. Different populations of the same species may have more, less, or no such distinctive chromosomes.

The somatic chromosome number of the representatives studied from the phylum Nemata varies from two in the rhabditid *Diploscapter coronata* to nearly 50 in *Meloidogyne* (rootknot) species or *Ditylenchus dipsaci* (stem and bulb nematode). Species for which the chromosomal numbers in males and females are equal exhibit a chromosomal complement consisting of a variable number of autosomes and one sex chromosome. The sex determination is of the type XX for females and XY for males, as is common in higher animals. In other species, where cross-fertilization occurs, sex determination may be of a different type whereby females are XX and males are XO. In these species the somatic chromosomal number of males is one less than that of females. In spermatogenesis such males produce sperm containing one sex chromosome (X) or no sex chromosome (O). Some animal-parasitic nematodes have been reported to have males with more than one Y chromosome and females with an equivalent number of X chromosomes. In amphimictic species with the XX-XY determination system, each gamete exhibits n number of chromosomes to produce a somatic cell nuclear complement of 2n, whereas in the sex determination system XX-XO the female gamete possesses n chromosomes and the male n-1 to give a somatic cell nuclear complement of 2n for females and 2n-1 for males.

It is in parthenogenetic species that significant anomalies appear in the chromosome complements. Although in botanical species polyploidy is not unusual (plant breeders commonly employ techniques to double, triple or quadruple the normal chromosome complement to develop new varieties), in higher animals the presence of one chromosome more or less or even a broken chromosome can produce serious consequences, including death. Parthenogenetic nematodes appear to be much more flexible in this regard, and perhaps can be best illustrated with *Meloidogyne* spp. (rootknot nematodes), one of the better studied parthenogenetic nematode groups. *M. hapla* populations, which reproduce mostly by meiotic parthenogenesis with occasional fertilization by males, have been reported with a varied haploid chromosomal complement, i.e., n = 15 or 16 or 17. In other populations n = 14 or 15, or n = 16 or 17, and in yet others n = 15 *and* 16 or 17. In populations of the same species which reproduce by mitotic parthenogenesis, the nuclear complement can be 2n = 45 or 3n = 45 or 48. In *M. javanica*, a related species, different populations can exhibit a chromosomal complement where 2n = 46-47, 47 and 3n = 43-48. Similarly, *M. incognita* populations may exhibit 2n = 47 or 2n = 32-36 and 3n = 40-46. *M. arenaria* populations have been observed to contain 2n = 36 or 51-52-53 or 56 and 3n = 50-56. What significance the disparity in chromosome numbers is to the biology of the species remains a matter of conjecture.

An interesting phenomenon, that occurs in invertebrate animals below and above nematodes in the evolutionary tree of development of life forms, entails the existence of n males and 2n females. This condition has not been observed to occur in nematodes. However, the permutable chromosomal complements exhibited by nematodes have led some nematologists to suggest further cytogenetic studies as to whether, in *Nemata,* males can be the result of unfertilized haploid eggs while 2n females are the result of fertilization with haploid males or by mitotic parthenogenesis. The likelihood of such events merit consideration.

Hybrid Forms

Intraspecific and interspecific hybridization is known to occur in *Nemata;* however, when it has been observed, the success rate has been much reduced from normal. For example, when females (15 chromosomes) from a population of *M. hapla* unable to reproduce on strawberry were exposed to cross-fertilization by males (17 chromosomes) from a population able to reproduce on strawberry, a very small proportion of the progeny were able reproduce on strawberry, suggesting that hybridization had occurred. This was confirmed by cytological evidence that the female progeny did have 15 bivalent and 2 univalent chromosomes.

In a different species, *Caenorhabditis elegans*, females of a population unable to reproduce above 18° C were fertilized by males of a population able to reproduce at higher temperatures. The progeny could reproduce at temperatures above 18° C. In contrast, crosses between "races" of the stem and bulb eelworm (*Ditylenchus dipsaci*) produced mixed results; depending upon the kind of cross, some progeny were and others were not able to reproduce on the new host. For example, crosses of populations of *D. dipsaci* living on onion or red clover with populations from dandelion or thistle did result in fertilization , egg laying, and embryogenesis. The hybrid eggs, however, usually died; those that did survive usually disappeared after several generations.

Interspecific crosses have been demonstrated with *Pratylenchus* species amongst others. Reciprocal crosses between *P. fallax*, which is able to reproduce on host A and host B, and *P. penetrans,* which is able to reproduce on host A, exhibited clear-cut hybridization, depending on the nature of the crosses. If *P. penetrans* females were crossed with *P. fallax* males, progeny would reproduce on host A but not B; however, if *P. fallax* females were crossed with *P. penetrans* males, progeny would reproduce on hosts A and B. In either type of cross the resulting population levels were much reduced from those of normal crosses, and rapidly died out. These results are typical for interspecific crosses with the possible exception of crosses between *Heterodera schachtii* and *H. glycines,* which appear to be highly successful. These kinds of observations, particularly of interspecific successful hybridizations, pose some perplexing questions for nematode taxonomy. Species designation in animals is based heavily on reproductive isolation, which means that two species, no matter how similar morphologically, cannot produce viable hybrids. But of course, there is always the exceptional mule.

Mutations

Mutagenesis is probably as common in nematodes as it is in all other organisms. The nematode literature is replete with reports of occasional bizarre individuals exhibiting morphological aberrance, females with nonfunctional secondary male characteristics, and vice versa. In less extreme situations, the question of mutation becomes extremely ambiguous. The conventional definition asserts that a genetic mutational event has occurred if "suddenly" the progeny differ in one or more characteristics from the parents. The question is unambiguous when the event results from a mutagenic treatment, such as temperature, radiation, or application of chemical agents. There is, however, a broad gray area between extremes, where the characteristics of an initial population can change to exhibit different characteristics-not abruptly, but within a relatively short period of a few generations. In such a case the acquisition of new properties by a population is believed to be the result of a natural selection process. The very low proportion of the initial population able to cope with the new set of environmental conditions outcompetes the remaining population less able to cope, thereby resulting in a population with new characteristics. Although a mutational event may have occurred concurrently with the environmental change, it is more likely to have occurred some time in the distant past and, not being disadvantageous, remained in the population gene pool as an incidental or benign trait. It is believed that the many populations of different species which exhibit diverse characteristics, some to the point of being considered races, have arisen by means of this process.

The science of genetics took an explosive leap forward with the adoption of *Drosophila melanogaster* (fruitfly) as a study organism. Mutants could be developed easily in the laboratory by mutagenic treatments including temperature, radiation, or application of chemical agents. Crosses of individuals with different characteristics could be conducted readily under controlled conditions, the mechanics of gene transfer could be described, and the loci of genes controlling individual characteristics could be mapped on different chromosomes. Similarly, studies involving biochemical genetics sprang forward with the adoption of *Neurospora crassa* (fungus), which was much more suitable for metabolic or physiological investigations involving discrete biochemical reactions. In recent years, a somewhat more complex organism, *Caenorhabditis elegans* (a free living nematode), has been adopted as a study animal, as it is more suitable to the integration of diverse morphological and biochemical changes and the genetic criteria that bring them about. As a consequence, a wide array of mutant lines of *C. elegans* have been developed. Some incorporate mutational events that affect biochemical reactions involved in metabolism and physiological processes, morphological features, organ structure and function (including fertility, gamete generation or sensory structure and function), and environmental responses (including those to temperature, chemotactic agents or osmosis), among others. Moreover, many of the controlling gene loci have been identified on the chromosomes, and others are in that process; gene mapping is a vigorous ongoing program. With other nematodes similar studies are virtually nonexistent; nevertheless, such findings provide some insight as to what processes and what events might be hypothesized for other nematodes. Direct, across-the-board transfer and application to other species of findings with *C. elegans* must be regarded with some skepticism in as much as *C. elegans* separated out very early (probably early Paleozoic) from the phylogenetic line of other nematodes. Clearly, it is rather risky to correlate events or processes directly to other nematodes that are products of 300 million years of independent evolutionary development.

Sex Determination

Extrinsic factors, through unknown mechanisms, appear to be involved in nematode sex determination. Hermaphroditic nematodes are sometimes referred to as "intersexes" because one individual possesses male and female functions, whether it is a male that produces eggs or a female that produces sperm. More frequently, reports describe unusual individuals exhibiting usually nonfunctional, secondary sex characteristics of the opposite gender. Such individuals can be females with posterior spicules, and less frequently, males with partial vulval structures.

Sex reversal is an altogether different phenomenon that has been observed to occur in *Meloidogyne* spp. (plant-parasitic rootknot nematodes). In these nematodes, hatched larvae destined to be females, but developing under the environmental stress of crowding and restricted nutrition, undergo sex reversal to become males. The normal condition for males of rootknot species or populations in which they occur frequently is to have one testis while the females have two ovaries. Under environmental conditions in which some females undergo sex reversal, the males have two testes and the females two ovaries.

There is no question but that unequal numbers of males and females are common in nematode populations. What underlying mechanisms account for the disparity in numbers of each sex remains a mystery. It is common knowledge that slightly more human males are conceived than human females, and this is sometimes explained as a result of the somewhat greater activity of the male producing gamete. Although slight differences in the numbers of each sex are common in nematodes, there are many populations in which the number of males can vary from very few to very many. In some parthenogenetic species several males may develop along with a preponderance of females. In the animal-parasitic *Strongyloides fuellerborni*, parasitic females produce two types of eggs, one that develops into free living males and the other into free living females. The environmental conditions surrounding the developing nematode appear to be strongly influential in determining the eventual proportion of females and males. This observation came early in the development of Nematology when it was noted that mermithid nematodes infecting insect hosts were generally females when few in number but mostly males when in high numbers. The explanation involved the nutritional status of the nematodes; that is, if nutritional elements were abundant, females resulted; if nutrition was deficient, males resulted. Subsequently, similar observations were made with plant-parasitic nematodes. If small host roots were heavily inoculated with infective larvae of *Heterodera* spp. (cyst-forming nematodes) or *Meloidogyne* spp. (rootknot nematodes), larger numbers of males developed than if the inoculum were very light. So far, results of *in vitro* culture studies, in which nutrition was modified by various means, have been consistent with the observations of more natural situations. Extrinsic factors other than nutrition also can modify the eventual sex ratios, such as pH (hydrogen ion concentration) and temperature. *Aphelenchus avenae* (a fungal feeding nematode) under normal circumstances reproduces parthenogenetically into females, with an occasional male. Hatched or unhatched second stage larvae normally develop into females at temperatures up to 28° C, but into males at temperatures above 31° C. Males developed at temperatures below 28° C if the population was reared in the presence of CO_2. However, not all *A. avenae* populations are temperature determinant of sex, and other populations that are amphimictic rather than parthenogenetic have high numbers of males.

A surprising modification occurs in a plant-parasitic *Meloidodera* sp. that is exposed to gamma irradiation. Normally 1.5% of hatched second stage larvae develop into males, but over 18% of larvae absorbing 10 kilorads of radiation develop into males and with 20 kilorads of absorbed irradiation, over 27% males resulted. The irradiated males consisted of not only normal, single testis males, but also ample numbers of double testis males, indicating that irradiation-induced sex reversal had occurred.

Embryogenesis

Embryonation begins with a fertilized egg or a mature parthenogenetic egg and progresses to produce a fully-developed, first stage larva. After fertilization the time interval required to achieve the first cleavage division varies in different nematodes according to the ambient temperature and the peculiarities of each species. The time interval to the first cleavage division is about a half-hour for *Caenorhabditis elegans*, 4-6 hours for *Ditylenchus dipsaci* (the stem and bulb nematode), 10-15 hours for *Meloidogyne* spp. (rootknot nematode), 26-35 hours for *Deontostoma californicum* (marine nematode) and 38 hours for ascarids (animal parasites). The second cleavage divisions may sometimes be synchronous but subsequent cleavage divisions are rarely so. For example, in *Parascaris equorum* (animal parasite) the second cleavage divisions result in four cells assembled in a D-shape because the P_1 cell undergoes a transverse division while the AB cell divides longitudinally. In *Meloidogyne naasi* only one of the two cells formed after the first cleavage division divides again, to give rise to a three-celled embryo. This process goes one step further in *Ditylenchus destructor* (plant parasite) when one of the two cells resulting from the first cleavage division divides twice, while the other does not, to produce a five celled embryo.

Embryogenesis involves a determination of cell lineage. In nematodes, with the exception of *Caenorhabditis elegans*, embryogenesis cell lineage has been determined in the early stages; by the 16- or 32-cell stage, cell distinction becomes very difficult, divisions occur in rapid succession, and lineage becomes uncertain. Subsequent development is usually described in more general terms in which the sequence of stages—blastula, gastrula, morula, and tadpole—lead to the fully developed first-stage larva.

Remarkably, some of the classic studies of embryonic development were conducted with nematodes about a century ago. Cell lineage was determined by these investigators for upwards of 100 cells, and resulted in a schematic representation of the development of founder cells and the eventual tissues derived from them (Fig. 8.6). This general pattern has been accepted as being applicable, with perhaps minor modifications, to many nematodes. A prodigious effort in recent years has established the complete cell lineage of *Caenorhabditis elegans*. Several interesting observations have emerged from these studies. The elimination or killing of certain cells of a 45- to 60-cell embryo appears to have little effect on the future development of adjacent cells; the death of many cells not only occurs but is necessary for normal development. The somatic cell complement of the newly hatched l_1 larva consists of some 550 cells and 4 germinal cells, about 810 for the mature hermaphrodite with about 2,500 gonadal cells and about 970 in the mature male. The haploid DNA content has been estimated at 80 million base pairs, the lowest DNA content of any known animal. The increase in cells from the newly hatched larva to the adult is an obvious consequence of

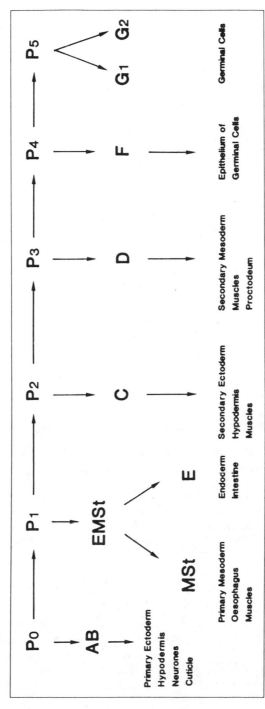

Figure 8.6. Schematic representation of early steps of embryogenesis and origin of nematode tissues. P_0 indicates the fertilized ova; P_1 to P_5 indicate a sequence of stem cells each of which represents the remainder of the embryo. AB, EMSt, C, D, F, G_1, G_2 represent the founder cells from which the various body tissues derive. Adapted from various sources.

the post-embryonic development of new structures present in the adult, the vulva, vagina, uterus, spicules, etc., and their associated muscles, nerves and connective tissue.

Behavioral Aspects

Pheromones

Pheromones are substances secreted into the environment by one individual and detected by a second, usually of the same species, eliciting a specific reaction behavior, or perhaps controlling a developmental process in the second. They are, in essence, a means of communication between two individuals.

Sex pheromones are known to play an important role in the reproductive biology of species which require fertilization by males. The best-studied phenomenon, demonstrated some 25 years ago, involved sex attraction. Single gender populations were placed on a semi-rigid medium on either side of a dialysis membrane (a membrane that permits the passage of smaller molecules but not large ones) and it was observed that if the genders were the same the nematodes remained randomly distributed; however, if the genders were different, high numbers of nematodes were found adjacent to the membrane. Currently there are upwards of 30 nematode species in which attraction pheromones have been demonstrated. In all of them the male is attracted to the female. However, there are also a few in which the female is attracted to the male. Moreover it has been found that this pheromonal activity can take place between different species. For example, in the plant parasitic cyst-forming species, *Globodera rostochiensis* and *Globodera tabacum,* males and females attract each other; however, those of the more closely related species, *Heterodera schachtii* and *H. cruciferae,* do not.

Nematode pheromones would appear to be water soluble, perhaps both volatile and nonvolatile. The sources and nature of these attractants are uncertain; in some species they are believed to derive from the dissolved cuticular material of a molting female, in others from the hypodermis or from vulval secretions and in others from the caudal gland of the male. Usually the attraction is between the sexes; rarely do members of the same gender attract each other.

A different aspect of the reproductive biology of nematodes may be mediated by a pheromone communication, in this case from a host to a nematode. It has been known for some time that in livestock species, sheep, pig, and cattle, there is a peri-parturient, a spring, or a lactation-induced rise in nematode egg output in the feces. Similar phenomena have been reported in other vertebrate and invertebrate host-nematode parasite systems. It appears that nematode reproduction is in some way keyed to the hormone levels in the host. A somewhat different phenomenon has been observed in laboratory mice infected with intestinal nematodes that involves rhythmic nematode egg deposition. To illustrate, the peak of egg production of the rodent pinworm, *Syphacia obvelata,* occurred at a period when the host showed minimum activity; whereas, the peak of egg production by the nematode *Nematospiroides dubius* coincided with the optimum general and feeding activities of the mouse host. It is uncertain whether a pheromone, or some other factor, is keying this egg production pattern.

Copulation

The purpose of copulation, of course, is the transfer of sperm from the male to the female since environmental bathing fluids, particularly water, are substantially spermacidal. The transfer process must be very intimate to avoid external exposure and sperm damage. To accomplish this process efficiently, accessory reproductive structures of males provide sensory, mechanical, and conducting means for the transfer of sperm. The mode of copulation is dependent upon the accessory features of both male and female and, as previously discussed, these are in great diversity among nematode groups. To illustrate, in *Aphelenchus avenae,* with relatively featureless sexual regions, the male gently explores the female vulva region with his tail until, perhaps by chance, the cloaca appears over the vulva at which time the spicules are thrust into the vulva. Moreover, an adhesive substance forms in the region of body contact to exclude any external interference. In other nematodes, for example *Panagrolaimus rigidus,* males, upon touching a female, immediately coil their tails to form a loop about the female, and with the aid of sensory structures slide upwards and downwards and about the female body until the cloaca is placed over the vulva and the spicules are extended into the vulva. In *Aspiculuris tetraptera* that same process occurs, but the anterior end of the nematode male bends back to press his genital region against the female.

Other constrictions may also be required. For example with *Nippostrongylus brasiliensis,* copulation requires normal adults not only to be in contact but also to be attached to the rat intestine. In other nematodes, *Ditylenchus destructor* (plant parasite) and *Nematospiroides dubius* (animal parasite), the copulatory pair are held tightly together by the clasping action of male copulatory bursa. It is interesting to note that the former nematode species copulates with a body alignment head to head, whereas with the latter it is head to tail. In other nematodes, e.g., *Oesophagostomum* species (animal parasite), the male positions its tail tip directly over the vulva and clasps a female with the caudal bursa so that the bodies of the male and the female are at right angles to one another. It is evident that modes of copulation in nematodes can be extremely diverse, with some perhaps as yet undiscovered.

Vipary

By far the largest proportion of nematodes are oviparous; eggs pass down the oviduct to become fertilized by sperm from the sperm receptacle and exit the vulva to develop outside of the nematode body. In other nematodes ovoviviparity occurs; that is, the egg begins development in the female body and may proceed to the second larval stage encased in an eggshell before being expelled. Occasionally, in very old and weak females the eggs may hatch internally to release motile larval forms. Viviparity is less common but occurs, for example, in the nematode causing trichinosis and in the guinea worm. In these cases the egg does not acquire a distinctive shell, and so embryonates to produce larvae that are retained in the uterus until expelled live.

Evolutionary Considerations

It is clear that *Nemata* exhibits multiple modes of reproduction consisting of parthenogenesis, hermaphroditism, and pseudogamy—but syngamy, requiring the cross-fertilization of females by males, is by far the most prevalent. The quandary appears to be: is sex in the process of evolution or regression? The polemics regarding the virtues, advantages and disadvantages of sexual versus asexual reproduction have been ongoing since the time of the Greek philosophers. The arguments usually revolve around several themes, one of which is the great cost in energy, time and resources that sex demands. Males and females may develop elaborate ornamentation that is presumed to impress the other gender with exceptional distinctiveness, even though these features may hinder survival. A somewhat different argument protests that the cost that sex levies on the reproductive potential of most species is high when the male half of the population offers nothing other than genes to the progeny, whereas asexual females all can reproduce and thereby increase the reproductive potential twofold. A different prevalent view maintains that the cost of a sexual union is more than compensated for by the greater genetic variation in progeny. Intuitively this appears to be so. After all, the cross of a poodle with a dachshund or a horse with a donkey gives rise to progeny that are different from the parents. On the other hand, it has been difficult to provide convincing evidence that genetic recombination from a sexual union offers any evolutionary advantage. Nematodes and other organisms reproducing by means other than cross-fertilization between two individuals appear to be just as adaptable as sexually produced ones.

Currently a different theme is emerging, based on arguments totally different from those of the past, to explain the great advantage provided by the sexual mode of reproduction that more than compensates for its high cost. To quote Richard E. Michod, evolutionary biologist:

> This theory has to do not with the adaptability of a species as a whole but with the integrity of the genetic material in the cells of each plant or animal. Sexual reproduction, it is becoming increasingly clear, plays a crucial role in the repair and maintenance of genes. During the manufacture of germ cells (eggs and sperm), a key stage in sexual reproduction, any damage the organism's genes have suffered is healed.

Deoxyribonucleic acid (DNA) is the principal molecule for the storage of information necessary to recreate a living organism. DNA consists of two strands helically entwined, each of which is made up of a specific combination of four organic basic constituents, each coupled to a pentose sugar (nucleosides) and tied together into a long chain by phosphoric acid molecules. The somatic cell multiplies by mitosis so that each daughter cell contains a copy of each chromosome pair of the mother cell. While undergoing mitosis, DNA can suffer an occasional change in the nucleoside sequence that gives rise to mutation. This event, occurring naturally within the cell, is unrecognized as an error and, if not lethal, is transferred to daughter cells. Drastic damaging change occurs when DNA is exposed to various kinds of radiation or mutagenic agents. While organisms have defensive mechanisms to counteract effects of the exposure, the nucleus eventually suffers damage. This damage, however, is recognized as an aberration and a remedial action is taken in response. Unless the damage is lethal, mechanisms are in place that may repair some or all of the damage. Excision repair, as this is called, is an ongoing process in most cells. Enzymes cut out the damage to a strand section and the resulting missing section is regenerated using a complementary strand as a guide.

Perhaps more to the point with this discussion of the value of sex is the process of meiosis, whereby a diploid germinal cell divides ultimately to produce haploid eggs or sperm, i.e., each with one copy of each chromosome. Each chromosome pair of the germinal cell doubles to form a tetrad and a measure of redundancy in genetic material. Damage to segments of chromosomes can be snipped out by enzymes and replaced by a corresponding strand from a sister chromosome. The missing strand segment can then be regenerated as in the excision process. Recombination of genetic material may also occur between the chromosome pairs before division, i.e., segments of sister chromosomes may be exchanged so that each consists of a gene mixture with portions deriving from each parent. Sex therefore provides a powerful additional mechanism to ensure that genetic maintenance functions at a highly efficient level.

Aging is sometimes explained as a consequence of damage accumulated over time that eventually overwhelms the limited capacity for self-repair. The demise of somatic cells therefore becomes inevitable, while germinal cells with highly efficient repair mechanisms remain, in a sense, immortal. Non-syngamous reproduction, which continuously recycles the same genetic, material can be expected to behave more like a somatic cell. No matter how free of harmful mutations, once this type of reproduction begins the accumulation of damaging mutation begins. Without the supplementary repair mechanism—and the addition of new genetic material to mask harmful recessive mutations—that sex provides, asexual species may be doomed to extinction, as appears to be the case. With respect to nematodes the conclusion would appear to be inescapable that those populations reproducing by parthenogenesis, hermaphroditism or psuedosyngamously, and unable to maintain an appropriate level of cross-fertilization, are also doomed to eventual extinction despite the short-term advantage in reproductive potential of the non-syngamous process.

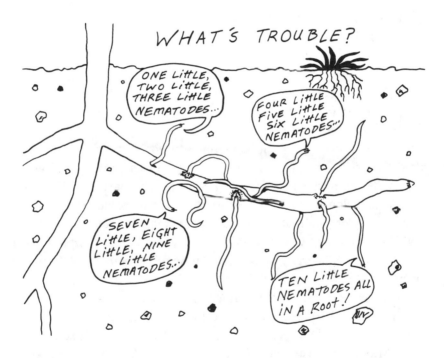

CHAPTER 9

Environmental Biology

The environment can present a myriad of obstacles to the growth, reproduction, and survival of any organism. Nematodes, like all other organisms, must cope with a range of problems and hazards including: temperature extremes, dehydration, flooding, ionic and osmotic stress, toxic chemicals, pathogens, predation, food and gender seeking, oxygen needs, light and locomotion for survival. Imagine the magnitude of these difficulties to creatures living life in the darkness of soil or mud or in the organs or tissues of host plants and animals; they have surmounted all these obstacles with remarkable success to become the most abundant of multicellular animals on earth.

Sensing

Naturally, before a nematode reacts to a potential threat or opportunity it must realize that either exists. Sensilla is the general term applied to nematode sensory organs including amphids, papillae, setae (these latter two terms are sometimes used interchangeably), and deirids (a special set of cervical papillae). Other sensory organs include phasmids, the post anal sensory organs of Secernentea, ocelli of some marine nematodes, and the gustatory sense organ located in the buccal cavity in stylet region of a plant parasitic nematode group, *Longidorus* species. Amphids were recognized early as distinct morphological features, paired laterally in the head region of the nematode. Whereas in ancestral species the amphids were believed to be located posteriorly in the head region, in the later derived species they have moved forward in a process called cephalization, to the labial region. Amphids will occur in a range of forms and shapes, from pore-like to multispiral (Fig. 9.1). Although the various forms can be used to identify certain groups of nematodes, they do not appear to have phylogenetic significance. Inside the amphid external opening lies the amphidial pouch which may be cuplike and of various shapes or a long tube that is straight, bent, or curved in various ways. Sensory neurons project into the channel

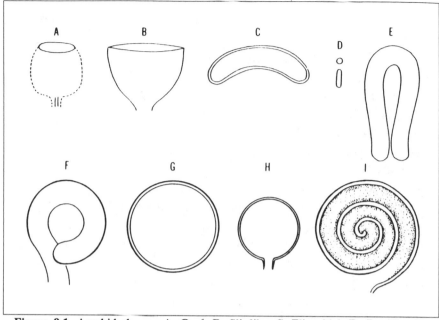

Figure 9.1. Amphid shapes: A. Oval. B. Slit-like. C. Elipsoidal. D. Porelike. E. Horseshoe. F. Unispiral. G. Circular. H. Circular, broken. I. Multispiral. After Maggenti with permission from Springer-Verlag.

and vary in number according to the species: *Dirofilaria immitis* (dog heartworm) has nine, *Caenorhabditis elegans* has twelve, Panagrellus silusiae has thirteen, and *Paratrichodorus minor* has twenty three. Amphids are generally believed to recieve signals chemically, a conclusion derived primarily by analogy to similar structures with well defined functions in other organisms. It has been reported that a *C. elegans* normally responds to certain solutes in solution, whereas its amphid-less mutant does not; unfortunately, however, such evidence must be viewed as circumspect until the mutant has been shown to suffer no other disorder than the absence of amphids. Furthermore, amphids of different nematode species have been reported to exude substance through the amphidial opening, mucous in the case *C. elegans*, anticoagulant from *Ancylostoma caninum* (dog hookworm) and *Syngamus trachea* and acetylcholine esterase in *Necator americanus* (hookworm). Clearly, the function of amphids is not very well resolved.

Most nematode sense organs are traditionally referred to as papillae (minute nipple-like projections from the cuticle) or setae (longer projections from the cuticle, sometime bristle-like protuberances, that articulate about the cuticle junction). Examples are tubiform setae, ambulatory setae, or bristle setae. Sensilla have been categorized into different groupings, e.g., exteroceptors, sense organs reflecting conditions of the external environment and interoceptors, reflecting those of internal conditions, another categorization is Type I, exhibiting a nerve process to a particular organ, and Type II, exhibiting a nerve process to the inner surface of the cuticle, or mechanoreceptors, sensing tactile events and chemoreceptors, sensing the chemical agents in their surroundings. A range of sensilla types are illustrated in Fig. 9.2. Those sense organs with external openings, e.g., amphids, sensilla basiconica (Fig. 9.2 C), and perhaps sensilla coeloconica (Fig. 9.2 D) and sensilla ampullastoma (Fig. 9.2 E), are believed to sense chemicals, whereas the others (Fig. 9.2 A,B and F) are believed to be mechanoreceptors responding to tactile stimuli. Many such sense organs have complex subcuticular structures incorporating associated support cells. Moreover, in some genera, e.g., *Caenorhabditis, Capillaria,* and *Heterakis*

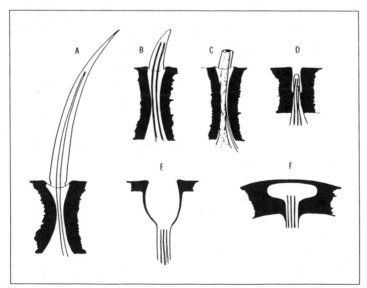

Figure 9.2. Forms of Sensilla found in Nemata: A. Sensilla trichodea. B. Sensilla basiconica. C. Sensilla basiconica, associated with glands. D. Sensilla coeloconica. E. Sensilla ampullastoma. F. Sensilla insiticus. After Maggenti with permission from Springer-Verlag.

a papilla is alleged to exhibit both mechano- and chemoreceptor function.

Other more specialized sensory organs include the gustatory organ observed in some *Longidorus* species, which is somehow involved in modulating the feeding process, and ocelli observed in some marine nematodes. The ocelli are paired and located anteriorly, partially embedded in the esophagus. They incorporate a pigmented spot with a lens-like structure just forward of the pigmentation. Ocelli are complex structures incorporating nerve processes, associated support cells, a pigmented area, and a lens-like structure. The pigmentation appears to be a melanin-like substance with a light shielding, rather than a light sensitive, property. Morphologically, ocelli are reminiscent of eye structures in higher order animals. But directional light responses have yet to be demonstrated. While the pigmented areas are paired and usually associated with lens-like objects, a second pair of pigmented regions not associated with lens-like structures may be observed posterior to the primary set. Indeed, in some nematodes tiny pockets of pigmentation are generally distributed throughout the esophagus. Although nematodes are known to respond to light, specific sensory organs for this purpose have not been identified. Neither has it been shown what particular sensillum is responsible for any specific sensing function.

While mechanoreceptors are presumed to be protected from the external environment by a cuticular covering, chemoreceptors that presumably require an external outlet to the environment are not. It has been shown for at least two nematodes attracted by carbon dioxide solutions that a ten minute bath in dilute solutions of many modulating agents alters the capacity of the CO_2 sensor to detect the CO_2 concentration gradient. Depending upon the kind and the concentration of the modulating agent, CO_2 sensing can be reduced or enhanced. Generally, lower concentrations enhance and higher concentrations reduce the nematodes' responsiveness. Modulating agents are able to improve the CO_2 sensory responses to enhance nematode attraction to a CO_2 source at very low concentrations (10^{-7} to 10^{-9} M). Moreover, these sensor modulation effects appear to be reversible, i.e., if treatment with the first modulating agent either enhances or reduces the CO_2 sensing activity, treatment with a second modulating agent of opposite properties can reduce or enhance the CO_2 sensing action. In some cases reversibility can be ascribed to oxidation-reduction systems or solubility product considerations; in other cases there is no plausible explanation. In general, it appears that CO_2 sensing capacity is effected by changes in the conformation of the CO_2 receptor brought about by the action of the modulating agents in solution. These observations appear consistent with recent findings on human olfactory system mechanisms involving hundreds of protein receptors for the detection of a wide array of compounds, a problem also encountered by nematodes. Perhaps the olfactory research to map cilia receptors and match them with odors they recognize will serve as a guide for similar research with nematodes matching sensilla receptors to their function. Much remains to be learned about sensing and sensor organs in nematodes.

Ionic Regulation

Nematodes, like all other organisms in nature, utilize "semipermeable" membranes to separate internal solutes from those of the bathing medium. The membrane serves as a barrier that permits the passage of selected solutes (usually small molecules or ions) through the membrane but inhibits the passage of large ions and organic solutes, including peptides and proteins. Water, however, passes readily through the membrane in either direction. The laws of thermodynamics require solvent in a sealed container to manifest a stable characteristic free energy level; in a sealed container a solution (some concentration of solute in the same solvent) must also manifest a stable but higher characteristic free energy level. If the two containers are uncovered and placed in a closed box which permits the free exchange of vapors above the two solutions, the solvent-solution system is rendered unstable. The free energy of the solvent is less than the free energy of the solution; therefore the system can only become stable when the solution achieves the lowest possible free energy level. For this to occur solvent from its container must vaporize, move through the gas phase and dissolve in the solution until all of the liquid solvent has evaporated and the vapor pressure above both containers is equal and the lowest free energy level of the solution is obtained. Similarly, when solvent and solution are separated only by a semi-permeable membrane (no vapor phase connection), solvent must pass through the membrane into the solution until the lowest system free energy level or equilibrium is attained. The difference of the chemical potentials of the solvent molecules in both solutions is the driving mechanism creating excess pressure (osmotic pressure) in the solution. At equilibrium the vapor pressure above the solution under the influence of osmotic pressure is thermodynamically required to be equal to that of the pure solvent. For a nematode in equilibrium with the bathing solution the internal osmotic pressure created by solutes in the body fluids must be equal to the osmotic pressure of the bathing solution plus the pressure created by the elastic cuticle resisting further stretching by the internal pressure.

Water passes freely through the membranes of the nematode integument, but most salts and organic solutes do not, unless the integrity of the membrane is disrupted by heat or organic solvents. Nevertheless, fat soluble organic solutes eventually are able to penetrate the integument (most probably by dissolution into and transport via the lipid layers of the membranes). By virtue of the characteristics of semi-permeable membranes, a nematode immersed in a bathing solution of greater osmotic pressure (hypertonic) than that of the internal contents will withdraw water from the nematode; if the bathing solution is of less osmotic pressure (hypotonic) the bathing solution will lose water to the nematode. The bathing solution is considered isotonic when it neither withdraws water from the nematode or loses water to it. While marine nematodes live in an environment whose osmotic pressure varies very little, other nematodes live in aquatic environments in which the osmotic pressure can vary substantially, e.g., nematodes living in soil environments, brackish water, plant and animal host tissues and intertidal zones. Nematodes in soil must contend with high osmotic pressure solutions when the soil is dry and very low osmotic pressures when it is flooded with rain water. Nematodes in brackish water or intertidal zones must cope with similar variations in the environmental osmotic pressure effected by changes in salinity, while plant and animal hosts must cope with differing osmotic conditions in the course of migration through tissues. Laboratory experiments have demonstrated that nematodes placed in hypertonic solutions quickly lose water and shrink, whereas others, particularly marine nematodes, placed in hypotonic solutions quickly take up water and swell. If the bathing conditions are not too drastic, many nematodes are able to regulate, i.e., they tend to recover to nearly their normal size in five to eight hours. Nematode analyses have shown that after such regulation, the internal content of salts is greater than normal. Over long periods of mild osmotic stress nematodes appear to be able to adjust to the changed conditions and resume normal activity. This is probably accomplished not only by transport through the nematode integument but also via the gut through excretion of excess water or salts. The integument permeability of marine nematodes is perhaps one hundred times greater than that of soil born bacterial feeding nematodes or plant-parasitic nematodes. While some of the latter two nematode types may have similar permeability, others do not, since for example, several soil-borne bacterial feeders or predators can be separated from plant-parasitic forms by immersion in hypertonic solutions, allowing time for regulation then followed by a subsequent immersion in distilled water. While the plant-parasitic forms quickly resume their normal state, the others take in excess water and explode. The observations to date suggest that our understanding of nematode integument permeability, ionic or solute transport and mechanisms of regulation and adaptation to osmotic stress is in need of substantial improvement.

Excretion

Analyses of solutions in which different nematode species have been incubated have revealed a wide array of products, including organic acids, fatty acids, nitrogen bases, urea, ammonium and carbonate ions, a range of cations and anions, amino acids, peptides, enzymes, and bacteria, among other components. A major problem of animal metabolism involves the detoxification or elimination of excess nitrogen and different animal groups have developed different mechanisms for accomplishing this task. How this is accomplished in nematodes is largely a matter of speculation, although it appears that several mechanisms may be involved, depending perhaps on the species or the environmental niche occupied. It is extraordinarily difficult to obtain any secretion or excretion from most nematodes that is free of contaminants; therefore, analyses are unable to differentiate between or correlate with any specific secretion or excretion. Sources for such products are many and varied, for example the stoma, anus, excretory pore, amphid, hypodermal and caudal glands, and perhaps other avenues, including reproductive organs when present. Emanations from all these sources have been noted through microscopic observations.

Defecation in nematodes has been a poorly studied process. In most nematodes defecation appears to be a simple pressure-driven process. Feeding involves active esophageal pumping to force nutrients through the alimentary canal against the pressure gradient. At some threshold pressure the nematode simply relaxes the sphincter muscle at the intestinal-prerectal junction and activates the anal muscles to provide an opening to the outside. A portion of the intestinal contents are ejected to reduce the internal pressure to the normal range, at which point the sphincter again activates and closes the intestinal-prerectal junction. Overall, the nematode swells slightly upon feeding and shrinks upon defecation.

Some nematodes have an additional valve between the prerectum and rectum so that defecation occurs in steps. The sphincter muscle at the intestinal-prerectal junction relaxes, allowing the intestinal contents to flow into the prerectum; at this point the sphincter closes and the prerectum-rectum valve opens, allowing the contents to move into the rectum and, with the activation of the dilator muscle opening the anus, voids to the outside. In certain nematodes there occurs a certain kind of peristaltic process in which a wave of somatic muscular contraction moves posteriorly down the hind gut to force excretory products out of the anus.

The pressure driven process of defecation can be demonstrated with *Ascaris* (a large intestinal parasite) by placing the animal in a hypotonic solution. The rapid uptake of water increases the internal pressure to such a high level that when the anus is held above the liquid and the sphincter opens, the fecal jet released can fly 100 centimeters. Interestingly, the laxative effect that bicarbonate solutions have on higher animals appears to occur also in nematodes.

Behavior

Behavioral patterns in nematodes are varied and wide-ranging. The deportment of a nematode, as is the case with most animals, involves a response to a stimulus, usually external, which may be transient or long-acting. Nematodes, like other poikilothermic (cold-blooded) animals, depend upon an appropriate environmental temperature to function optimally. Although such animals do not function as well when temperatures are below or above the optimum, there are characteristic high and low temperature thresholds at which normal activity ceases while the nematode remains alive. Within the active range nematodes do function, though it has been shown with several nematode species that if they are reared at some temperature for several generations, and succeeding generations are given a choice, they prefer and function best at the rearing temperature. Whether this response is a consequence of natural selection or some other factor is open to question.

Of all the behavioral phenomena expressed by nematodes, the orientation and reaction (taxes) to different stimuli has been studied most thoroughly. Positive taxis means an orientation and movement toward the stimulus, and negative taxis means an orientation and movement away from the stimulus.

A positive phototaxis (orienting and moving in relation to a light source) was reported some seventy years ago in an observation of old world hookworm larvae. Over the years it has been shown that a number of nematodes exhibit positive phototaxis, others are indifferent to photostimulation, and others exhibit negative phototaxis. Unfortunately, many of the early experiments failed to separate radiation frequencies producing visible light from those of the long wave infrared radiation generating heat. In subsequent studies, when this distinction was made, the observations were less clear-cut and often in conflict with the earlier results. Nevertheless, strong phototaxis responses do occur: *Panagrellus silusiae* is negatively phototropic, as it accumulates on the dark side of a culture dish while *Rhabditis* species, which often contaminate mushroom beds, climbs to the top of the highest particle of the bed and on themselves when exposed to illumination. Larval stages of *Dictyocaulus viviparus* (lung worm of cattle) move away from the dung pile by the aid of the fungus *Pilobolus kleinii* but when illuminated the larvae climb up the erect hyphae to accumulate on the sporangium. When the sporangium explodes to disperse black sporangia, the nematodes go along and become dispersed over a two to three meter area. Several other animal-parasitic nematodes exhibit a similar behavior. Some nematodes, *Haemonchus contortus* (animal parasite) and *Aphelenchoides ritzema-bosi* (foliar parasite) appear to do best in decreased light (intensities of 50–100 foot candles).

Different and unusual responses have also been noted. The gravid female of *Mermis subnigrescens* (insect parasite) exhibits a red spot in the head region. The wave length of light striking this spot modulates the rate of uterine contraction.   Adults of the filarial nematode, *Litomosoides carinii,* react to strong light by violent motion. Other nematodes, upon exposure to light, increase their initial activity but then, decrease activity to very low levels on continued illumination. A recent report indicates a novel response to light by several mermithid nematodes; in this case, the nematodes oriented perpendicularly to an incident light ray and moved in this orientation until they left the incident beam. The mechanisms by which light induces such reactions remain a mystery. A photo response yet to be considered with nematodes involves the influences of photoperiodism on the resumption or shutting down of life cycle processes with seasonal changes.

Temperature Responses

As has been indicated, poikilothermic nematodes function within a characteristic temperature range, with the optimum somewhere between the extremes. In contrast, those nematode parasites that infect homothermic (warm-blooded) animals function best at the hosts' body temperature.   Not all poikilothermic nematodes have identical temperature ranges and optima—the temperature range may be shifted downward or upwards depending upon the species characteristics. Not only can the temperature ranges of two species within one genus be different, but also different life functions, e.g., hatching, mobility, invasion, and growth may have different optimum temperatures. These general temperature effects notwithstanding, thermotaxes (reactions to temperature) are also exhibited by nematodes. Some of the animal-parasitic nematodes, e.g., old world and new world hookworms, *Strongyloides stercoralis* and other parasites from tiger and ostrich, serve as the best example of positive thermotaxes. In laboratory demonstrations such nematodes, mixed with very small insoluble particles, were placed in the dish covered with a cover slip. When the cover slip was touched at a point with a hot glass rod, nematodes swam to the heat source and stayed there while the insoluble particles flowed past with the convection stream; this response could be elicited repeatedly. Some animal-parasitic nematodes, e.g., *Nippostrongylus brasiliensis*, *Rhabdias bufonis* (from frogs) and *Camallanus* (from turtles) exhibit "suicidal" thermotaxes. They persist in moving to higher and higher temperatures until they die. Similar responses are known elsewhere in the animal kingdom and occur with certain mites and plerocercoids. Some plant-parasitic nematodes, e.g., *Pratylenchus penetrans*, *Ditylenchus dipsaci*, and *Tylenchorhynchus claytoni*, can move up heat gradients of a fraction of a degree per centimeter, while others can not. The temperature taxes discussed are thermopositive; occasionally one is negative, e.g., *Dorylaimus saprophilus*, which moves away from a heat source. At least one nematode has resolved its problem with thermotaxis to suit its own purposes. *Terranova decipiens* (from cod muscle) will migrate up the thermogradient to 32.5 C or down a thermogradient to 32.5 C, its preferred temperature of activity and survival.

Chemical Responses

Nematodes residing in soil, in thick muds, or in animal and plant tissues spend all or part of their lives in total darkness, under conditions in which light and temperature differences play minor roles. Nematodes in such environs must be able to perceive external conditions in terms of quality (organic and inorganic solutes and ions) and quantity (concentration). Chemosensing, discussed in chapter 5, is believed to be the major avenue by which this is accomplished by nematodes. Laboratory experiments have demonstrated that a wide range of substances, including anions, cations, alkalis, acids, sugars, amino acids, adenosine monophosphate (AMP), cyclic guanosine monophosphate (GMP), and reducing agents, among others, can be attractive depending on the nematode species characteristics. Moreover, a number of the same substances which attract at low concentrations repel at high concentrations. Gases such as carbon dioxide attract a number of nematodes while oxygen attracts others. In nature, complex mixtures of unknown substances, such as are released from roots, growing bacterial and fungal colonies, and adult nematode females, can attract various species of plant-parasitic nematodes, free living nematodes, or males of the same species.

For the present, it appears that chemoattraction in nematodes is likely to be a response to a summation of nonspecific stimuli emanating from some complex source. Unfortunately, the processes by which a nematode distinguishes a food source, prey or predator, friend or foe, suitable or unsuitable environment and male or female of the same species remain a mystery. Unless a better understanding of chemosensing and chemotaxes is achieved, it is unlikely that there will be a reasonable explanation for a range of striking natural phenomena. For example, how do many plant-parasitic nematodes accumulate in the region of elongation of a growing root or at the site of an emerging adventitious root? How does a foliar nematode climb the plant stem to penetrate the apical meristem of a growing point or a young leaf? How does an animal-parasitic nematode penetrate the skin or intestine to enter the bloodstream? How does it move into a muscle to encyst, or move to the lungs, up the trachea into the pharynx, and down the esophagus to the intestine to continue its development? How do microfilariae establish a circadian rhythm? How do they accumulate in blood-sucking insects in greater numbers than can be explained by the quantity of ingested blood (if the microfilarial blood concentration were equal to that of blood from a finger prick)? How do the microfilariae that develop into third stage larvae migrate to the salivary glands and proboscis region of the mosquito or other blood-sucking insect and down both sides of the proboscis to the feeding site on a new host? How do marine nematodes accumulate and remain in fungal mats placed on the sea floor?

Touch Responses

Nematode body surfaces are generally endowed with what appear to be mechanoreceptors, located on setae (Fig. 9.2 A,B,F). Setae come in various forms and lengths; in marine nematodes it is not uncommon for setae length to be of the order of a body width. It has long been known that touching a nematode body, no matter how lightly, can produce body movement responses. Observations of nematode pairs preparing to copulate suggest that tactile responses are utilized by nematodes to achieve the appropriate positioning for copulation. In those nematodes that aggregate or swarm, tactile responses appear to aid in the formation of entangled clumps of nematodes. It seems reasonable that a nematode without a visual or acoustic sensing system would rely on chemosensing and tactile sensing to move about in its niche. Tactile sensing, for example, would be extremely useful in detecting obstacles and constricting pore spaces in a soil environment.

While mechanoreceptors can be viewed as absolutely indispensable to a nematode, it is not known which seta does what or what functions distinguish different types of setae. In some nematodes these setae are connected together via a peripheral nerve net. There remains much to be learned about whether the net is commonplace among nematodes and, indeed, how the entire tactile sensing system functions.

Geotaxes

Geotaxes, i.e., nematode movements in response to gravity, have often been evoked to explain nematode movements down through a soil column or upwards on a leaf blade or stem. Although gravitational force acts on nematodes as it does on any other particle, whether animate or inanimate, this force is exceedingly small due to the small size and mass of the animals. The density of nematodes is slightly greater than that of water so that the downward force acting on an aquatic nematode is due to the mass of the nematode less the mass of the corresponding volume of water. The resultant downward force is, therefore, virtually negligible in comparison to the surface tension forces of water and the counter frictional forces exerted by the nematode involved in movement (see locomotion). Consequently, the movements of nematodes up a stem or down a soil column are, for all practical purposes, independent of gravity.

Aggressive Behavior

Aggressive responses to stress, heretofore unrecognized behavioral phenomena in nematodes (but common to all organisms) are arousing great interest and concern, particularly as such behavior impacts applied nematology and helminthology. Nature evolved the process of adapting in order to cope with change early in the history of life forms. Evolution has been and continues to be fueled by modification, the flexibility and adaptability of species; species unable to adapt to environmental pressures of whatever origin disappear, an observation consistent with the fossil records. The capacity to adapt is inherent in most organisms; moreover, the environmental stresses driving the process are not limited to climatic or habitat modifications, but include such factors as pests, diseases, nutrients, hosts, and chemotherapeutics, among others.

Pest-like organisms have been part of the planet's environment for eons. Those forms that were unable to adapt have disappeared. Those that were flexible evolved into the current complement of weeds, microorganisms, insects, nematodes, and others. To modern man their organismal relationships took on an anthropological hue, i.e., organisms simply seeking food became pests and live nutritional sources became hosts. Pests that became dominant and overwhelmed the host destroyed the food source and disappeared. Hosts that dominated and overwhelmed the pest caused the pest to disappear. The relationships between organisms that have survived are dynamic, competitive ones

the small society   by Bill Yates

Figure 9.3. A popular cartoon "the small society" illustrating the vagaries of nature as they apply to evolution and the endeavors of mankind. After Bill Yates with special permission of King Features Syndicate Inc.

in which each component alternately may achieve a modest advantage but never becomes overwhelmingly dominant. This adaptive process in nematodes has probably been active since the Paleozoic era. The essential point is that nonadaptability to stress in an organism is tantamount to extinction. Consequently, the greater the capacity for flexibility and adaptability under stress, the greater the probability for survival (Fig. 9.3).

This phenomenon was recognized many years ago by the famous German chemist Paul Ehrlich, the father of chemotherapy, who envisioned "magic bullets" of drugs to cure many diseases of man, but who became frustrated by his subsequent observations that drug resistance followed the development of new chemotherapeutic agents "like a faithful shadow." The widespread use of antibiotics during this last half century has dramatically raised the specter of drug resistance development to nearly catastrophic proportions in modern medicine. In a parallel situation, the use of modern pesticides for weed, insect, and plant pathogen control has resulted in dramatic increases in pest resistance—to the point that hundreds of pesticides have become useless. Until recently, nematodes had been essentially ignored with respect to their capacity to adapt to pesticides or other forms of environmental stress; now there is abundant evidence that nematode populations adapt to nematicides and other forms of environmental stress, as do most other organisms. This capacity for change is commonplace in all nematodes, whether plant and animal-parasitic or free living bacterial or fungal feeders. In short, this means that if a nematode population is subjected to a persistent environmental stress, whether climatic (temperature, light, moisture), chemical (pesticides, salinity, fertilizers, pollutants) or nutritional (hosts, prey), for some threshold period in excess of five generations, the probability is excellent that the original nematode population will modify for survival and adapt to the new conditions. Moreover, this adaptability can be expected to be reflected by changes in biological characteristics and physiological processes.

Bioelectric Phenomena

That animals respond to electric fields should be evident to the avid fisherman who collects his own earthworm bait electrically by plunging two electrodes into soil several meters apart and connecting them to a power supply. Animal reactions should also be plain to the handyman who inadvertently receives a shock while conducting minor electrical repairs or to anyone who walks across a carpet and receives a shock upon touching a door knob. A number of animals, protozoans, mollusks, and fish migrate to one or the other electrode in an electric field; in fact, Departments of Fish and Game routinely depend on this response in counting or sampling fish populations. Some organisms routinely use electrical fields for defense, such as the electric eel, which stuns its tormenters. Others, such as sharks, locate prey by following the weak electric fields generated by small fish. Nearly a half century ago a number of nematode species were observed to migrate toward a cathode (negative electrode) after being placed for some eight hours in a direct current field generated by a battery. Laboratory experiments with shorter electrode distances and higher direct current electrical fields, on the order of ten volts per centimeter, confirmed the original findings. These observations led to odd control experiments where electrodes were placed in or dragged through a field via tractor power (connected to very large direct current generators). The only effect noted was that if the current was high enough, the heat generated by the huge DC current passing through the soil killed nematodes. To clear the nematodes and many other organisms in a very small field it would be necessary to connect the entire electrical output of a Niagara Falls. Experiments also revealed that some nematode species move to the anode (positive electrode) preferentially. Moreover, it was observed that modifying the hydrogen ions (pH) of the electrified medium, or treating nematodes with cationic or anionic detergents, could modify the rate or the direction of migration. Although dead nematodes did not migrate in an electric field, not all live ones did either, but a significant portion did. Whereas fish, or sharks, are able to detect a very weak electric field, perhaps with specialized sensors, and move rapidly towards it, nematodes, in the light of current knowledge, do not. The most likely explanation for nematode migration in an electric field involves simple electrophoresis, the process by which charged molecules in solution drift (are attracted) to the electrode of opposite charge. In a solution of very low conductivity the electric field induces a charge separation at the extremes of the nematodes' body that polarizes the worm opposite to the polarity of the electric field. The driving force generated by the electric field is too weak to drag a nematode through a soft agar gel or an aqueous sand matrix; nonetheless, a wriggling nematode subjected to a persistent driving force migrates preferentially in the direction of the attracting electrode. Attempts to apply this notion by charging growing plants in a fashion to repel nematodes have been unsuccessful because of circuit junction incompatibility, i.e., an inability to connect a plant to a power supply without destroying plant tissue at the junction.

More recent laboratory exploratory experiments have revealed an unusual electric field phenomenon with potentially useful applications for control of living nematodes. A single vermiform nematode (*Xiphinema index*) was placed in a drop of very dilute electrolyte on a microscope slide with a microelectrode near each end of the nematode. When connected to a power supply generating one volt of direct current (D.C.) or 60 cycle alternating current (A.C.), the nematode remains active for over a half hour. However, if the power supply generates an R.F. electric field of one volt at 40 Khz (40,000 cycles) the nematode dies in about 30 seconds. Not only does the nematode become straight and inactive, but the internal contents can be seen to become increasingly granulated. The bioelectric properties of radio frequency (R.F.) fields are poorly understood. For example, a 200 Hz electric field is more lethal to humans than the normal household 60 Hz field, whereas a radio frequency field is not lethal to humans and, in fact, is used in hospitals to monitor patient pulse and respiration frequency.

In another case of interesting phenomena, when a dense packet of nematodes is placed as a dense spot on a horizontal agar plate and centered directly between two poles in a vertical magnetic field, and a horizontal D.C. electric field is generated, as previously described, not only do the nematodes move as prescribed by the electric field but also in a direction perpendicular to it. The path of the nematodes is not linear but curved; in fact, the path is described by the right hand rule used in physics to describe the curvature of a charged particle moving through a magnetic field. In particle physics very strong magnetic fields are required to bend very high speed charged particles as in particle accelerators; it is striking that a nematode moving in the direction of an electric field, at the rate of about a centimeter or so an hour, can be deviated by twenty-five to fifty percent of this distance in a perpendicular direction by the magnetic field. Although no ferromagnetic organelles have yet been observed in nematodes, physicists have suggested that some factor other than a charged particle moving in a magnetic field (as in cyclotrons) may be involved in explaining the exaggerated deviation—the charge of the nematode and the strength of the magnetic field are much too weak. Much remains to be learned about bioelectric phenomena in *Nemata*.

Survival Mechanisms

Nematodes lifespans vary greatly; in some species a lifespan may be a few days, while in others it may be a few years. Under ideal conditions, when all life cycle constraints are met, life processes proceed continuously, cycle after cycle. In the real world,, however, interruptions are commonplace; brought about by either environmental changes (temperature, moisture, photoperiod, etc.) or nutritional changes (absence of host, prey, microorganisms). Although literature reports suggest that some nematodes (e.g., certain plant-parasitic species) require a rest period before initiating the next cycle, this notion is often suspect since these observations are usually made in nature. When some of these nematodes are brought into the greenhouse, they cycle continuously. It is likely that in many cases these observations are a consequence of some external interruption of the kind just discussed. Without question, nematodes can survive substantial adversity, waiting to resume normal life processes when conditions become favorable. They are known to survive ambient freezing temperatures, desiccation and absence of food sources for varying periods.

Nematodes function best at some characteristic optimum temperature; above this temperature, body functions quickly deteriorate as enzyme denaturation increases and membrane function falters.

Below the optimum temperature enzyme reaction rates decrease and the overall nematodes' functions become more sluggish. For many nematodes at a temperature threshold of about 15°C the major life processes, e.g., feeding, migration, and reproduction, virtually cease; the nematode is alive but in a dormant-like state with primarily the internal life-sustaining functions operating. For some terrestrial nematodes this temperature threshold may be as low as 10°C. In this "dormant" stage many terrestrial nematodes can survive temperatures of −10°C (16°F) for weeks. When nematodes do freeze in nature or in the laboratory, they die primarily because with slow freezing, ice crystals form and grow to disrupt membranes and organelles. However, some nematodes, if protected with certain agents and frozen quickly, as in liquid nitrogen, can survive for years. Marine nematodes do not suffer the extreme variations in temperature with which terrestrial forms must cope; nevertheless their reaction to a low temperature threshold is believed to be similar although the optimum is often shifted downward to correspond to that of ambient seawater. In Antarctica however marine nematodes have been found to function well at temperatures of −2°C (29°F) year round.

In Chapter 7, which discussed dispersion, it was indicated that many nematodes could be moved by wind (such as in dust storms). Such nematodes are dry, of course, and in a state of anhydrobiosis (lacking water) as an aspect of the more general term cryptobiosis (Greek: hidden life). The desiccation of soils and plant material is a commonplace occurrence in nature, and one with which many terrestrial nematodes have evolved a way to cope. Some vermiform nematodes can be dried very quickly to a brittle body form, and yet retain the ability to revive when immersed in water. Most, however, require a gradual desiccation process lasting over several days to achieve this state. For those nematodes in which the onset of anhydrobiosis has been studied, the nematode loses water and begins to collapse and shrink much as it would in a salt-generated hyperosmotic solution. With continued drying, radial body folding becomes more pronounced (reminiscent of the leg warmers used by dancers) and the body begins to curl ventrally. The end result is a tight, ventrally curved nematode with cuticular folds resembling a partially extended concertina. Such a nematode is totally inactive in terms of any current physiological measurement such as respiration or enzyme activity, and although a nematode in a state of anhydrobiosis may have insufficient water to support any physiological reaction it must retain sufficient water or water substitute to preserve the integrity of the membranes, organelles and proteins. Although anhydrobiosis in nematodes has been poorly studied, it has been shown that gradual desiccation effects the production of substances not normally present. In *Aphelenchus avenae* there is an accumulation of glycerol and trehalose (a non reducing disaccharide); in *Ditylenchus myceliophagus*, glycerol and adonitol (a pentose sugar alcohol); in *Anguina tritici* trehalose and inositol (a cyclic alcohol); in *Ditylenchus dipsaci*, trehalose. It appears that these substances provide additional chemical stability to the water tightly bound to the polar groups of membranes and proteins. While the carbohydrates have been shown to be superior in maintaining the integrity of the membranes for dry conditions, inositol and glycerol may be able to protect the functional integrity of the proteins. As membranes and proteins dry, they tend to unfold, exposing sulfhydryl (–SH) groups, which can cross link to other proteins, especially in the presence of oxygen, to disrupt the integrity of both proteins. The presence of oxygen stimulates the production of highly reactive free-radicals that instigate different cross molecular bond formations in lipids, carbohydrates and proteins to cause additional degradation. Conversely the addition of sulfhydryl protecting substances and free-radical inhibiting substances helps to maintain the functional integrity of the nematode components. Those nematodes (*Plectus* species) which can withstand quick drying appear to be preadapted, by some unknown mechanisms, for desiccation (at the cellular level).

Some nematodes have evolved an alternate life cycle to ensure the survival of the species; *Strongyloides stercoralis*, an animal parasite, operates by way of the parasitic cycle so long as conditions are favorable, but shifts to a free living cycle taking place totally in soil, when conditions change. Nematodes can survive starving conditions for varying periods of time; longevity under such conditions is a function of rate of metabolism and the quantity of depot storage products—usually lipids and some glycogen. To illustrate: a freshly hatched rootknot larva maintained at optimum storage temperature remains active for about thirty days; however, whereas initially its gut was dark and packed, after thirty days it appears as a barely visible, translucent ghost. In contrast, a sugar beet nematode larva maintained under the same conditions maintains a dark gut after thirty days; in fact, sugar beet nematode larvae have been reported to remain viable in moist soil for at least two years. This situation is sometimes referred to as arrested development, inasmuch as a life cycle cannot continue until a host is present. In some animal-parasitic nematodes this response pattern can be modified. To illustrate, larvae of hookworm species that infect tissues of a paratenic host are unable to develop further; however, when such larvae are extracted from the tissue they are found to be active and infective long after other larvae maintained in a solution at the same temperature have died. A similar phenomenon occurs in seals, nematode larvae penetrate the flippers of males and females and migrate throughout the body. Larvae in the female seal migrate to the mammaries and suckling pups become infected via the milk. Nematode adults are found only in the intestine of suckling pups, never in the gut of males or females. Different variations of these kinds of arrested development patterns also occur in other animal-parasitic species.

Perhaps the most striking examples of arrested development involve the "resistant stage." The discussion of reproductive biology in Chapter 8 revealed that the nematode egg constitutes a self-sufficient, independent unit whose intact eggshell prevents the passage of solutes and most solvents. The effectiveness of the egg as a resistant stage survival unit can be best appreciated by considering the eggs of *Ascaris lumbricoides* (intestinal round worm of man) and those contained in a cyst of the sugar beet nematode, both of which can survive at least thirty years in soil.

Under stress, many microbivorous nematodes, such as rhabditids, are able to form a special resistant nonfeeding juvenile stage, commonly called a dauer larva. The dauer is characteristically morphologically and physiologically different from the normal third stage developmental juvenile. The cue for redirected development to dauer formation comes during earlier developmental stages and appears to arise as a consequence of nutritional deficiency or some other environmental stimulus. The process begins during the second stage with the collapse of the gut and the closure of the oral opening. Dauers can be motile or nonmotile; some climb blades of grass or other high points to attach to vertebrates and be transported elsewhere; others enter animal organs, for example the head glands of ants, the metanephridia of earthworms, or Malpighian tubules of beetles. While plant-parasitic nematodes do not form dauer larvae, various stages are particularly resistant. In *Anguina* seed gall nematodes, the second stage larval form is resistant and in *Ditylenchus dipsaci* (stem and bulb nematode), it is the fourth stage pre-adult. While all stages of *Ditylenchus dipsaci* can tolerate desiccation, the fourth stage tolerates harsher conditions for longer periods. In a drying host plant the nematode accumulates preferentially in the most resistant stage. It is a normal nematodes' tolerance for adversity which, together with special characteristics of resistant stages that enable it to be so tenacious and persistent in nature.

As an additional survival note, nematodes appear to be extremely insensitive to radiation. In the limited number of nematodes studied, forty kilorads of absorbed radiation (0.1 rad is the accepted maximum dose per year for humans) were necessary to sterilize pre-adult larvae of *Ditylenchus dipsaci*. Several hundred kilorads were needed to kill the same nematode, and several other nematodes require equally high radiation doses to bring about death.

Hatching (Eclosion)

All nematode species, other than viviparous ones, expel their unembryonated or partially embryonated eggs into the environment for continued development. The expelled egg embryonates to the fully formed first stage larva, which in some species (animal parasites) hatch to continue development; most, however, remain within the eggshell, molt, and develop into fully formed second stage larvae before hatching. Hatching, therefore, is referred to as the process of emergence of a larva from its protective eggshell. Hatching is referred to as "spontaneous" when it proceeds without pause, as when the second stage larva, upon achieving full development, immediately initiates the emergence process to relieve itself of the eggshell. In a number of nematodes the entire development process stops just before hatching.

Fully morphologically developed second stage larvae remain quiescent within the eggshell until the intervention of extrinsic factors or stimuli which initiate the hatching process. This phenomenon is different from those in which environmental influences (temperature, moisture, carbon dioxide, oxygen) slow down or speed up normal physiological processes. Some nematode species, e.g., *Nematodirus battus* (sheep intestinal parasite), require a cold exposure before they are able to hatch and infect a new host. Although our understanding of the hatching process is rather meager, the role of extrinsic stimuli, usually from potential hosts, has been an area of long-time interest, particularly since these effects relate to parasitism in animals and plants. The stimulation of hatching in animal parasites has perhaps best been studied for ascarids (intestinal round worms). The fully developed second stage larvae, quiescent within the eggshell of the ascarid egg, upon ingestion passes downward to the small intestine. There the hatching process begins, but the stimuli which initiate eclosion remain a mystery. It has been demonstrated, however, that the fluids in the alimentary canal between the mouth and the intestine play no role in the process, for if the eggs are surgically implanted directly in the intestine they readily begin the eclosion process. The host appears to have no role in digesting the eggshell; moreover, once the eclosion process has begun the egg can be removed from the host without hindering the process. Laboratory experiments have shown that carbon dioxide can initiate the hatching process and that while a somewhat alkaline pH and a reducing environment can improve the process, the presence of CO_2 is mandatory. The hatching fluid bathing a second stage larva within the egg expands in volume and affects the egg wall to increase permeability and the absorption of water. It is postulated that enzymes weaken the remainder of the shell, whereupon the increased pressure of absorbed water bursts the egg, releasing the second stage larva as a motile form. Interestingly, if hatching fluid is withdrawn from the egg and used to bathe a fresh egg, the hatching process begins in the fresh egg.

Researchers have pursued most aggressively the nature of stimulated hatching in plant parasites with cyst-forming nematodes, particularly those attacking potatoes and sugar beets. It has long been known that if mature cysts were placed in water, relatively few larvae would emerge. However, if a comparable batch of cysts were placed in water in which there were also roots of a vigorously growing host plant, larval emergence would be substantially greater. Substances emanating from the immersed roots (root exudates) can greatly stimulate hatching. The great motivation for these kinds of studies came from the great potential for nematode control; if the hatching agent were found to be a simple, inexpensive compound then it could be applied to a field to force nematodes to hatch and be subject to starvation or more effective killing by nematicides. So great was the motivation that several English nematology laboratories pursued studies of the hatching process and the isolation of the hatching factor for nearly half a century, unfortunately, with little success. In this process an enormous array of biologically active agents including vitamins, amino acids, alkaloids, carbohydrates, cations, anions, organic acids and other substances were screened for hatch factor activity. In consequence of all this work in Europe and North America, a number of substances were found able to stimulate hatching somewhat, but none (alone, or in combination) approached the effectiveness of natural root exudates. Zinc ion had good hatch activity, but not as good as natural materials. Corollary studies in North America suggested that the hatch factor activity was rather nonspecific and not restricted to host plants, for the root exudates of a number of non-host plants were equally effective for stimulation of hatching. The emergence of vermiform second stage larvae from such cysts involves a complex process in which the quiescent larva within the egg becomes active. It then targets one end of the eggshell and attacks that target area by repeated extensions and withdrawals of its stylet, first weakening the shell and inflicting a line of perforations (much as the perforations in a stamp book) that eventually break open to release the active nematode. A curious complexity in some of these species (which often can benefit from hatch factor activity) arises from the observation that a freshly produced cyst isolated from a growing culture will hatch as well in water as it will in root exudate. However, if it is aged or matured in some special way, for example, gradual drying at very high humidities at temperatures of about 5°C over a period of several months, then the stimulatory effect of the hatch factors in a root exudate becomes readily apparent. While an explanation of the hatching stimulant activity remains an open question, it appears that hatching involves a series of interrelated physiological reactions, each requiring its particular set of factors and cofactors and which, depending upon the rearing and environment of the nematode (nutrition, host plant, soil solutes), become depleted or limiting during the "aging" process and when supplied by the root exudate stimulate emergence. The eggs of rootknot nematodes, under certain conditions, appear to benefit from the stimulation of root exudates. However, the effect is not nearly so striking as with cyst formers. The vigorous activity of the nematode in seeking to escape from its eggshell invokes a high metabolic activity and therefore a requirement for an abundant supply of oxygen.

CHAPTER 10

Feeding Characteristics and Disease Symptomatology

While all representatives of *Nemata* must feed to reproduce and propagate the species, the feeding characteristics are wide ranging and varied. Some groups feed exclusively on microorganisms, or on prey that include nematodes, tardigrades, and other micrometazoans. Others feed by parasitizing plants or animals, and some species use nutrition obtained from totally different sources depending upon the stage of the life cycle.

However, all nematodes do not necessarily feed during each stage of their life cycle. All nematodes embryonate utilizing the nutritional reserves provided by the egg; some nematodes in later segments of the life cycle may repeat this process by developing through one or two additional stages, utilizing the reserves accumulated during a preceding feeding stage. *Meloidogyne* species (rootknot nematodes) embryonate and develop into the fully formed second stage larvae utilizing the reserves initially deposited in the egg. They feed as parasitic second stage larval forms, stop feeding through the development to third and fourth stages, but resume feeding as adults. While some animal-parasitic nematodes feed exclusively on animal tissue (*Trichinella spiralis*), others spend part of their life cycle in soil feeding on micro-organisms. The stomas of microbivorous nematodes and the feeding apparatus of most plant-parasitic nematodes are retained much the same through all stages of the species life cycle. However, this is not necessarily true for some animal parasites. In Strongylids, for example, the stomas of the early stages, which resemble the small pouches of microbivorous forms, become relatively cavernous in the adult stage; in mermithids, a small juvenile stylet is lost.

Microbial Feeders

The stomas of these types of nematodes generally have a small cup-shaped pouch as a buccal cavity. They graze a bacterial colony by taking in cells with a vacuum-like action created by a peristaltic-like wave in the esophageal muscles. The same type of action moves the food material posteriorly through the esophageal-intestinal valve and into the gut.

A smaller group of microbivorous nematodes utilizes a totally different feeding apparatus; the pouch-like buccal cavity is replaced by a stylet (stomatostyle). As previously described, the stylet is a pointed, hollow, tubelike arrangement that can be extended to penetrate fungal hyphae and other large cells, such as diatoms and algae. The feeding apparatus in this group is very similar to that used by plant-parasitic nematodes. There appears to be a practical correlation between stylet size and hyphal size; if the stylet is large and robust and the hyphal filament very slender, the stylet is unable to penetrate the hypha to withdraw the internal contents. Or, if the stylet is small and slender and the hyphal filament is large and robust, the stylet is also unable to penetrate the hypha to withdraw the internal contents. The nutritional matter represented by internal contents of fungal and algal cells is normally taken in through the hollow stylet and propelled back to the intestine by the pumping action of the esophageal musculature.

Plant-Parasitic Feeders

The feeding apparatus of all plant-parasitic nematodes functions with the use of a protrusible hollow stylet or a protrusible solid axial spear with an expendable feeding tube. While all plant feeders have a stylet or the equivalent feeding apparatus, not all stylet-bearing nematodes are plant feeders. Some feed on fungal hyphae or algal cells and others on insect larvae.

Disease symptomatology is usually understood to refer to a characteristic host response to infection. Unfortunately, as any farmer knows, nematode infected plants usually show no symptoms diagnostic for of nematodes. They show only general, nonspecific characteristics that could be the result of any of a number of problems, including deficiency in water, compacted soil, nutritional disorders, microorganismal or viral pathogens, insects, or nematodes. Most commonly, heavy parasitic nematode infections are required for the host to generate localized responses—usually at the nematode attack site—that can be considered somewhat characteristic for the species or genus.

Most root-attacking phytoparasitic nematodes are particularly interested in the root tip region, extending back from the root cap some 5–10 mm and feed upon different root tissue zones (Fig. 10.1). At the microscopic level, such nematodes, depending upon species, may or may not induce characteristic local responses of root cells about the attack site (Fig. 10.2). Several genera (perhaps the best known include *Heterodera, Globodera, Meloidogyne*) induce the formation of giant cells by the host. The infective larvae cruise along the root system until a suitable root tip site is found, whereupon they penetrate in the region of elongation of the root, orienting acropetaly (facing the plant top) in the cortex. Shortly after feeding, the motile larva swells and becomes sedentary. Thereafter it is obliged to feed on a limited number of plant cells adjacent to the head, as it is only capable of limited bending of its head region and extension of its stylet (Fig. 10.3 B). The continued feeding induces high metabolic activity in the cell and the generation of amino acids, proteins, organic acids, chromatin material, and carbohydrates. As a consequence of all this activity, these cells increase in volume perhaps a thousand fold to become giant cells.

At the macroscopic level a few nematodes produce root growth disorders which can be discrete (galls as in *Meloidogyne* or *Nacobbus* species) or amorphous (masses as in *Xiphinema* species). In the case of *Meloidogyne* species (rootknot nematode), the gall is a consequence of hypertrophy (cell enlargement) and hyperplasia (increased cell division) in a root region of some ten to fifteen cell diameters about the giant cells and the head of the nematode.

Plant growth regulators are known to be involved in these kinds of plant growth disorders. It has been demonstrated that the galls and the second stage larvae of several rootknot species exhibit elevated levels of different auxins (indoleacetic acid derivatives) or the same derivatives in different relative proportions but characteristic of the species. Most probably other plant growth regulators are involved in this type response. It is of interest to note that *Meloidogyne hapla*, infecting tomatoes, for example, induces very small galls, whereas the related *M. javanica* and *M. incognita* produce galls on the same host that are one to two orders of magnitude greater in size. Further-

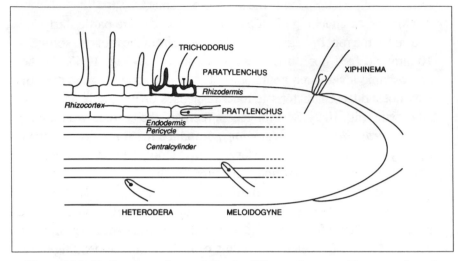

Figure 10.1. Preferred root tip attack sites by different phytoparasitic nematodes and the root tissue chosen for feeding. After B. Weischer with permission.

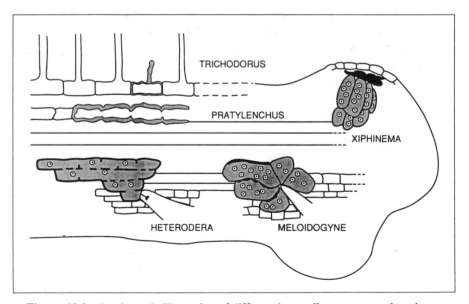

Figure 10.2. A schematic illustration of different host cell responses at the microscopic level immediate to the nematode feeding site for several nematode species. After B. Weischer with permission.

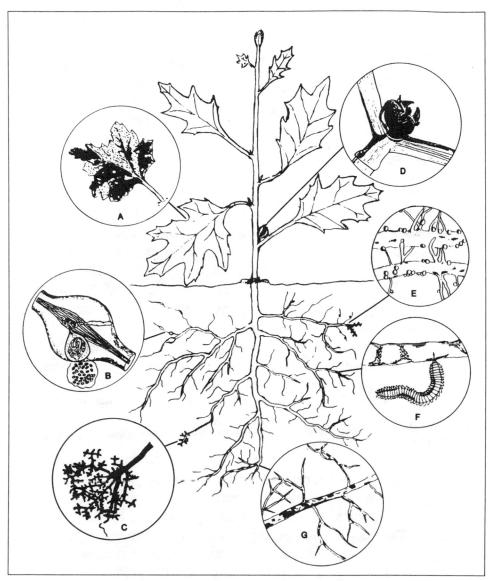

Figure 10.3. A schematic plant exhibiting symptoms and nonsymptoms resulting from infection by diverse nematodes. Adapted from various sources. A. *Aphelenchoides ritzema-bosi* infecting chrysanthemum leaves. B. *Meloidogyne* species (rootknot nematode) infecting various hosts. C. *Trichodorus* sp. (stubby root nematode) in high populations. D. *Anguina* sp. seed galls deriving from infected flower buds. E. *Heterodera* sp. and other cyst-forming species indicating cysts attached to the roots. F. *Criconemella* sp. (ring nematodes) attacking roots but showing no particular site symptoms. G. *Pratylenchus* sp. (root lesion nematodes) exhibiting root lesions after long-term infection of roots.

more, if these three species infect cabbage root, *M. hapla* produces miniscule or essentially invisible galls, while the other two species produce galls that are about the size induced by *M. hapla* on tomato roots instead of the huge galls normally produced (Fig. 10.4 A,B). Perhaps an explanation for this subtle observation lies in the fact that cabbage roots contain indoleacetic acid (auxin) degrading enzymes and that *M. hapla* second stage larvae also exude an indoleacetic acid degrading enzyme, as do a number of diverse nematode species, not including *M. javanica* or *M. incognita*. The degrading enzymes produced by *M. hapla* reduce the effect of the indoleacetic acid giving rise to small galls in relation to those of *M. javanica* or *M. incognita*. A different degrading enzyme present in cabbage roots reduces the effects of auxins produced by any of the three. Unfortunately, nothing is known about the role of plant growth regulators in the formation of the amorphous root tip masses produced by *Xiphinema* species, the galls produced by *Nacobbus* species, or other nematodes that produce root growth disorders.

Several genera of above-ground plant-parasitic nematodes also produce growth disorders (Fig. 10.4 C,D). *Ditylenchus dipsaci* (stem and bulb nematode) causes stunting of alfalfa and clover. The nematode invades the apical meristem to produce a swelling which is sometimes referred to as a gall, but whose main effect is to inhibit the growth and elongation of the apical growing point. *D. dipsaci* is also one of those nematodes that releases an indoleacetic acid (auxin) degrading enzyme. Apparently, upon attacking the growing point the nematode releases enzymes that degrade the indoleacetic acid produced by the apical meristem for normal growth, thereby stunting the plant. This notion explaining the mechanism of stunting is supported by the fact that a nematode-stunted growing point supplemented by exogenous nondegradable synthetic auxin quickly resumes growth.

Foliar nematodes that invade the flower bud to eventually generate a large "seed" gall (Fig. 10.3 D) probably invoke plant growth regulators in the gall formation. However, there exists no evidence of any kind to suggest a possible mechanism.

A different kind of root system is often produced by lesion nematodes (*Pratylenchus* species). The nematode enters the root (Fig. 10.4F)

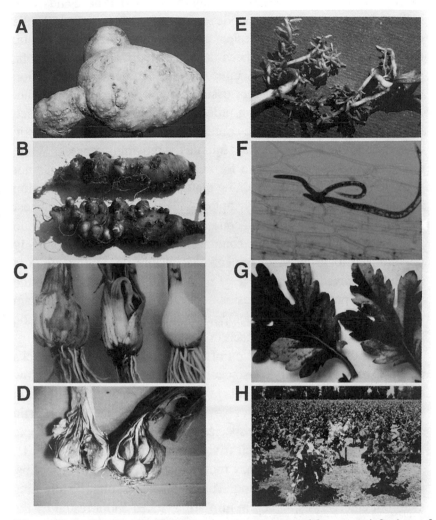

Figure 10.4. Photographs of disease symptoms generated by severe infections of different kinds of plant parasitic nematodes. A. Potato tuber infested with rootknot nematodes (*Meloidogyne* sp.). B. Carrot deformed by rootknot nematodes. C. Onion bulbs deformed by the stem and bulb nematode (*Ditylenchus dipsaci*). D. Garlic bulb and cloves attacked by the stem and bulb nematode. E. Maize roots parasitized by Oat Cyst Nematode (*Heterodera avenae*). F. Root lesion nematode (*Pratylenchus vulnus*) in an apple rootlet. G. Chysanthemum leaves infected by the foliar nematode (*Aphelenchoides ritzema-bosi*). H. Grapevine suffering from the virus caused fanleaf disease that is transmitted by *Xiphinema index* (dagger nematode). All after de Guiran with permission from INRA, France.

to feed and in the process destroys many root cells. The dead and dying cells darken so that as the nematode moves to feed on healthy cells, the dark spot expands to form a lesion, a brown to black area of necrotic tissue (Fig. 10.3 G). It has been demonstrated that in peach roots, grown in aseptic culture and infected with certain sterilized lesion nematodes, a darkening of root tissue occurs about the feeding site. Apparently, during the feeding process enzymes are released which hydrolyze amygdalin (cyanide containing glucoside) to liberate toxic cyanide ions that kill the cells and initiate the browning process. While this scenario is probably valid for most *Prunus* species, it does not apply to non-amygdalin containing plants. Not all hosts of the lesion nematode exhibit root lesion symptoms. Histochemical tests suggest that the darkening reaction is a consequence of hydrolysis of phenolic glycosides to release phenolic compounds which become oxidatively polymerized to form dark pigments. In nature, the dying tissue is secondarily invaded by a range of microorganisms, speeding up the process that produces black lesions. Most root tissues which contain very low levels of phenolic compounds do not exhibit characteristic lesions, however, the macro-effects of nematode attack remain.

By far the greater proportion of plant-parasitic nematode attacks create no macroscopically conspicuous characteristic symptoms at low or moderate infection levels. It is usually at extremely high infection levels that host plants may exhibit symptoms somewhat characteristic of certain particular nematode species. These distinctive macroscopic symptoms have resulted in their trivial common names (Appendix 1).

Trichodorus species (stubby root nematodes) attack the root tips, causing them to cease elongation. The host plant responds by initiating side root emergences, which in turn are attacked and arrested by the nematode. The root system that results consists of a mass of short, thick stubs—stubby root (Fig. 10.3C). These nematodes employ a remarkable feeding mechanism. While all other plant-parasitic nematodes withdraw their nutrients from plant cells through their hollow stylets, *Trichodorus* species cannot. The Trichodorid spear (odontostyle) is in essence a pointed solid rod, believed to have derived from a dorsal tooth of ancestral forms, that can only pierce a plant cell. To conduct cell nutrients into the alimentary canal it forms a feeding tube about the spear connecting the plant root to its oral opening (mechanism unknown). Continued spear action agitates the plant cell contents and clears the feeding tube of obstructions to maintain nutrient flow. Upon the cessation of feeding, the feeding tube is broken off at the oral opening and left attached to the plant root surface, while the nematode moves to a new feeding site to repeat the process.

A totally different nematode, the oat cyst nematode (*Heterodera avenae*) stunts maize roots to produce similar looking root symptoms (Fig.10.4 E). Clearly, diseased roots can at best be only indicative of which nematodes may be causative; the definitive diagnosis relies upon the consideration of other independent observations.

Ditylenchus destructor (potato rot nematode) received its common name by virtue of the rot it initiates in potato tubers, although it can attack and feed upon a wide range of hosts, including plant roots, fungi, conifers, and plant storage organs including fruits. The nematode enters the tuber through the bud eye to feed on underlying cells. As the site nutrients become exhausted the nematodes move into the surrounding healthy tissue, and the original site of dead cells becomes invaded by secondary microorganisms. The invaded area becomes darkened, probably by a process similar to that already described, and the nematode population feeds upon and grows in the white region just bordering the black area. Under humid conditions the black rotted area is moist and mushy; under less humid conditions the black rot becomes dry and brittle. The black rot symptom appears to occur preferentially in storage organs rather than roots and other tissues.

Aphelenchoides fragariae (spring crimp nematode) is a nematode that crawls up the moist surface of the plant, in this case strawberry, to enter leaf stomata (openings for exchange of gases) to feed on the parenchymal tissue between the leaf surfaces. Heavy infections effect chlorosis in portions of the leaf and plant growth disorders in terms of crinkling and crimp. In other host plants, these kinds of leaf symptoms may not occur. *A. ritzema-bosi* similarly produces chlorosis and drying of leaves of chrysanthemum, with less leaf growth distortion, but with very characteristic symptoms (Fig.10. 3 A, 10.4 G).

Tylenchorhynchus species (stunt nematodes) may feed ectoparasitically, i.e., externally from the surface or from a partially imbedded position, depending on the host root. At high population levels root symptoms are distinct from those of other root parasitic nematodes; such roots may not show discriminative lesions but may be shrunken, shrivelled, and stubbylike because root elongation does not normally occur. The end result is a sparse root system devoid of adventitious roots and rootlets that normally support plant growth.

Aphelenchoides besseyi (white-tip-of-rice nematode) is a foliar nematode that, like its relatives, can climb a moist surface to enter above-ground host plant tissue. While this nematode can invade the entire plant, it derives its name from the fact that at elevated infection levels the leaf tips of rice become chlorotic and then turn white, eventually dying and drying. However, it is by way of the floral parts and the eventual formation of seed galls that the nematode is dispersed and carried forth through the following growth season. Many foliar nematodes are not particularly discriminate feeders and can survive well on a wide array of plants and fungi. The diagrammatic representation of an infected plant (Fig. 10.3) illustrates some of the kinds of symptoms characteristically occurring at persistently high infection levels.

Predaceous Nematodes

Predaceous nematodes may be found in several diverse taxonomic groups whose other representatives may be microbial feeders or plant feeders. Although "carnivorous" nematodes occur in a marine environment, they are most abundant in terrestrial habitats. Cursory thought would lead to the belief that these nematodes would be ideal for biological control, inasmuch as they are happy to devour any animal they can overpower. They are opportunistic, but unfortunately, are unable to discriminate in prey selection and readily cannibalize their own kind. This means that the dense populations normally required for effective biological control are unlikely to be ever attained.

The feeding characteristics of predaceous nematodes are varied with different groups, and include the major mechanisms found in *Nemata*. Some species even combine several methods to achieve their nutritional goals. A common mechanism used for the capture and ingestion of prey involves the application of strong suction forces generated by an exceptionally muscular esophagus. Mononchus species (Fig. 4.1) exhibit these characteristics. This nematode has a large dorsal tooth which projects down into the stomatal cavity; upon placing its lips upon its prey, the esophagus creates a vacuum that sucks the prey, often whole, into the stomatic cavity. If the prey happens to be a nematode grasped at midbody, the suction forces are so great that the prey body bends in half and zips inward. Prey are ingested with such velocity that the larger forms are ripped open by the fixed tooth. The speed of ingestion is indeed remarkable; from cinematographic studies it was found that prey in contact with lips at one moment, disappeared into the Mononch in less than the blink of an eye.

A different group of predators employ a moveable, jawlike oral opening to capture prey. The stomatal lining may be dentate or denticulate with rasping plates to lacerate and rupture the prey for the release of the internal contents. *Selachinema* (Fig. 3.3 A) illustrates this feeding habit; the prey parts and contents are transported into the gut by the usual esophageal pumping mechanisms. Examination of the gut contents of these kinds of predatory nematodes reveals the presence not only of prey components, but also ciliates, bacteria, plant debris and fungal remains, among other particles. Most likely such extraneous materials are a consequence of accidental ingestion along with the prey. A different representative of this type of feeding group, *Ironus*, is reported to feed by holding the prey with its lips while the teeth lining the mouth cavity pierce the prey cuticle to allow the contents to be sucked out.

An alternate group of predators attack their prey and feed by use of a stylet, as do plant parasites. The nematode, e.g., *Seinura* species inserts its stylet through the prey body wall to inject secretions that cause paralysis and pre-digestion of the body contents, which are subsequently withdrawn. These types of predators are relatively large, and robust, and readily attack other nematodes, oligochaetes and occasionally mite eggs and insect larvae.

Actinolaimus employs stomatal teeth near the oral opening to catch its prey and a stylet to pierce the prey body wall, paralyze the victim, predigest, and withdraw the contents. *Nygolaimus* species employs a solid spear (odontostyle) to pierce the body wall of oligochaete worms.

They then suck out the worm contents, much like the plant-parasitic *Trichodorus* species.

The evolutionary origins of such diverse mechanisms for feeding by predaceous nematodes remains a subject of much speculation. The presence of solid spears, hollow stylets, single and multiple teeth or rasping plates represent perplexing questions in need of explanation.

Animal-Parasitic Nematodes

The feeding characteristics of animal-parasitic nematodes are varied and diverse, particularly as they involve bizarre life cycles. It is not uncommon for nematodes progressing through their life cycles, no matter how complex, to develop and proceed through several stages without feeding. Currently nonfeeding stages are identified by a lack of oral opening or a degenerate nonfunctional alimentary system; the presence of a nonfunctional anus is not an indication of nonfeeding, for several feeding nematodes are known to possess no functional anus. Although the absence of a functional alimentary system is strong presumptive evidence of nonfeeding, at least in the classical sense, it does not constitute incontrovertible evidence that some nutrition does not take place by some other means, such as through the body wall. Nematodes with complex life cycles, in which a segment involves development in a soil environment feed microbivorously with a feeding apparatus very similar to that of free-living nematodes feeding microbivorously. Certain *Tylenchus* and *Aphelenchoides* species that can live on the fungi in the frass of beetle tunnels have parasitic juvenile forms which live in the beetle Malphighian tubules. A *Deladenus species* which can feed and complete a life cycle on a fungus can switch cycles to feed on a larval *Sirex* (wood wasp) and develop into fertile females. These examples are merely indicative of similar processes occurring in a number of other nematode systems. In more complex cycles involving a primary host and an alternate host for different segments of the cycle, feeding on either host may be required for continued development.

Generally, the mechanisms by which nutrition is accomplished are poorly understood, with the exception of a few specialized cases. Consider nematodes which are swallowed by a host and then leave the intestine.   Some migrate through tissues until adulthood (guinea worm). Others enter into the bloodstream and migrate to the lungs, up the trachea, into the pharynx, and down the esophagus into the gut. A different type penetrates the skin, while another is injected into the bloodstream by an insect vector; both to be transported to other tissues or organs for development.

How do they feed in order to propagate the species? Some intestinal nematodes essentially swim in the intestinal chyme to take in predigested nutrients via their alimentary system while some take in additional nutrients through the body wall. Others, like Oxyuris species or hookworm types, take an intestinal mucosal plug into their stoma to extract blood for nutrition. An adult hookworm, for example, normally processes 2/3 ml of host blood daily so that a burden of 350 adults extract about 1/4 liter (1/2 pint) of host blood per day.   Others that migrate through tissues and organs and develop to adulthood probably feed by a combination of methods described for intestinal parasites. Nematode parasites of warm-blooded animals function continually at high temperatures and therefore with high metabolic rates; with extended life cycles of up to a year there must be a high level of nutrient uptake to support development, growth, metabolism and reproduction. The nature of the parameters facilitating the nutrition in such life modes remain a mystery. Similar problems are encountered by nematode parasites of invertebrates. Some insect parasites, such as mermithid juveniles living in an insect body cavity,are known to take in their nutrient supply through the body wall. *Bradynema* is known to have a thick, porous cuticle with a modified hypodermis in which the outer surface exhibits microvilli which probably serve for nutrient absorption. The giant, seven-meter *Placentonema* of the sperm whale must, in all likelihood, absorb nutrients through its body wall to supply the development of its 32 ovaries, each of which extends throughout most of the body length.

Two genera of nematodes, *Steinernema* and *Heterorhabditis,* which are often considered insect parasites, are really not parasitic. Although they penetrate the body wall, they carry within their gut specialized bacteria which are released into the insect. The bacteria attack the insect body contents and reproduce; the nematodes feed on the increasing bacterial population.

There are nematodes who evert their uteri out of their body to grow and develop (like *Sphaerularia bombi*) by absorbing nutrients directly into the uterine reproductive sac from the insect haemolymph.

Some insect parasitic nematodes feed with the aid of a stylet during some of their life cycle stages. Mermithid juveniles utilize a degenerate

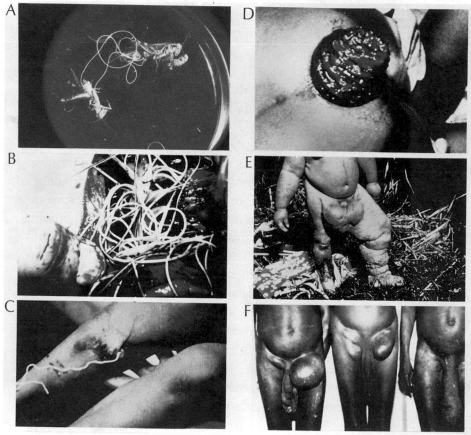

Figure 10.5. Photographs illustrating symptoms resulting from heavy infections of diverse animal-parasitic nematodes. C–F. Photos after Peters and Guiles with permission. A. Mermithid parasite of the grasshopper. Anonymous. B. *Dirofilaria immitis* in the heart of a dog killed by dog heartworm. After Kessel with permission. C. Adult guinea worm in a knee joint. After B. M. Greenwood with permission. D. Rectal prolapse resulting from heavy infections of whip worm (*Trichuris trichiura*). After F. Boltran with permission. E. Elephantiasis, gross swelling of an extremity from *Wuchereria bancrofti*. Anonymous, with permission from Peters and Gilles. F. Hanging groin and scrotal elephantiasis due to onchocerciasis. After O. P. Argo with permission.

stylet to attack and macerate insect viscera and fat bodies, but appear to absorb the released nutrients through the body wall (Fig. 10.5 A). A different insect parasitic nematode, *Noctuidonema*, uses a stylet that is approximately a third of its body length to feed on moths; these kinds of nematode parasites may be common in *Lepidoptera* (insect group).

Disease symptomatology of animal-parasitic nematodes, as with plant-parasitic forms, is rarely obvious in light to moderate infections. The symptomatology resembles that which can be attributed to a wide range of causes, including fungal and bacterial pathogens, nutritional disorders, and stressful conditions and may take the form of lethargy, debilitation, weakness, diarrhoea, poor growth, altered metabolic functions or a general malaise. It is with very heavy infections that symptoms may become prominent. Emaciation, abnormal muscular function, poor respiration, skin nodules as in the guinea worm (Fig. 10.5 C) or onchocerciasis (Fig. 10.5 F), which are mostly worm, tissue fluid and inflammation, a prolapsed rectum as in whipworm (*Trichuris trichiura*, Fig. 10.5 D), a dog heartworm packed heart (*Dirofilaria immitis*, Fig. 10.5 B), skin ulcerations as in dog (Fig. 10.6) or horse (Fig. 10.7), or gross edema as in elephantiasis (*Wuchereria bancrofti*), where extremities enlarge to grotesque proportions (Fig. 10.5 E). Closer examination of other nematode host systems reveal galls in the wings of bats, muscle encysted galls in trichinosis, or anemia in hookworm infections.

Cultivation

Many nematodes, particularly free-living forms, have for years been alleged to be saprophytic feeders. A saprophyte is defined as any organism living on dead or decaying organic matter. Although it has been observed that Ascaris species or related nematodes ingest such substances as charcoal, barium and other particles fed to the host, as well as mitochondria and other cell organelles, it is unlikely that these substances have much nutritional value. Similarly, the marine nematode, *Deontostoma californicum*, is able to ingest wax or plastic particles as well as other substances from which it is unlikely to derive much nutritional benefit—like the goat which is popularly alleged to ingest metal or plastic containers, cloth, paper and other sundry items. A nematode has yet to be shown to be able to survive on dead or

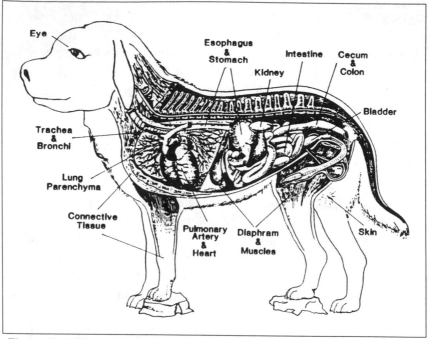

Figure 10.6. Nematode parasites of the dog with preferred organ sites of infection. Redrawn after Garbutt.

Esophagus & Stomach: *Spirocerca lupi* fibrous nodules in the wall of the esophagus and stomach. *Physaloptera* spp. stout worms in stomach.

Small Intestine: *Toxocara canis* & *Toxascaris leonina* large yellow-white intestinal worms. *Ancyclostoma caninum* reddish from blood, hookworms. *Ancyclostoma braziliense* whitish hookworms. *Ucinaria stenocephla* whitish hook worms. *Strongyloides stercoralis* (2.2 mm) females in the mucous membrane.

Cecum & Colon: *Trichuris vulpis* whipworms have anterior portion embedded in mucosa.

Trachea & Bronchi: *Filaroides osleri* occurs in submucosal nodules near the bifurcation of the trachea. *Crenosorna vulpis* (<2cm) occurs free in lumen. *Capillaria aerophila*.

Lung Parenchyma: *Filaroides milksi* (<15mm) occurs in nests embedded in lung parenchyma. *Dirofilaria immitis* occurs in pulmonary artery. *Strongyloides stercoralis* & *Toxocara canis* & *Ancyclostoma* spp. larvae progressing through their life cycle.

Pulmonary Artery & Right Heart: *Dirofilaria immitis* (<30cm) white heartworms often in large numbers; microfilaria in the blood. *Angiostrongylus vasorum* (<2.5cm) reddish gut.

Connective Tissue: *Dirofilaria repens. Dipetalonema reconditum. Dracunculus* spp. occurs in subcutaneous tissue that ulcerates, & upon wetting discharges a barrage of larvae, from a skin rupture.

Diaphram and Muscles: *Trichinella spiralis* occurs in diaphragm & muscles.

Kidney: *Dioctophyma renale* (<100cm) not too common.

Bladder: *Capillaria plica* embedded in bladder mucosa.

Eye: *Thelazia californiensis* eyeworm.

Skin: *Rhabditis strongyloides* occurs in mange-like skin lesions.

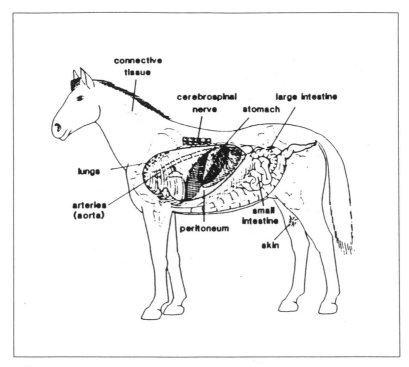

Figure 10.7. Nematode parasites of the horse with preferred sites of infection. Redrawn after Codrington.

Stomach: *Drascheia megastoma* (13mm) in the interconnecting galleries forming fibrous nodules in the stomach wall (chicken egg size). *Habronema* spp. (25mm). *Trichostrongylus axei* (<5mm) in the mucosa lining the stomach.

Small Intestine: *Parascaris equorum* (15-20cm) large yellowish white intestinal worms. *Strongyloides westeri* (<1cm) females in mucosa.

Large Intestine: *Oxyuris equi* (<15) larval stages in colon mucosa. *Probstmayria vivapara* (<3mm) completes full life cycle within colon confines. *Strongylus* (50 species).

Peritoneum & Peritoneal Cavity: *Setaria equina* (15cm) slender white worm, microfilariae in the blood. *Strongylus edentatus* larvae migrate in peritoneum.

Lung (Bronchi): *Dictyocaulus arnfieldi.*

Arteries: *Strongylus vulgaris* migrate in the blood. *Eleophora bohmi* found within large intimal nodules of the wall of the aorta or other vessels.

Connective Tissue: *Onchocerca cervicalis* & *Onchocerca reticulata* adults in the nuchal ligament mainly but also other ligaments.

Nervous system: *Strongylus vulgaris* usually aberrant. *Setaria* spp. aberrant but quite common in the Orient.

Skin: *Parafilaria multipapillosa* cause summer bleeding.

decayed organic matter. Those that appear to are most probably feeding on the microorganisms responsible for the decay. No nematode has been reared on the simple kinds of media used for the propagation of many bacteria and fungi. Several microbivorous nematodes have been reared on a complex chemical medium, but their growth and reproduction was very slow; moreover, they have been found to do better if certain undefined tissue extracts are incorporated into the medium. They invariably grow best feeding on their normal microbivorous food source. Furthermore, no nematode tissue has yet been propagated in vitro. With the exceptions noted above, all nematodes require prey, plant or animal host or microorganismal food sources to grow and reproduce. A truly saprophytic feeder should be easy to rear and culture; that has not been the case to date. The notion of saprophytic feeding should be discarded until it can be resurrected with good evidence. The nutritional requirements of nematodes are poorly understood and remain largely a matter of speculation; more so if one considers the complex life cycles of parasitic species whereupon some stages feed on microorganisms and later shift to animal or plant hosts or from alternate hosts to primary hosts. Until several diverse nematode species are cultured on nonliving media to enable an intense study of nutritional component needs, it is unlikely that our understanding of the nutritional requirements of nematodes will improve.

CHAPTER 11

Distinctive Interactions With Other Disease Agents

Generally nematodes occupying any habitat are simply a part of a community rich in microorganisms including fungi, bacteria, protozoa, viruses, nematodes and other micrometazoans. Each organism goes about the business of propagating its species essentially independent of other community members except as possible food sources. Diseases of nematodes, in the anthropological connotation of infection followed by recovery, have never been demonstrated. Perhaps this is because an immune system or active mechanism fighting against disease has yet to be substantiated. Diseased nematodes do occur, but the diseased condition is usually transient; a nematode attacked and penetrated by bacteria or fungi from within or without leads to a rapid proliferation of the microorganisms in the nematode's tissues and its quick demise, often in a day or two. In fact, these kinds of events serve as bases for the development of biocontrol technologies. Certain nematode species have been reported to contain bacteria-like particles, and others contain virus-like particles within their tissues. Whether such a relation is a consequence of the disease condition or some kind of mutualistic relation is open to question. All components of an environmental community incorporating nematodes, microorganisms, and micrometazoans can be considered opportunistic. Therefore if a component of the community, by virtue of its activities, creates an advantageous court, other organisms will invade and benefit. This is particularly evident for nematodes that have adopted the parasitic mode of living, for in attacking host cells to penetrate and feed they generate a site of weakness and injury that constitutes an infection court for secondary invaders. Should these latecomers be nonpathogenic, the damage to the host attributable to them is likely to be minimal.

With the addition of other pathogens to the parasitic nematode-host system the complexity of the interactions among the system components can escalate dramatically. Often the resultant effect of multiple pathogens is additive, i.e., each pathogen acts independently so that the resultant host damage is simply the sum of the individual damages. The responses produced by these kinds of associations are expected, inasmuch as they are based upon recognized properties of individual organisms. Unanticipated, and perhaps more important, are a range of "distinctive interactions" involving nematodes with other potential disease microorganisms. A number of these kinds of interactions entail the transfer of a disease agent from an infected host to a healthy one by a nematode, and may be viewed as the transport phase. Moreover in many systems there may be an additional response phase in the host that is more complex than that of each individual agent.

When the transport activity is purely phoretic there is little confusion, for it is understood that the second disease agent, smudged on the cuticle surface or taken internally into the alimentary canal, is transported or deposited elsewhere. Similarly, it is well understood that a nematode can serve as a vector (defined as actively transmitting a disease agent) by withdrawing a disease agent from an infected host and injecting it into a healthy host. In between these extremes there are many interactive systems in which transport can be interpreted as either phoretic or vectorial or neither, depending upon an individual's acceptance of the terms' definitions. In any event, these distinctive interactive complexes thrive and remain totally indifferent to the fuzzy anthropogenic categorization.

Bacteria

Microbivorous nematodes feeding on bacteria are not known to be particularly discriminatory regarding their food supply. Consequently, pathogenic bacteria can be ingested along with non-pathogenic species. Soil-inhabiting nematode representatives of *Panagrellus, Panagrolaimus, Pristionchus* and *Rhabditis* have been reported to ingest and excrete plant pathogenic bacteria such as *Agrobacterium, Erwinia* and *Pseudomonas* species. Correspondingly, other representatives of *Cheilobus, Diplogaster* and *Pristionchus*, often associated with excretia waste disposal beds, ingest and excrete animal pathogenic bacteria. Should such nematodes (phoretic carriers) inadvertently find their way into a new host site, animal diseases could result.

Whether nematodes as parasites of animal vertebrates are involved in the animal host acquisition of a bacterial disease is uncertain. There are several parasitic nematode-bacterial pathogen associations which are suggestive of "distinctive interactions." Occasionally *Ascaris* (intestinal roundworm) leaving the gut to enter other tissues and organs results in septicemic complications. Nematode-induced skin rashes and eruptions in the horse and dog, and eye infections of the dog, are often associated with characteristic pathogenic bacteria. Theoretically it appears possible that skin-penetrating parasitic nematodes can trigger the explosion of a bacterial disease. Hookworms, for example bathed with *Anthrax* bacillus or typhoid bacteria and smeared on the skin of a guinea pig quickly result in the demise of the host, as does *Strongyloides* bathed with chicken cholera kill a rabbit. The importance of this interaction in nature is open to question.

An interesting intimate relationship has developed between two genera of nematodes and a genus of bacteria, *Steinernema* with *Xenorhabdus nematophilus* and *Heterorhabditis* with *X. luminescens*. The nematodes penetrate the insect host via the body wall, alimentary canal or respiratory system and enter into the haemocoel, whereupon they release the bacteria carried within their gut by defecation. The nematodes feed on these bacteria that attack and reproduce on the internal contents of the insect which is quickly destroyed. Moreover these special bacterial associates appear to exert a suppressive activity inhibiting the growth of extraneous bacteria accidentally carried into the insect by the nematode.

Perhaps the better known "distinctive interactions" of bacteria occur with plant-parasitic nematodes. Probably the most common association involves the normal activity of the phytoparasitic nematode that facilitates the entry of the pathogenic bacteria. The nematode, in the act of penetrating and feeding upon the host root, creates a weakened site that provides access for the bacteria which are then able to invade, reproduce and disperse throughout the root tissue to generate the bacterial disease. In the presence of bacteria, but the absence of nematodes, the healthy root resists the invasion of the bacteria and the incidence of bacterial disease is very low or nonexistent. In many cases mechanical injury of the roots can simulate nematode activity to provide an access site for bacterial invasion and disease formation, as is observed for carnation wilt with *Pseudomonas caryophylli,* or a crown gall caused by *Agrobacterium tumefaciens,* or tobacco wilt caused by *Corynebacterium* species. While this mechanistic explanation for many "distinctive interactions" of this kind may be acceptable, exceptions do occur. For example in carnation wilt, *Meloidogyne* and *Helicotylenchus* species increase the incidence of wilt, whereas *Xiphinema diversicaudatum* does not and in contrast *Ditylenchus* reduces wilt incidence.

A totally different "distinctive interaction" involves a so-called "cauliflower disease" of strawberry which requires a foliar nematode, *Aphelenchoides ritzema-bosi,* and *Corynebacterium fascians* acting in concert. The nematode by itself produces leaf scars and causes long narrow leaves, while the bacterium by itself produces galled, distorted and poorly developed leaves. With both disease agents active the strawberry plant responds in a totally different manner, producing a cauliflower appearance. The crown produces auxiliary buds continuously, plants are stunted, and flowers become deformed with vestigial petals, enlarged sepals and the plants remain totally nonproductive of fruit.

A genus of seed gall nematodes (*Anguina*) couples with characteristic bacterial associates to generate yet another "distinctive interaction." In the normal situation the nematode climbs the plant to enter the floral bud, which it takes over and modifies for its own reproductive purposes to form a seed gall. With the presence in the soil of the appropriate bacteria, the nematode, in leaving the soil, carries these contaminates on its cuticle and into the floral bud. Initially both develop independently, but eventually the bacteria may outcompete the nematodes which die and what was to be a seed gall is filled with bacterial slime. In the absence of *Anguina* the bacterial disease is reduced or nonexistent. In the presence of the nematode the "distinctive interaction" can be devastating, as it is in Australia where *Anguina* species couple with a *Corynebacterium* species to produce a slime-filled seed gall containing the bacterially produced toxins that destroy sheep and other livestock feeding on the annual ryegrass host. In general the evidence suggests that there are probably more undiscovered nematode-bacterial interactive systems in nature than those discussed (Table 11.1).

Table 11.1. Distinctive Interactions of Nematodes and Bacteria That Result in Disease and Enhanced Plant Damage.

Disease	Nematode	Bacteria
Granville wilt of tobacco	*Meloidogyne*	*Pseudomonas solanacearum*
Bacterial wilt of tobacco	*Meloidogyne*	*Corynebacterium* species
Bacterial wilt of tomato	*Meloidogyne*	*Pseudomonas solanacearum*
Bacterial wilt of carnation	*Helicotylenchus*	*Pseudomonas caryophylli*
Crown gall	various	*Agrobacterium tumefaciens*
Cauliflower disease of strawberries	*Aphelenchoides ritzema-bosi*	*Corynebacterium fascians*
Sheep staggers	*Anguina agrostis*	*Corynebacterium rathayi*
Bacterial disease of insects	*Steinernema* sp.	*Xenorhabdus nematophilus*
Bacterial disease of insects	*Heterorhabditis* sp.	*X. luminescens*
Peach canker	*Criconemella xenoplax*	*Pseudomonas syringe*

Protozoa

Although "distinctive interactions" involving nematodes and protozoa have been poorly studied, reports suggest that the phenomenon occurs and may be of greater importance than is currently realized. "Black head" disease of domestic fowl is caused by *Histomonas meleagridis*, an amoeba that invades the internal organs of birds. The nematode parasite *Heterakis gallinarum* lives in the bird's alimentary canal and ingests the amoebae as it feeds. The amoebae invade the nematode's intestinal cells and reproduce to migrate eventually through the nematode body cavity to the reproductive system and therein enter the developing nematode egg. The infected eggs released by the nematode pass through the host feces to be eliminated in droppings, and are then ingested by a healthy bird that thereafter contracts "Black head." A similar relationship exists with the same nematode and different amoeboid organisms in other bird hosts.

Associations of a similar nature are believed to occur between the human pinworm, *Enterobius vermicularis* egg and *Dientamoeba fragilis,* or between the nematode *Toxocara cati* egg and the protozoan *Toxoplasma gondii.*

Fungi

Although it may be anticipated that if some animal-parasitic nematodes are able to carry pathogenic bacteria to or into a host, a similar relationship should prevail for fungal pathogens. Unfortunately the significance of these kinds of "distinctive interactions" in the animal host system remains poorly understood. Much better documentation is available for the plant host systems. These special nematode-fungal pathogen associations generally produce substantially increased severity of fungal disease, whereas in the absence of the nematode little or no fungal disease prevails. Rarely does the presence of a nematode reduce the severity of a fungal disease. The mechanisms by which such fungal pathogens become aggressive are varied and poorly understood. The enhancement of crop injury from disease agent coupling was observed over a century ago in a report indicating that, while rootknot nematode and Fusarium wilt were independent disease agents of cotton, substantially more damage resulted when both pathogens occurred together in the same field. Nearly a half century later, after the development of cotton resistant to Fusarium wilt, it was noted that wilt resistance of cotton cultivars was lost in the presence of nematodes.

Strangely, not all nematode parasites of cotton were able to facilitate a break in resistance. *Belonolaimus gracilis* and *Meloidogyne* species would; whereas *Trichodorus, Tylenchorhynchus* and *Helicotylenchus* species would not break resistance. In a similar system involving tomato cultivars resistant to Fusarium wilt, it was observed that the presence of *Meloidogyne incognita* resulted in a complete loss of resistance, but the presence of *M. hapla* resulted in only a modest loss, whereas with *Paratrichodorus minor* resistance was conserved. Other similarly interactive *Fusarium* associations with nematodes include *Radopholus similis* (banana wilt), *Tylenchorhynchus claytoni* (tobacco wilt, pea root rot), *Tylenchulus semipenetrans* (citrus root rot), and *Rotylenchulus reniformis* (cotton wilt).

Other disease complexes of a similar nature involving plant-parasitic nematodes and several different genera of fungi include but are not limited to *Verticillium, Phytophthora, Rhizoctonia* and *Botrytis* (Table 11.2).

It is known that the balance of microflora in the rhizosphere (soil region adjacent to roots) can be altered by the presence of nematodes, or indeed, by soil amendments. Root knot nematodes, for example, favor an increased level of *Fusarium* but suppress *Actinomycetes* (a different fungal group), whereas an amendment consisting of chitinous exoskeletons of crustacea fosters *Actinomycetes* and suppresses the pathogens. What is the nature of the resistance in a host cultivar that rejects fungal pathogens unless the roots are attacked by certain nematodes? Why does the genetic resistance of a host plant to a microfloral pathogen break down in the presence of certain nematodes, yet remain intact when different nematodes are present? Moreover, what transpires to cause normally nonpathogenic fungi to become aggressive and pathogenic in the presence of certain nematodes?

The converse situation also exists, whereby a root system infected by fungi suppresses some nematode populations (e.g., cyst nematodes on tomatoes or sugar beets) but not others. Incidences of such events, however, are less frequent. Rarely, plant-parasitic nematode populations increase more rapidly in the presence of certain fungal pathogens, as has been reported for root lesion (*Pratylenchus*) nematodes in the presence of *Verticillium* or *Aphanomyces* fungi.

In some cases the reported crop damage is probably additive, that is, the total damage is simply the sum of the damages caused by each disease agent acting independently. However, from the preceding discussions it is clear that different factors and interactive mechanisms are often involved. A wide array of diverse compounds present in root cells are known to leak from the roots to create a rhizosphere rich in nutrients for microorganisms. It has been suggested that the activity of pathogenic nematodes increases or decreases certain constituents, or adds new ones to the root exudate to enhance infection with pathogenic

Table 11.2. Distinctive Interaction of Nematodes & Fungi That Result in Disease & Enhanced Plant Damage.

Disease	Nematode Genera	Fungal Genera	Plant Host
Black shank	Meloidogyne, Pratylenchus	Phytophthora	Tobacco
Collar rot	Ditylenchus	Botrytis	Onion
Collar rot	Pratylenchus	Trichoderma	Celery
Damping off	Meloidogyne	Rhizoctonia	Cotton, Soybean
Damping off	Meloidogyne	Pythium	Cotton
Early yellowing	Rotylenchus	Fusarium	Peas
Root rot	Tylenchorhynchus	Fusarium	Peas
Root rot	Tylenchulus	Fusarium	Citrus
Sore shin	Meloidogyne	Rhizoctonia	Tobacco
Wheat rot	Pratylenchus	Rhizoctonia	Wheat
Wilt	Meloidogyne	Fusarium	Tobacco, Tomato, Cotton, Carnation
Wilt	Belmolaimus, Rotylenchus	Fusarium	Cotton
Wilt	Tylenchorhynchus	Fusarium	Tobacco
Wilt	Radopholus	Fusarium	Banana
Wilt	Heterodera	Verticillium	Potato
Wilt	Meloidogyne	Verticillium	Cotton
Wilt	Pratylenchus	Verticillium	Tomato, Eggplant

fungi. Observations from experiments, such as the addition of leachings from a nematode-infested plant to a plant growing normally in a fungal-infested soil, in order to generate a root rot disease, are consistent with this notion.

The degree of complexity that can be anticipated in "distinctive interactions" involving fungi is perhaps best demonstrated by a split root experiment. In this case, the root system of a host plant was divided equally before planting each half into a different soil-filled container. After the plant was established, nematodes were added to one soil container and the fungal pathogen to the other. The root lesion nematode (*Pratylenchus*) normally attacks and reproduces on the host, whereas the fungal pathogen (*Verticillium*) does not. In the split root experiment, both the nematode and the fungus invaded the plant, thereby indicating that the nematode-infected root portions generated a susceptibility factor to the fungal pathogen that was translocated to the other root system where there were no nematodes. Evidence suggests that nematode modification of normal host physiological processes is more important than previously suspected in disease susceptibility and expression.

A different nematode-fungal interaction of substantial significance involves a mycorrhizal association between plant roots and certain fungi. A mycorrhizal complex is usually one of these two forms: endomycorrhizae, in which fungal hyphae penetrate deeply within the root, but usually do not cover the root surface, and ectomycorrhizae, in which the hyphae penetrate superficially between cells near the root surface and form a fungal mantle which covers the entire root surface. The resulting symbiosis benefits the fungus as it derives its organic nutrient primarily from root cell leakage, while the plant benefits from the fungus' capacity to better scavenge and solubilize inorganic nutrients from the mineral soil components. The improved growth provided by a root-mycorrhizal association is perhaps best known with coniferous forests; however, similar associations are known to occur for a wide range of trees, shrubs and other plants.

Nematodes interact with the mycorrhizal system either as plant parasitic forms feeding on the plant or fungal feeding forms grazing on the fungi. Fungal feeding nematodes reduce the fungal mass and the effective benefit to the plant; indeed, in high populations they are able to inhibit mycorrhizal formation. In contrast, parasitic nematodes feeding upon the plant roots can disrupt root function and interfere with the formation of the symbiotic mycorrhizal complex. Evidence suggests that mycorrhizal fungi are able to shield or protect plant roots from attack by some pathogenic fungi. It has been suggested that mycorrhizal fungi may serve in a similar capacity to protect plants from parasitic nematodes; the evidence for such a function is as yet not particularly convincing.

In summary, "distinctive interactions" involving nematodes and fungi are many and varied. Unfortunately the mechanisms, parameters, and even the nature of most of the interactions are poorly understood.

Viruses

Of all the "distinctive interactions" comprised of nematodes and other disease agents, those that most clearly cast the nematode in the role of a vector are those that involve virus transmissions. Nematodes as vectors for virus transmission was first reported (1941) for an animal system. The swine lung worms, *Metastrongylus elongatus* and *M. putentotectus,* become infected by swine influenza virus in a diseased host. During development the virus is incorporated into the nematode eggs which, upon release into the soil via feces or nasal discharge, are ingested by earthworms. The nematode eggs embryonate and develop through three stages in the earthworm, which serves as an intermediate host. Viable virus particles are retained within the nematode so that, upon ingestion of the earthworm by a healthy pig, the pig becomes infected with a latent form of the virus. The swine influenza virus remains in its latent form until the swine is subjected to some triggering stress, e.g. cold temperature, a second parasite, or some other debilitating factor, which stimulates the virus into activity for the development of the swine influenza.

Since these early findings, numerous attempts at defining the parameters and confirming the virus transmission hypothesis as a principal method of infection have been unsuccessful, and now the notion is viewed with some skepticism. Subsequently, under artificial laboratory conditions, *Trichinella spiralis* was found able to transmit the lymphocytic choriomeningitis virus when encysted larvae were surgically removed from guinea pig muscle and then fed or injected into healthy guinea pigs. Similarly, Newcastle disease virus could become incorporated into the avian nematode parasite, *Ascaridia galli,* when both disease agents were present in the chicken. While some animal viruses clearly can be transmitted by animal-parasitic nematodes, the importance of this mechanism in nature is open to question.

In contrast the evidence is unequivocal that certain groups of nematodes can serve as vectors for the transmission of virus particles from viruliferous plants to healthy host plants (Table 11.3). It is perplexing that all the alleged plant virus transmissions by nematodes

Table 11.3 Nematode Vectors of Plant and Animal Virus Diseases.

Disease Virus	Nematode Vector	Common Hosts
Polyhedral shaped (Nepovirus)		
Arabic Mosaic (AMV)	dagger species	cherry, cucumber, grape, raspberry,rhubarb, hops
Artichoke, Italian Latent (AILV)	needle species	artichoke
Cherry Leaf Roll (CLRV)	dagger species	cherry, blackberry, elm, rhubarb
Grape Fanleaf (GFV)	dagger species	grape
Grape Chrome Mosaic (GCMV)	dagger species	grape
Mulberry Ringspot (MRSV)	needle & dagger species	blackberry, raspberry, red currant, strawberry, cherry
Strawberry Latent Ringspot (SLRV)	dagger species	black curant, cherry, celery, peach, plum, rose, raspberry, strawberry
Tobacco Ringspot (TRSV)	dagger species	bean, blueberry, gladiolus, grape, tobacco
Tomato Black Ring (TBRV)	dagger species	celery, artichoke, lettuce, peach, potato, raspberry, strawberry, sugarbeet, tomato
Tomato Ringspot (TRSV)	dagger species	blackberry, cherry, grape, peach, raspberry, tobacco
Tubular rod shaped (Tobravirus)		
Pea Early Browning (PEBV)	stubby root species (5+)	pea, alfalfa
Tobacco Rattle (TRV)	stubby root species (12+)	artichoke, bulbs, lettuce, pepper, potato, tobacco
Other Viruses		
Brome Mosaic (BMV)	dagger & needle species	grasses, cereals
Carnation Ringspot (CRSV)	dagger species	carnation
Prune Necrotic Ringspot (PNRSV)	needle species	prunus species
Swine Influenza	*Metastrongylus* species	pig
	Strongylus species	rat
Lymphocytic Choriomeningitis	*Trichinella spiralis*	carnivores
Encephalomyelitis	*Strongylus* species	horses
Newcastle disease	gapeworms (*Syngamus*)	chickens
Polio	pinworms (*Enterobios*)	man

are associated with five nematode genera in the order *Dorylaimida*. The Dorylaimids constitute an order in the class *Adenophorea* which separated from the class *Secernentea*, containing all the other plant-parasitic nematodes about five hundred million years ago (Fig. 2.1). Although by far the greatest proportion of plant parasitic nematodes are found in the class *Secernentea*, none of those has been found to transmit or vector a plant virus or subviral particle. As a consequence, the only four plant parasitic nematode genera known to vector plant viruses include *Longidorus, Xiphinema, Paratrichodorus*, and *Trichodorus*. Of unknown significance is the fact that *Longidorus*, *Paralongidorus* (allegedly) and *Xiphinema* species transmit nepoviruses (polyhedral particles approximately 3×10^{-8} meters in diameter) while *Trichodorus* and *Paratrichodorus* transmit only tobraviruses (straight tubular particles). Equally mystifying is the fact the first group of nematodes, those transmitting nepoviruses, has a stylet-based feeding mechanism, whereas the latter transmitting tobraviruses, uses a solid spear-based feeding mechanism.

In the process of feeding on a virus-infested plant the nematode takes in with the ingested nutrients virus particles which adhere specifically to the walls of the esophageal lumen. A viruliferous nematode feeding upon a healthy plant injects some of these virus particles, along with the digestive fluids of the dorsal esophageal gland, into the healthy cell to infect the plant. Only a few species in these genera are able to transmit viruses; most do not. Moreover there appears to be a high specificity as to which nematodes transmit which viruses; that is, a virus-transmitting nematode is unable to transmit just any virus. In recent years the complexity of the system has been supplemented by the observation that all nepovirus or tobravirus particles are not identical. It appears that the virus' ribonucleic acid (RNA) genome is subdivided into two complementary fragments, each in a different particle. Both must recombine in a plant cell for an infection to progress.

It is readily apparent that nematodes are involved as an integral component in a wide range of "distinctive interactions" involving microorganisms, viruses, plants and animals. The most common incidences appear to involve plants (Fig. 11.1).

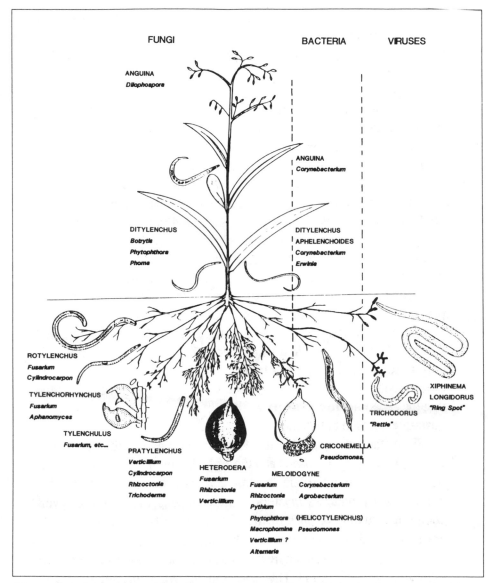

Figure 11.1. Schematic representation of the more significant "Distinctive Interactions" of plants involving nematodes with the major disease agent groups Fungi, Bacteria and Viruses. Adapted from de Guiran, INRA, France.

CHAPTER 12

The Control of Nematodes

The demographics of parasitic diseases are of sufficient significance to compel any thoughtful individual to pause and reflect. Is it possible to be indifferent when one of three human inhabitants of earth is burdened with parasitic organisms; when one of four Americans is infected with *Ascaris*, *Trichurus*, *Enterobius*, *Ancylostoma*, or *Necator* (nematodes); and annually worldwide some 50,000 people die from hookworm infections? Can any thoughtful individual be unconcerned about the toll taken by the parasitic nematodes of domestic livestock, pigs, cattle, sheep, fowl, and pets or wildlife, including reptiles, fish, birds and warm-blooded animals? Is anyone so foolish as to remain apathetic toward a tax of ten to fifty percent of total agricultural plant production lost to nematodes, depending on the pest control capability of each nation? Moreover, these tributes must really be supplemented by the corollary economic tolls of medical care, lost work time, poor quality food stuffs, reduced production and loss of earnings, among others. Most people, particularly the victims, need not be persuaded that the capability to control parasitic nematode populations is not only desirable but also beneficial.

From their origins plant life forms grew, developed, reproduced and evolved in the absence of any biological knowledge except perhaps by one Entity. Any problems that arose in the process were resolved in good time by nature's mysterious mechanisms to sustain an ever-changing dynamic balance of life forms. With the advent of human endeavor and accumulation of biological knowledge, mankind discovered that many of nature's mechanisms were not consonant with his egocentric interests. This collision of will with nature, and its infinite number of inner connective processes and relations, has taken on the specter of a comedy of errors. The adversarial approach seeking control agents to eradicate pests, in defiance of nature's counteractive measures, has been thwarted more often than not. As observed by the Nobel Laureate, Richard Feynman, "You can't fool nature."

Animal Parasites

In dealing with parasitic diseases the immediate medical goal is to eliminate the agent from within the host, whereas the principle long term goal is to break the cycle of reinfection. Few individuals will quarrel with the premise that for any potential disease situation the simplest and most effective method of control involves the evasion of the infective agent; but because of ignorance, indifference, or economic considerations the practice often founders.

Perhaps a prime example of the old adage, "an ounce of prevention is worth a pound of cure," is most evident in the control of parasitic diseases. Not only has preventive medicine been a prime component of the control practices by parasitologists of the past, it remains the method of prime reliance for the reduction and prevention of parasitic diseases. The consensus of parasitologists purports that, by large measure, parasitic diseases can be reduced drastically or prevented by the implementation of modern sanitary practices incorporating the use of sanitary facilities, education and personal hygiene. Sanitary facilities are very important for the provision of non-contaminated water and for the disposal of solid wastes of human or animal excreta harboring the infective stages of a wide array of parasitic disease agents. Education that explains and encourages the adoption of hygienic practices is a basic component of an effective program. The use of protective clothing and foot covering to prevent skin penetration, clothing to reduce insect vector transmission, washing with soap to reduce infective stage anal-to-mouth transmission, and sanitary housekeeping and food preparation practices to reduce sources of infection, are all essential to the interruption of the infection cycles of parasitic nematodes.

A supplementary strategy advocated by the World Health Organization, which has achieved moderate success, calls for the reduction or elimination of intermediate hosts that are involved in the transmission of disease agents. The policy begins with a modification of intermediate host habitat to render it non-suitable, or at least much less suitable, for the multiplication of the intermediate host. If this step is insufficient it is usually followed by broad pesticide application, particularly if the intermediate host is a flying insect vector. The incidence of Malaria and filarial parasitic nematode infections has been reduced drastically in some areas, and moderately in others, by reducing mosquito populations. In different regions of the world the same practice has been used to reduce *Simulium* black flies which transmit the filarial nematode causing onchocerciasis. Unfortunately, such projects to reduce or eliminate the reservoirs of infection are hampered by political instabilities in different regions, by the lack of fiscal support for the operations, and by the development of pesticide resistance in the target pests.

These broad programs are effective in reducing the incidences of parasitism in indigenous regions. Still, they are of little benefit to the parasitized victim. At this point, the only recourse available to the victim is therapeutic intervention. In the course of pharmaceutical efforts of the last half century a number of compounds (Table 12.1) have been found to be helpful. All have been discovered by trial and error, that is, through the empirical testing of a wide range of compounds, whether from synthetic or natural sources. Early on, distinctions were made between alimentary canal parasite residents and those resident in other body tissues, with the hope that a greater selection of substances would be available to render intestinal parasites narcotized or moribund long enough for them to be expelled with the feces of the host. While some compounds were effective for this purpose, they showed no particular advantage over newer developed compounds with a more general action. Many compounds are broad spectrum; others are not. Some compound classes are believed to have the same mode of action, while others are believed to have different modes. Most of the compounds are very toxic and the margin of safety, for tolerance by the host and the demise of the parasite, is very small. Therefore the selection of the therapeutic substance is predicated not only by the kind and heaviness of the parasite burden but also by host health.

Fortunately this situation has been alleviated somewhat by the increasing potency that has evolved in modern broad-spectrum anthelmintics. The effective dosage beginning with phenothiazine in the early 1940's was about 600 mg per kilogram of body weight; this has been decreasing with newer materials, such as Invermectin in the 1980's to 0.2 mg per kilogram body weight. The potency of the newer

Table 12.1. Classes of therapeutic compounds available for medical treatment of animal parasitic nematodes. Abstracted from Campbell.

Alimentary System Site	Period of Introduction	Body Tissue Sites
bephenium	—	arsenicals
benzimidazole	mid 1970's	benzimidazole
invermectin	early 1980's	diethylcarbamazine
levamisole	early 1970's	invermectin
morantel	early 1970's	levamisole
nitroscantate	—	suramin
organo-phosphate	late 1950's	—
phenothiazine	early 1940's	—
piperazine	—	—
pyrantel	mid 1960's	—
pyrvinium	—	—

drugs is such that optional delivery systems may be entertained. Slow release systems, skin patches and the like, maintain a less erratic dose level within host body tissues and thereby increase the margin of safety and convenience, and also decrease the risk in applications to livestock and human populations in poverty-stricken third world countries.

The important nematode parasites of livestock can be controlled rather effectively with the currently available anthelmintics; however, a similar statement cannot be made for man and his pests. The filarial nematode parasites constitute a major disease group in need of improved therapies. Current therapeutics are highly unsatisfactory in that they are risky, inconvenient and costly; moreover, they are unsuitable for the commonly accessible stages, for example the pre-adult stage in onchocerciasis, or the lymph-dwelling adults of the filarial nematode which causes elephantiasis. It is important to recognize that certain forms or stages of better-known parasitic nematode diseases of man or other animals remain untreatable, as do some of the rarer nematode parasitic diseases, e.g. trichostrongyliasis, anisakiasis, angiostrongyliasis and toxocariasis.

A partial immunity, or perhaps tolerance, for certain parasitic nematode infections appears to exist in the human native populations of endemic regions. This view has been nourished by field observations, wherein immigrants from non-infected areas suffer substantially more, with a given parasitic nematode burden, than the native population. This has also been confirmed by several laboratory animal experiments. In general, the notion of preventive prophylactic treatments remains essentially a vision, perhaps to be resolved in the future. The trends of society on a worldwide basis appear to be moving in a direction of increased commerce, recreation, and environmental concern—activities facilitating the worldwide dispersion of parasitic nematodes and other disease agents, and a corresponding increase in the incidences of unprovidential parasitism; at the same time parasitology and helminthology are being de-emphasized in many universities. It is generally recognized by the ranking parasitologists that in industrialized nations most physicians receive perfunctory training in parasitology, and concomitantly too great a proportion of teaching hospitals lack the necessary expertise for clinical diagnosis of parasites. Unfortunately, in the tropical and sub-tropical areas endemic to parasitic diseases the establishment has neither the means nor the funds to support a medical community able to deal with the serious problems.

Plant Parasites

Chemical Agents

The collapse of the German sugar beet industry (caused by the sugar beet nematode) in about 1870 stimulated a serious search for chemical agents which could be used for nematode control. About a decade earlier, *Phylloxera* (root aphid) was causing great damage to European grape root stocks. Entomologists eventually discovered a soil fumigant, carbon bisulfide (CS_2), which was efficacious for *Phylloxera* control. As a matter of course, therefore, carbon bisulfide was applied to sugar beets fields infested with the sugar beet nematode, but the results were not particularly promising. Shortly after the turn of the century, carbon bisulfide testing was resumed in the Southern U.S.

for the control of the rootknot nematode; again the practice did not prove to be particularly encouraging. A number of other chemicals were tested including formaldehyde. Cyanide, among other substances, was found to be nematicidal but too expensive and totally unsuitable for field applications.

Some of the old-timers could tell hair-raising stories about nematicidal trials, particularly those with carbon bisulfide. Carbon bisulfide is highly flammable and even explosive in the appropriate air mixtures. In a field application, liquid carbon bisulfide was run down through tubes attached to the back of chisels that were inserted into and dragged through the soil with a tractor. The carbon bisulfide flow was regulated according to the speed of the tractor, so as to deliver the desired dose. The principle of the delivery system, with perhaps somewhat cruder controls, was essentially similar to that employed by modern devices. Apparently it was not uncommon to look back at treated portions of the field to see fires and explosions along the treated strips and when these disturbances appeared to catch up with the tractor, the fumigant supply was turned off and the tractor moved quickly to avoid ignition of the carbon bisulfide reservoir tanks.

Fumigation as a means of nematode control began in earnest in about 1930 with a report that chloropicrin (trichloronitromethane) was highly efficacious in controlling rootknot and the reniform nematode on pineapple in Hawaii. The declaration, by the U.S. Army, of chloropicrin (tear gas) as a surplus war gas available for disposal led to the fumigation of pineapple fields with chloropicrin as a routine operation. With the depletion of the surplus chloropicrin stocks, and with no available substitute, fumigation as a practice lapsed until World War II.

As a consequence of war manufacturing, Shell Chemical Company had been accumulating enormous quantities of glycerol as a byproduct and was in search of a means of disposing the surplus, preferably at a profit. As part of the search program, a sample of glycerol was chlorinated to give a mixture of chlorinated aliphatic hydrocarbons which was made available to diverse groups for testing. The pineapple growers in Hawaii, desperate for a substitute for chloropicrin tested the crude chlorinated mixture, principally 1,2-dichloropropane and 1,3-dichloropropene (DD), and found it extremely efficacious for nematode control. Fumigation, primarily with DD, quickly became an accepted nematode control practice wherever nematode problems arose. Within a short period, a number of chemical agents were developed as fumigants, the major ones being methylbromide (MeBr), ethylenedibromide (EDB), 1,2-dichloropropane and 1,3-dichloropropene (DD), dibromochloropropane (DBCP), and a purified 1,3-dichloropropene (1,3-D). Concurrent with the development of newer fumigating agents was the development of non-fumigant nematicides which were water soluble materials. Insecticide manufacturers seeking to broaden their markets tested their stable of products for possible use in nematode control. The major non-fumigant products which have survived include Metham Sodium, Aldicarb, Carbofuran, Fenamifos, and Oxamyl. With the possible exception of methylbromide the fumigants are not acutely toxic, whereas the non-fumigant nematicides, with the possible exception of Metham Sodium, exhibit extremely acute toxicity towards mammals.

Fumigant applications usually involve injection of the active ingredient, pure or as a solution, into well-cultivated moist soil by means of tractor-drawn equipment at a spacing and depth that would allow diffusion to treat a volume of soil down to a predetermined depth. The injection chisels are usually followed by a pulverizing and packing device to seal the surface layer or, in the case of highly volatile fumigants such as methylbromide, by tarping with plastic sheets to reduce the rate of loss from the soil surface. Depending upon the local situation, some fumigants could be applied as emulsifiable concentrates in irrigation water.

Non-fumigant nematicides have been applied in the granular form to reduce the toxic risk to handlers and operators. The active agent is absorbed into granular particles which are subsequently coated with a sealing layer to protect against dust inhalation and prevent accidental contact. The granules are incorporated into soil by cultivation, then irrigated to release the activity and distribute the active agent. In an alternate application, dilute solutions can be injected directly into irrigation systems, whereby the water is distributed to plant root zones via various forms of emitters.

The major fumigants are all phytotoxic, with the possible exception of DBCP at low dosage rates; therefore they could only be used for pre-plant treatments. The exception, DBCP, could be used at low dosage rates around perennials, including trees and grapes, to keep the nematode populations under control. The mode of action of fumigants is uncertain, but is generally believed to involve the disruption of membranes, whether of cells, nuclei, or organelles. Nematodes that survive are escapees that the vapors for some reason do not reach.

The major non-fumigant nematicides, other than Metham Sodium (VAPAM), are not toxic to plants; nor, for that matter, are they efficient killing agents for nematodes. Some nematode populations may be bathed by one millimolar (mM) solutions for 24 hours, with 4 out of 5 nematodes remaining viable. Furthermore, immersion in solutions approximating levels recommended for field applications leaves moderate numbers of nematodes viable; in fact, taking a population that was immersed in such a manner for one week and then washing with water for 48 hours permitted up to 80% recovery of the total population.

The alleged mode of action of many non-fumigant nematicides is the result of cholinesterase inhibition. The fact that so many nematodes can remain viable for long periods in solutions of such high concentration, of which one drop on the skin of a mammal would be disastrous, suggests that the alleged mode of action is likely to be a minor component of the overall activity that renders a compound useful for nematode control. Moreover, it has been demonstrated recently that repeated field application of these types of compounds leads to the formation of adapted populations of nematodes that can tolerate the subsequent treatments of the same or related nematicides. The behavioral modification of plant-parasitic nematodes subject to repeated stress with non-fumigant nematicides is a complex phenomenon, rather than the simple development of pesticide resistance. The relations that appear to be involved include:

1) Selective pressures from subnematicidal exposures can result in nematode populations with a lower or higher fitness for reproduction;
2) Nematodes can be selected for, and/or can be conditioned to be more sensitive to nematicidal doses;
3) Nematode stressing can yield resistant populations with indifference to nematicidal doses;

4) Nematode stressing yields cross-susceptible and cross-resistant populations;

5) Nematode stressing can yield populations that show an habituation to nematicides;

6) There are real differences between nematode species in their responses to different nematicides.

Unfortunately, a nematode population well-adapted to some nematicides can be totally intractable to subsequent treatments of all of the major non-fumigant nematicides. Such a phenomenon is not unique for nematodes; pesticide resistance is a common occurrence in insects, plant pathogens and weeds—in fact all pests.

All nematicides have been found to be most effective in light sandy soils; heavy clay soils, peat soil, or others high in organic matter have usually been a problem. There is little question that fumigants, in suitable situations, were highly reliable and effective; whereas, in general, non-fumigants provided more erratic results and less effective control.

Within the past decade, remarkably rapid changes have occurred in plant-parasitic nematode control practices. Plant nematode control, which was believed to be well in hand then, has ceased to be so now. All of the fumigant nematicides previously discussed, with the exception of methyl bromide, are no longer marketed for use; three have been banned by regulatory action and the fourth withdrawn by the manufacturer, who concluded the cost of fulfilling the expanded test requirements for re-registration could not be recovered from sales. The situation is similar with non-fumigant nematicides. Carbofuran has been withdrawn by its manufacturer for reasons already stated. Aldicarb, Fenamifos and Oxamyl have had their use conditions restricted substantially. It appears to be inevitable that with a continuation of this trend the use of traditional nematicides as a means of nematode control will soon become a memory. So long as the regulatory restrictions of the past were modest or non-existent, pesticide manufacturers were inclined to invest in the development of new effective nematicides, inasmuch as the proprietary rights obtainable enabled the manufacturer to recover the costs of development and manufacture, and earn a profit. The current cost for procuring test data and other documentations for the fulfillment of all of the requirements necessary for the registration of any drug or pesticide is on the order of $30 million. Clearly, for a total nematicide market of somewhat over a $100 million, the exploration for registration and manufacture of new proprietary nematicides becomes an economically non-viable venture. The reality exists that economic forces restrict the investment of venture capital only to profitable enterprises. The current situation with nematicides is similar to that existing with medications for rare human diseases; the latter problem area eventually was partially resolved by the institution of government sponsored "orphan drug" programs.

Abandonment of chemical agents for pest control is not a practical option. To a grower-producer, such an option would result in the limitation of crops, the development of an intractable pest level, an even higher cost-return ratio, and great economic vulnerability in terms of reduced production, higher prices, loss of crops, conversion to crops of marginal profitability, and an accumulation of useless production equipment. The increased market demand, coupled with the decreased production, would accelerate the process (ongoing in Europe as well as North America) to rely on imports to make up the shortfall. Strangely enough, the constrictions on pesticide use for domestic production do not yet apply to imports.

To the consumer with a tunnel view, the abandonment of pesticides constitutes a terrific and emotionally satisfying idea; after all, no consumer, or grower for that matter, wishes to be poisoned. What consumers discount, or fail to recognize, is that natural pesticides can constitute 5 to 10% of plant dry weights, or that all consumers normally ingest, by weight, 10,000 times more natural pesticides than synthetic ones. Moreover, the hazards of naturally occurring pesticides are not to be disregarded; there is an abundance of such substances that are carcinogenic and mutagenic. Nor should it be overlooked that some of the most toxic substances known to man (aflotoxins) are produced naturally on certain foodstuffs infested with particular microflora.

While it was totally unanticipated, it is now abundantly clear that the over use and abuse of traditional nematicides (fumigants and non-fumigants) has led to our current clutch of problems, including ground water contamination, soil pollution and foodstuff residues. Alternative technologies are helpful (as will be discussed later); but with few exceptions, they are unlikely in the foreseeable future to fill the void left by the withdrawal of traditional nematicides. While the public clamor for new and improved drugs to treat pain, disease and other infirmities continues unabated, there exists tremendous apprehension and even terror of pesticide agents, even though their normal use poses less of a health threat than the side effects of some prescribed medicinal drugs, including anthelmintics or for that matter many of the naturally occurring pesticides.

While a mild apprehension conveys a healthy awareness in the informed consumer, exaggerated concern or excessive dismay is not only unfortunate, but counterproductive to the achievement of the general goals of society. An informed society ought to be mindful of the fact that all organisms function and relate to all other organisms by a system of checks and balances involving chemical compounds and chemical reactions. The problems associated with the overuse and abuse of nematicides need not be; the opportunities and the potential for the development of chemical agents with different modes of pesticide action have never been greater. It is a question of taking advantage of research findings in corollary areas of biology and adapting and refining those most appropriate, and least hazardous, in a sensible non-threatening nematode management program.

Experience of the past has revealed that no single agent by itself will ever provide a sustainable nematode control technology. Recent research with biochemical inhibitors of various kinds has demonstrated the potential that may be achievable by this approach. Of course, inhibitors must be selected to target nematode reactions vital to the pest, but of little consequence to the host. Preferably, the search should not be restricted to those inhibitors of traditional biochemical reactions, but should include, for example, the more unusual types, such as reaction complexes or apparatus that can generate short-lived free radicals to interfere with nematode chemistry. Pessimism directed to the non-hazardous chemical control of nematodes is really unwarranted.

Biocontrol Agents

The use of biological agents to control pestiferous nematodes remains an especially attractive notion, despite the fact that a half century of research has resulted in no generally effective technology. This approach applied to other pests, particularly insects, has provided remarkable successes in a few suitable systems. Unfortunately, the few successes have been far outnumbered by the failures, and some outright disasters when the supposed "biocontrol agent" became an even worse pest.

Soil-borne nematodes, like all other organisms, are subject to risk according to the general law of nature, "eat or be eaten." In a complex community, such as a terrestrial or terrestrial-like habitat, there resides an incredible diversity and abundance of life forms, many of which would consider nematodes as appetizing morsels. Such life forms consist of different species of bacteria, fungi, protozoa, micrometazoans (including predacious nematodes), tardigrades, collembola, flat worms, oligochaetes, mites, and other arthropods.

Bacteria have often been found within plant-parasitic nematodes; however, the bulk of the observations are subject to an element of doubt. The nature of the bacterial association, whether it is parasitic, symbiotic, or saprophytic (invasion after death of the nematode from some other cause), is seldom clearly established. For bacterial species to be directly useful as biological agents in nematode control, they need the capacity to invade live worms, with the possible exception of certain saprophytic feeders that produce toxins causing death to nematodes that absorb the toxins.

There exists one clear parasitic bacterial association with plant-parasitic nematodes initially observed a half century ago. This agent was reported as *Duboscquia penetrans* (mis-identified as a protozoan), renamed much later after additional study as *Bacillus penetrans*, and finally redescribed a few years ago as *Pasteuria penetrans* (Fig. 12.1B). The bacterial spore attaches to the nematode cuticle, sends a spore tube through the nematode integument, after which it proliferates within the nematode body and overwhelms it to eventually release new spores for reattachment to a new host. According to one researcher

"*P. penetrans* is the most specific obligate parasite of nematodes yet discovered." Unfortunately, until this organism can be cultured commercially on a monoxenic medium the criteria for practical applications are unlikely to be established.

Fungi that attack nematodes directly are widespread and include varied forms, e.g., nematode-trapping fungi (Fig. 12.1C,D,E), endoparasitic fungi (Fig. 12.1F), egg and cyst parasitic fungi, and indirectly other fungi that produce toxins injurious to nematodes. There are more than a hundred fungal species considered to be nematophagous (feeding on nematodes). Interest has focused on fungi that are able to attack plant-parasitic nematodes, although the same or other fungal species may also target microbivorous nematodes. Microbivorous nematodes may be attacked by these fungi from without, that is, by spores or mycelium attaching to the cuticle and penetrating, or from within by ingestion of the infecting particle and penetration of the alimentary system. However, plant-parasitic nematodes can only be invaded through the cuticle, since the stylet aperture is too small to permit the entrance of fungal spores or hyphae. For unknown reasons these fungi can have different habitat preferences; some are rhizospheric in that they prefer the habitat adjacent to a growing root, whereas others are non-rhizospheric, indicating they are satisfied with the conditions in soil away from plant roots or rootlet extensions.

It has been estimated that a normally fertile field soil may contain on the order of: 10^9 bacteria, 10^5–10^8 actinomycetes, 10^5–10^6 fungi, and 10^4–10^5 protozoa as reproductive units per gram of soil, in addition to large numbers of nematodes and other micrometazoans. The resultant proportion of life forms in such a habitat can be expected to be in dynamic equilibrium. A foreign life form, unless extremely suitable to the habitat and added in massive numbers, is unlikely to be competitive and will therefore disappear. Potential exceptions arise in select environmental systems wherein specific unfilled niches exist that are well adapted for the particular introduced species. Experimental observations have indicated a general succession of fungal species, beginning with an intense microbial activity in a soil heavily supplemented with organic amendments. As the initial microbial activity subsides, the microfloral browsers (e.g., nematodes) ascend in dominance, followed by trapping fungi. The succession of fungal species continues at irregular intervals, sometimes weeks or months after the initial explosion of microbial activity.

The trapping fungi, representatives in the class *Phycomycetes* or *Moniliales*, demonstrate rather surprizing characteristics to sate their predacious habit. Upwards of two dozen species from these groups exhibit adhesive conidia or adhesive hyphae which, upon contact with

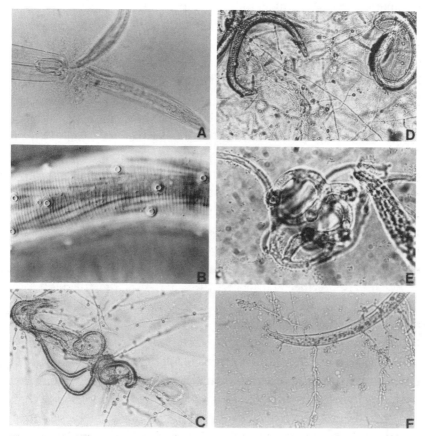

Figure 12.1. Biocontrol agents attacking nematode prey. A. A predacious nematode (*Monochus* sp.) left, attacking a prey nematode. B. Bacteria (*Pasteuria penetrans*) spores attached and developing on a prey nematode surface. C. A fungus (*Dactylaria* sp.) using sticky knobs to trap nematodes. D. A fungus (*Dactylella* sp.) using sticky knobs to trap nematodes. E. A fungus (*Arthrobotrys* sp.) using constricting loops (center) to trap nematodes. F. Fungal hyphae exiting a parasitized nematode. Fig. 12.1 B after B. Jaffee with permissin. Fig. 12.1 A, C, D, E & F after R. Mankau with permission.

a nematode, adhere to the cuticle and send a germ tube through the integument for the spread of mycelium throughout the animal. Over a dozen species in the genera *Dactylaria* and *Dactylella* ensnare nematodes by means of adhesive knobs atop short stalks arising from the mycelial network (Fig. 12.1 C,D). While small nematodes remain anchored to the hyphal network, larger nematodes may tear away from the mycelium; however, the knob remains attached to send a germ tube through the integument to infect the nematode. Over two dozen different species, primarily from the genera *Arthrobotrys*, *Dactylaria* and *Dactylella*, ensnare nematodes by forming adhesive and non-adhesive loops through modifications of hyphal filaments. Nematodes attempting to pass through the loop either stick to the adhesive inner layer of the loop or become wedged in non-sticky loops to allow any of the three cells forming the loop to initiate the germ tube penetration of the nematode integument. Over a dozen other species, primarily from the genera *Arthrobotrys* and *Dactylaria* form a highly specialized non-sticky loop. Any nematode, small or large, endeavoring to pass through the loop and thereby touching the inner wall of the loop stimulates the three loop cells to enlarge abruptly to ensnare the nematode. The constricting loop is activated in a fraction of a second. Once ensnared by the adhesive hyphae, knob or loop, the nematode, whether it breaks away from the mycelial net or not, is invaded by the attached fungal fragment. Despite their spectacular characteristics, trapping fungi have so far been found useless as biocontrol agents for field control of nematodes. Their ubiquitous occurrence in field soil, their ill-defined nature of nematode predation, their fastidiousness which resists easy culturing of the more promising species, and the enormous capacity of soil to resist practical efforts at modification, all create immense obstacles to their development as biocontrol agents.

A different approach which is gaining acceptance involves a survey of fields in nature infested with plant-parasitic nematodes where, despite a regime of repeated host cultivation, the nematode population remains at a relatively constant low level. Perhaps one of the better known occurrences involves several English fields infested with the Oat Cyst Nematode (*Heterodera avenae*), which maintain low population levels despite repeated planting of host cultivars. In similar fields elsewhere, high populations of nematodes developed to decimate the host cultivars planted. The Oat Cyst Nematodes in the former fields were heavily parasitized by naturally-occurring soil fungi, whereas in the latter fields the nematode populations showed little or no parasitization by soil fungi. While cursory observation points to the fungal parasite as a biological agent, clear-cut evidence is lacking. Nevertheless such fields are likely to be more useful in the search for an effective biological agent. Such situations are natural developments; the effect is taking place in a wide area, measurable in hectares rather than pots; it is an established system that functions in a natural soil rather than in a highly modified synthetic mix. Many of the obstacles to the practical application of most of the previously discussed parasitic agents would be circumvented by selecting for biocontrol agents which appear to be indigenous and functioning on a field scale. Such fungal parasites appear to invade live eggs, larvae and/or adults, much as saprophytic fungi would invade dead organisms.

It is unfortunate that the spectacular mechanisms exhibited by trapping fungi, while fascinating and intellectually stimulating, have been in practice total failures. Despite the lack of success to date, it would be reasonable to anticipate the development of several effective nematode management systems based on biocontrol agents, as have been found for insect control.

Although a wide range of organisms other than bacteria and fungi are known to be ready and willing to consume nematodes as a food source, their potential for use has been virtually ignored. The portion of a given nematode population that is eliminated by any of the predators in the community remains unknown. For example, a plant-parasitic nematode population in the absence of a host is known to perish at a certain rate, depending on the species and the conditions; however, what portion of the perishing population is attributable to the action of predators, whether fungi, nematodes (Fig. 12.1 A), mites or tardigrades, and what portion succumbs to starvation, or what portion succumbs to abiotic environmental factors—these questions remain a total mystery.

Plant Resistance

The notion of selecting plants for desirable characteristics is as old as agriculture itself. Our hunter-gatherer ancestors most probably selected those plants from the wild that produced, in abundance, the most tasty fruits, seeds, root organs, or edible plant parts, for harvest and consumption. Their followers, the early farmers, are likely to have used similar criteria for choosing plants to cultivate, and continued the practice to improve their crops by selecting the better producing plants from their domesticated stock. Despite their ignorance, they were empirically utilizing modern genetic principles to infuse more desirable traits into their crops.

Until the late nineteenth century, crop improvement was a matter of empirical trial and error and a measure of good fortune. Modern animal and plant breeding was founded upon the remarkable observations of an Austrian monk, Gregor Johann Mendel. His report outlining the manner of inheritance of certain traits in the progeny resulting from the crossing of two plants manifesting two different traits was ignored for thirty-five years. Fortunately, at the beginning of the twentieth century his work on the inheritance of tallness and dwarfness in pea plant crosses, together with the notion of the inheritance of the dominant or recessive character, was rediscovered and confirmed by several botanists. Since then plant breeders have produced some remarkable crop improvements in terms of quality and quantity of fruits and seeds, color, size and conformation of flowers and leaves, and adaptation to diverse environmental regimes including heat, cold, drought, wetness, high and low light intensity, soil type and salinity.

The results of plant breeding for pest resistance have been substantially less than spectacular. This is not a consequence of a failure of plant breeding technology, but of a misguided theoretical presupposition. Breeding goals that involve host adaptation to abiotic factors provide candidates to occupy unfilled ecological niches, and therefore work in concert with nature by supplementing its efforts; whereas host breeding for pest resistance is largely antagonistic to natural mechanisms and processes, whose express purpose is not to permit undue favoritism in the relationships of two organisms. Man's intervention in favor of one partner in the relationship automatically triggers nature's mechanisms in defense of the threatened organism, as noted earlier. Nature's balancing mechanisms are not rigid, but incorporate some flexibility that allows for variations in the relationships.

Some incidences of host resistance are multigene based, that is, some two to twelve genes must be present and active in the host tissue for the full expression of resistance; however, most frequently resistance is based upon a single dominant gene. All multigene-based resistance in a host constitutes an inherent bias in natural mechanisms in favor of the host, thereby rendering the simultaneous mutagenic development of corresponding genes for aggression in the pest much less probable. The mutagenic development in the pest of an aggressiveness gene to counter the single-gene based resistance in the host is highly probable, and as noted from past experience can be anticipated to arise in from five to ten generations.

To summarize, as a plant breeder modifies a gene component to favor the host, the genetic constitution of the pest population modifies to neutralize this stress pressure. It is not surprising, therefore, that most cultivars based on single-gene resistance to nematodes become useless in a few years when planted repeatedly on a single plot of infested land. It should be clear that man's attempts at host breeding for resistance did not cause the adaptive response in pests, but simply revealed its existence and made it of abundant concern. The capacity of a nematode to adapt, best studied in parasitic nematode-plant systems, has been in place for eons. Current information indicates that, in plant-parasitic nematode species of worldwide importance, there are at least two, and usually more, representative populations (races, pathotypes, biotypes) differing in host preferences already present in nature. In fact the stem and bulb nematode, *Ditylenchus dipsaci,* consists of more than twenty such populations, and the Oat Cyst nematode, *Heterodera avenae*, consists of more than a dozen such populations. The existence of a multitude of populations in every nematode species, with diversity not only in host preference but also in a range of inheritable characteristics, is probably the rule rather than the exception.

Traditional breeding techniques are preferred because they do not exclude multiple-gene based resistance, provided that resistance genes exist in the gene pool of the nominal species. For host species in which resistance is limited or absent, recombinant DNA techniques (biotechnology) can be used to transfer a resistant gene from a non-host, particularly when traditional cross-fertilization is unachievable. Single-gene based resistance can be very effective against a non-aggressive pest population. The risk arises from an undue reliance upon the use of such a cultivar in a nematode management program. To illustrate with an extreme example, should the gene for resistance to a nematode in an infested field be transferred by recombinant techniques to each cultivar of a given four-year crop rotation cycle, one could anticipate with high probability that the resident nematode population will have developed sufficient aggressiveness by the end of the cycle to render the initial resistance inserted into the cultivars useless. Plant resistance to nematodes is not all that common, and is therefore an extremely important trait which must not be abused, but employed conservatively and judiciously for long-term benefit.

Cultural Methods

Diverse cultural practices to improve crop production empirically have probably been employed since the beginnings of agriculture. Crop rotation (planting different crops in sequence usually over a three to four year period before replanting the first crop) was found to be especially beneficial in maintaining a better soil mineral nutrient balance, a better soil particle structure, and facilitated the dissipation of crop root toxic exudates and the suppression of soil-borne pest and disease agents. Inadvertently some of these practices were likely to have provided some degree of nematode control, although farmers of the time were unaware of the existence of nematode pests.

Despite the manifold benefits derivable from a crop rotation, there may be serious drawbacks to a practical implementation. Periods of fallow allow nematode populations to diminish by natural processes of attrition, but provide no practical economic return; moreover in regions subject to intense wind and water erosion, fallow may cause more damage than benefit. Crops in a rotational program must be economically useful; an agricultural unit is unlikely to survive by attempting to grow crops that are unprofitable, notwithstanding the fact that they may be helpful in depressing nematodes and other pest populations. Inasmuch as each agricultural region has available a limited number of profitable or marginally profitable crops from which to choose, a totally satisfactory crop rotation program is largely an illusion. The development of profitable crop cultivars resistant to nematodes has been immensely helpful; however, as previously indicated, overuse of such a cultivar is likely to be self-defeating.

Early planting is a practice which takes advantage of the temperature differential that permits plants to grow well while parasitic nematodes do not. If a crop is planted early in the season, so as to germinate and grow more slowly at the lower temperatures at which the nematode is marginally active, crop growth is favored and the harvest may be early with little yield loss. Although helpful, this practice is often hampered by unfavorable crop habits, and the ever-changing environmental conditions occurring each Spring.

The use of trap crops has a long history, and that of toxic crops is somewhat shorter; however theoretically and emotionally satisfying, the concepts have been useless as practical methods. In either case a better part of a growing season is sacrificed for no economic return. Most frequently the trap crop is a susceptible crop which must be left in the soil as long as possible to maximize the number of nematodes which penetrate and infect, but it must be removed just before nematode reproduction begins. Inasmuch as nematode life cycles are not on precise time scales, but subject to the vagaries of photoperiod, temperature, and other factors, a miscalculation in timing of trap crop removal can be disastrous by leaving a higher nematode population than would have been there naturally. Toxic crops suffer similar disadvantages, including the loss of a cropping season, and may enjoy modest efficacy against certain target nematodes, but could provide a good host to build up populations of other nematodes that may be in the soil. The prospect for crops toxic to nematodes has been stimulated by recent advances in insect control wherein recombinant technology has placed the *Bacillus thuringiensis* toxin gene in tobacco to discourage insect pests. Pests in areas subjected to repeated use of *B. thuringiensis* have developed resistance. This technology has not been demonstrated with nematodes, nor has it been determined how rigorous the criteria for registration will be, particularly in the case of comestible crops.

Freezing, heating and desiccation are cultural practices that have been very useful for certain problem conditions. While it has been previously stated that most nematodes probably can survive in a desiccated state for an extended period, with few exceptions they must arrive at that state in a slow, gradual fashion. Abrupt or rapid drying, therefore, is highly lethal to most nematodes, though hard to achieve with the enormous masses of organic material or soil in a large field and therefore variable in effectiveness. Nematode activity ceases at some low threshold temperature characteristic of the species; however, many nematodes remain viable and revivable although exposed to subfreezing temperatures. At low enough temperatures arrived at slowly, nematodes die. In some temperate regions, where winter temperatures persist at below freezing for extended periods, nematodes will be killed.

Heat treatments are one of the more effective methods to eliminate nematodes from moderate masses of soil or organic matter, and are free of toxic hazards and pollution of the environment. Years of temperature testing have demonstrated that no terrestrial or marine nematode survives a temperature of 52°C (125.6°F) in a moist atmosphere for one half hour. Unfortunately, heat treatments are very costly and so practical only for high value crops. Nurseries, for example, bury steam lines in their planting beds to pasteurize the soil for elimination of weeds and soil-borne pests including nematodes and plant pathogens. Hot water treatments, carefully controlling temperature and length of exposure, are used to eliminate nematodes from planting stock with minimal injury to plant tissue. The application of this technology to disinfect garlic cloves from the stem and bulb nematode (*Ditylenchus dipsaci*) for use as planting stock was critical to the survival of the garlic industry of California.

A variation of the heat treatment concept is basic to "solarization" as a means of field pest control. Solarization involves sealing a moist field with a transparent plastic tarp to create a "greenhouse effect" over the soil, allowing solar radiation to penetrate but preventing heat radiation from emerging. The heat accumulating in the soil from the intense solar radiation for long periods (usually 6 weeks or so) heats the upper layers of soil to destroy nematodes, weeds and other pathogens.

Unfortunately, the heating occurs primarily in the region near the soil surface and so is most effective for shallow rooted crops in areas where the summers are too hot for normal agricultural production and the treatment therefore does not interfere with normal crop sequence.

Good crop care is indispensable for optimal crop production, but even more critical for fields infested with nematodes. The discussion of the earlier section covering nematode dispersion emphasizes the value of good crop care to avoid new nematode introduction by way of contaminated farm machinery, nursery stock, soil, tools or irrigation water. Phytonematodes stress a crop—the higher the population the greater the stress; therefore it is essential to create the most favorable growing conditions possible to gain the highest yield. This means the elimination in so far as possible of all controllable stresses, e.g., nutrient deficits, insect pests, pathogens, weed competition and water deficits. Mulching, for example, is often recommended to reduce weed competition and soil water loss.

Plants normally have excess capacity to overcome minor adversity (water uptake, mineral uptake, photosynthetic activity, etc.); as the stresses on the plant increase the reserve capacity to compensate for limiting processes diminishes, after which the physiological functions begin to shut down, probably in the order of priority for survival. The photosynthetic rate appears to be one of those functions. Although several reports involving nematode stress of bean and grape cultures suggests no change in those functions, other preliminary observations with tomato and sugar beets, suggest otherwise and are consistent with similar observations on plant stress with plant pathogens or insects. How a nematode invasion of roots can effect a photosynthetic rate taking place in a leaf many centimeters away is open to speculation. Application of Occam's Razor Philosophy would suggest a simple hypothetical explanation for the infected root. In a healthy root the high concentration of accumulated photosynthates constitutes a feedback mechanism to regulate photosynthetic rate in the leaves, whereas in a heavily infected root, photosynthetic accumulation does not occur because of increased utilization by the infected root. Photosynthesis therefore proceeds at a high rate; however, if the demand of photosynthates by the roots is greater than photosynthesis can supply, the plant suffers. Even higher photosynthetic rates might be achievable if the substrate component supply was not limiting; therefore, supplementary nutrition of the above-ground plant portions with mineral and organic substrates, or reaction co-factors, could perhaps be useful to increase photo-synthetic rates and to maintain them longer to counteract the stress on the plant. Recent evidence suggests that such a hypothesis may have practical merit, although unequivocal supporting evidence is lacking.

A brief overview of the nematode control technology in the last century not only attests to a total lack of program design for development of effective control options, but also the complete absence of any theoretical hypothesis for achievement of long-term sustainable control. Pre-World War II technology relied heavily upon crop rotation, the use of resistant plants, and other cultural manipulations with unremarkable success. The practice was helpful as a preventive measure, but in cases of heavy infestations was economically ruinous. With the discovery of fumigant and non-fumigant nematicides, applied nematology overwhelmingly jumped on the bandwagon of chemical agents' success, essentially relegating alternate technologies to the dust bin. Fascination with nematicides continued for several decades until it turned into an abhorrence relationship with the recognition of the role of nematicides as polluters and health hazards. With advocation for the abandonment of chemical nematicides came the frantic search for alternate control technologies. Consequently, there was little option other than to return to the old inadequate pre-war technologies in a desperate hope to upgrade and embellish them with sophisticated instrumentation and techniques to make them more effective. As might be anticipated, different advocate groups arose to promote their specialty—whether recombinant DNA resistant gene transfer, use of biological control agents, or integrated pest management to rearrange old technologies in a more effective sequence. In retrospect it is clear that there is a compelling need for an alternate philosophy for sustainable long-term nematode control to replace the traditional "knee-jerk philosophy" of the past. For the development of the proactive philosophy for nematode control, several fundamental tenets merit acknowledgement:

i)   The expectation that any single agent or method will be effective in controlling all nematodes is essentially fantasy.
ii) Sustainable nematode control can be accomplished; however it must be applicable to the local pest and cropping systems.
iii) Successful sustainable nematode control will be predicated upon an identification and intensified development of original, non-traditional biotic and abiotic agents and mechanical, physical and biological techniques and devices whose spectra of activity are based upon different modes of action. With the development of some half dozen agents from any of the control categories discussed, an effective sustainable management protocol can be devised to avoid adaptation, aggressiveness, and an intractable nematode control situation.
iv) It is essential that the philosophy and strategy of nematode management be conceived to work in concert, rather than in conflict, with natural principles and processes to avoid continual repetition of the ineptitudes, failures and mistakes of the past.

Microbial Feeders

There has been little interest or economic need to control microbivorous nematodes, with the exception of a few species that plague the mushroom industry. Mushroom beds are usually maintained in dark, humid, moderately-temperatured barns for extended periods to allow the mycelium to grow abundantly before the application of a surface treatment to stimulate the formation of fruiting bodies. A mushroom bed infestation by certain cosmopolitan mycophagus nematode species (*Ditylenchus myceliophagus*) quickly decimates the mushroom culture. Nematode control has usually been in the form of preventive measures, including pasteurization of bed containers and fungal growing medium, and sanitation measures to disinfect barn floors and support members. Partial nematode control was achieved with the incorporation of a predacious fungus with a commercial mushroom spawn, inasmuch as nematicidal treatments were unacceptable. The problem was eventually resolved by modification of mushroom bed containers. Since nematode eradication is impossible the few residual nematode escapees would eventually migrate up the always wet wooden structural members of the barn and the bed containers to infest a spawn bed. In the modification the bed container consisted of plastic bags filled with the mushroom growing mixture and placed on shelves in the same sheds. Though the barn remained very humid, the outer plastic bags' surfaces remained dry, thereby preventing the nematode from climbing the container walls to infect the spawn bed.

Insect Control

Although, in the light of current knowledge, most nematodes are innocuous and the rest are pestiferous, there are a few species that are helpful in resolving society's insect problems. The incidence of entomogenous nematodes in insects is a common occurrence, encompassing perhaps some twenty orders of insects. Perhaps all nematode infections of insects, with few exceptions (the pollinating insects), may be considered beneficial to man by helping to control insect populations. Despite the abundance and diversity of nematode infections of insects, very few genera have received moderately intensive study. Probably the most highly promoted and publicized nematode genera include *Steinernema, Heterorhabditis,* and *Romanomermis.* The insurmountable problems appear to include the delivery of the nematodes in sufficient proximity to the target insect and their survival until host penetration occurs. Notwithstanding over 65 years of promotional effort towards utilizing nematodes for insect control, practical applications of the technology remain only in the "potentially useful" category.

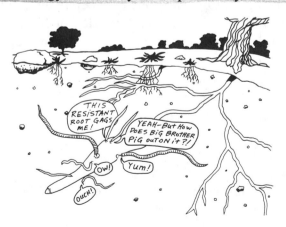

CHAPTER 13

Impact on Man

Academic purists of zoological bent may become interested in nematodes simply because they are curious creatures. Most of us, however, require a little more incentive and stimulation before devoting energy and time to improve our understanding of nematodes. Perhaps the greatest motivation comes with the appreciation of how such an organism can affect our health or well-being. The following discussion evinces concepts and considerations regarding three major nematode groupings to pique the interest of the pensive reader.

Plant Parasites

No plant-parasitic nematode has yet been found to be a disease agent of humans or other vertebrate animals. Infested plant tissue, upon ingestion, simply passes through the alimentary canal and is excreted without causing harm. On occasion, a plant-parasitic nematode may be associated with a livestock disease syndrome (the "sheep staggers") that kills sheep in Australia. This disease syndrome is associated with a seed gall nematode, which plays an essentially passive role by transporting a bacterium into a seed gall it induces. The bacteria in the seed gall grow luxuriously to overwhelm the nematode. It is these bacteria that produce the toxin that causes the "staggers disease;" in the absence of the bacteria, the nematodes pose no problem for livestock.

In general, the impact of plant-parasitic nematodes on humans is indirect and a consequence of the reduction or total loss of production of food and fiber from plants. For food plants, perhaps the major nematode pests worldwide are rootknot nematodes (*Meloidogyne* sp.), so-called because they induce a formation of galls or knots on the roots, or, at high concentrations, effect grotesquely gnarled roots and the eventual death of the plant. This genus consists of upwards of fifty species, with a host range of thousands of plants including, with few exceptions, most of those producing food and fiber. Representatives of the genus are cosmopolitan in distribution and apparently indigenous to many areas of the world. For example, an Egyptian nematologist, responding to a small independent farmer's complaint of poor tomato crops, pulled up a young tomato seedling root system from the field to explain that the galls on the roots were caused by a nematode that would eventually destroy his crop. The farmer remarked that he did not believe this to be so, simply because neither he, his father, nor his grandfather had ever seen a gall-free root system, and that he could therefore be certain that the galled root system was the healthy condition.

A different pest, the reniform nematode, has nearly as large a host range and distribution as some of the major rootknot nematode species. It is particularly important in tropical and subtropical regions and attacks many of the major crops grown in these regions. The citrus nematode is found in all citrus-growing areas of the world. It can reduce tree growth and production drastically, as in Iraq, where it is normal for 20 year old orchards to be comprised of dwarfed trees with poor fruit. Virtually all banana plantations in the subtropical regions of the world are heavily infested with several kinds of nematodes. The nematode control practices are not very effective, so that the fruited plants must be artificially supported in the upright position. Nematode infection sites serve as courts of infection for fungi and bacteria, which rot the plant base and weaken the root support system so that without artificial propping, the plant is toppled to the ground by wind and rain.

A diversity of cyst-forming nematodes are known to plague a wide range of major crops critical to the world's food supply. The sugar beet cyst nematode, which collapsed the German economy in the 1870s, continues to be a problem wherever sugar beets and crucifers are grown. A related cyst nematode attacks potatoes everywhere in the world that potatoes are grown commercially, except for the United States fields in which it does not yet appear. A different cyst nematode attacks corn, or maize, in Latin America; it is particularly devastating to corn production in the central highlands of Mexico. Another cyst nematode damages grain in North America, Europe, Asia, and Australia. A related cyst nematode attacks soybeans in all major production areas of the world.

Two totally different groups of plant-parasitic nematodes pose an unusual threat. Although in high-level infestations they can weaken plants and reduce crop production, they are perhaps a greater problem at low levels of infestations, in which they can serve as virus vectors. They have the capacity to feed on virus carrying plant hosts, harbor the virus internally, and migrate to a healthy plant root to inject the virus while feeding. While the nematode population may be too low to cause any problem, the transferred virus causes a decimation of a planting in a few years.

Plants which are sources of fiber are affected by various parasitic nematodes as well. Cotton is perhaps the major worldwide source of fabric fiber, but in certain regions of the world other source plants, e.g., flax for linen, jute, sisal, and others, are of economic importance. With the advent of synthetic fibers, the demand for natural fibers has diminished, and correspondingly the price of raw material has fallen. Cotton has faired best in this economic environment, while most other fiber plant industries have weakened. These depressed industries can no longer support high inputs of care, fertilizer and pesticides to maintain production; consequently the crop damage effected by nematodes and other pests is rising.

Fiber also comes from trees, which provide lumber, paper pulp, and fuel to meet society's needs. The forest industry has existed principally as a gathering process, harvesting trees fortuitously provided by nature. It has become abundantly clear that if the industry is to survive, forest tree production will need to change to a farming process in the foreseeable future. Pest problems and disease management in forestry appear to remain an incidental concern. In particular, the role of nematodes associated with forest trees remains essentially unknown. There is no active forest nematologist in the western hemisphere, and the rest of the world fares little better. However, the few pioneering studies available suggest that nematode parasites of forest trees may be as devastating to forest production as their relatives are to agriculture. A grassland range biome study in the central United States reported that the soilborne fauna (primarily nematodes) extracted a quantity of energy from that fixed by the photosynthetic activity of the vegetation equivalent to that removed by grazing livestock. Is it rational to believe that natural biological forces that apply to rangeland and agricultural plants do not apply to forest land trees? Apparently, the forest industry continues to maintain its typical, shortsighted indifference to most pest problems, particularly those that are soilborne.

The development of monocultural practices has enabled agriculture to become sufficiently efficient and productive to meet the food and fiber needs of growing populations. In the U.S., 3% of the population constitutes the farming community that supports the remaining proportion of urbanites; in other industrial countries the ratios are similar. Unfortunately, the monoculture practice which has been so bountiful for society is ideal for the development and dissemination of high populations of parasitic nematodes and other pests. With the best use of modern control and pest management practices, an average production loss of approximately 10% can be attributed to plant-parasitic nematodes. With poor farming practices, the loss may increase to 100%. The consequent reality is that production losses in Third World countries are generally much greater than for industrialized nations.

Environmental conditions tend to be of minor relevance to the incidence of pest problems; however, individual nematode species or other pests do have preferred environmental requirements. Within a broad latitude of host, climate, and soil conditions, usually one or more nematode pests will find suitable niches. To illustrate, the Peruvian high desert is an extremely arid place, with less than 1 mm average yearly rainfall. With an incipient rainfall this land bursts into activity. Water is absorbed. Seeds germinate. Plants grow, bloom and produce seeds; a process that may consume months in other areas is compressed into a few short weeks. A nematologist fortuitously having occasion to visit such an area during its "bloom" period noted that plant roots were heavily infested with a rootknot nematode species. In a totally different area, the Alma-Ata Valley of Kazakhstan, a region of the former Soviet Republic, the resident nematologist observed that several different nematode species were causing agricultural pest problems on the valley floor. A survey revealed that the nematode had dispersed from higher elevations. Following the nematode species distribution up the mountain range, he observed the presence of a rootknot nematode species and a stem and bulb nematode surviving happily on wild host plants above 3,000 meters in elevation.

Since plant-parasitic nematodes of some kind can be found most anywhere, they lend support to the notion of some evolutionists that pests in general may be a component of the evolutionary process that shapes and influences the development and multiplication of plant life forms.

Man does not have the technology to eradicate plant-parasitic nematodes once they have become well established. Under ideal conditions, they may be controlled or managed to tolerable levels. It is in this connection that quarantine regulations play a role. Clearly, if a pest species is not present in a particular area, it is far more effective and less costly to prevent its introduction than to attempt to control or manage it after it has dispersed. Quarantine restrictions may be imposed on a national, state, provincial, or regional basis to protect agriculture and livestock as well as other local indigenous wildlife species. In some states, a certified nursery program serves as an extension of the quarantine concept. A certified nursery program acts to ensure the healthiest quality stock plants that practical technology permits by requiring a rigid protocol for plant propagation. Similar preventive quarantine programs are in place to prevent the introduction of animal parasites and disease agents with the potential to infect domestic livestock or wildlife in general. Unfortunately, the quarantine program is not a rigid barrier. Undetected pests slip through the inspection (usually inadvertently), and if they are not eradicated in the very early stages, quickly colonize and disperse to become a problem. Quarantine practices, of course, are effective only for human based activities, i.e., export, import, transport and travel; they are totally ineffective in preventing introductions by natural forces, such as strong winds or floods that can move incredible amounts of infested soils.

Free Living Nematodes

Free living nematodes have no direct effect on man; so far as is known they are generally benign. For example, during the "hippie" back-to-nature era of the 1960s, a woman consulted an emergency clinic regarding a genital inflammation. The diagnosis revealed a population of bacterial feeding nematodes in the vagina as a result of her use, as a hygienic sanitary napkin, of dried moss and fern in which there were nematodes in a desiccated state. The nematodes revived and propagated on the bacterial population but were incidental to her problem.

The effects of free living nematodes on society are generally indirect, but may function in diverse ways. It was discovered long ago by botanists that the plant rhizosphere (the soil zone immediate to the roots of plants) harbored very high populations of microorganisms compared to soil far removed from roots. The microorganisms feed on the secretions, excretions, and sloughed off tissue of the living roots. It is inevitable that soilborne animals able to feed on microorganisms would also congregate in this zone, as would predators feeding on the microbivorous animals. Should these root emanations be allowed to accumulate in the absence of microorganismal activity, there would result a distortion in the balance of nutritional mineral cations and anions to reduce plant growth, an accumulation of organic constituents that would become toxic to the plant and, for leguminous plants, a reduced ammonia and nitrate availability from atmospheric nitrogen fixation, along with other manifestations. Sufficiently high populations of microbivorous nematodes could lower microorganismal populations and reduce plant growth. In fact, the late Russian nematologist, A. A. Paramonov, considered such nematodes as exibiting a form of plant parasitism since they cause reduced plant growth. How important microbivorous nematodes are in plant growth and production remains to be seen.

A significant aspect of this general phenomenon involves mycophagous (fungus-feeding) nematodes. Foresters have long known that certain fungi (mycorrhizal fungi) form symbiotic relationships with certain forest trees. The association is mutually beneficial in that the fungus utilizes as a nutrient the organic emanations from the roots, while the tree benefits from the leakage of mineral ions from the mycelium of the fungus, and its capacity to scavenge additional nutrients from soil particles and rock. In recent years evidence has been accumulating that similar relationships occur in perennial and annual agricultural crops. Many fungal feeding nematodes are delighted with mycorrhizal fungi as a food source, and so thrive in forest plantings. A high population of mycorrhizal fungi feeding nematodes may well disrupt the symbiotic relationship advantageous to the tree, and thereby reduce its rate of growth. Despite the ominous potential of the situation, little is known about the parameters and dynamics of the feeding relationship—and the forest industry persists in its disinterest.

Despite the fact that the overwhelming majority are free living forms, pathetically little is known about such nematodes' role in nature's order of things. Whatever their role, they have not been perceived by mankind to interfere with his endeavors, as have the plant or animal-parasitic forms. As a result, these microbivorous nematodes have been conveniently ignored. Keeping in mind that free living nematodes live happily in diverse habitats, e.g., in melt water at the foot of polar glaciers, in the benthos of polar seas at subfreezing temperatures, in deep ocean trenches, in the intertidal zones, in rivers, ponds, and lakes, brackish bodies of water and soil, deserts, mountains, growing moss, and even hot springs, it does not seem reasonable that such a diversity of nematodes exists as an artifact or an incidental error of nature. Realistically, such nematodes are an integral component of the interlocking chains of nutrient conversions. They function in nature's scheme of recycling carbon-containing substances, mineral nutrients, and nitrogenous compounds. They control explosions of microflora and microfauna and maintain the balance in life forms that constitute the dynamic, biological complex of nature. Free living nematodes functioning in such a fashion far exceed in importance the plant and animal-parasitic forms by sustaining an earth with the features that are familiar to us. It must be emphasized that though they are perceived as benign by mankind, they constitute a vital component in a preservation of the balance of life processes of our world.

Animal Parasites

Animal-parasitic nematodes are of concern to man for obvious reasons. They infect and bring about disease conditions that range from benign to incapacitating and lethal to man himself, to the livestock he raises, and to other animals he closely associates with, including wildlife and pets. The behavioral and physiological properties of animal-infecting nematodes are varied and generally poorly understood; as a result, avenues of infection periodically occur that could not have been foreseen. It is perhaps useful to consider several areas of human endeavor in order to illustrate potential problem sources and the difficulties in effecting protective preventive measures.

In commerce and industry, even industrialized nations have difficulty maintaining all livestock and poultry in a healthy and disease-free condition. In lesser developed countries the situation is substantially less satisfactory, and in the worst cases the number of sickly and diseased animals can be greater than the healthy. A relatively low proportion of diseased animals may constitute a mild economic problem that can be minimized by inspection and non-human consumption of meat products (e.g., sterilized pet food). In very poor countries the high proportion of diseased stock not only constitutes a grave economic problem, but if the animals must be destroyed there is the potential for disease, malnutrition, and starvation. In rural Latin America, Africa, and elsewhere the more healthy stock goes to market at higher prices for the more affluent of the population, while the bulk of unhealthy stock goes to the underground economy for the poor at reduced prices. Well cooked diseased meat would likely cause little risk; however, poorly cooked meat and the contamination of utensils and food preparation surfaces with raw infected meat, coupled with poor sanitary practices, lead to parasitism and other health hazards. Moreover, unhealthy livestock produces poor quality by-products, e.g., wool, leather, feathers and down. For industrialized nations this is a minor problem, but for nonindustrialized countries depending upon these products for their own use or for earning foreign exchange, the problem becomes major.

Increasingly, industrialized nations are unable to meet their internal demand for meat and meat products from domestic sources, and must resort to importation. While the meat from major world suppliers poses little risk, that provided by others can be suspect insofar as parasites are concerned. Though domestic and imported meat carcasses are inspected visually, only the heavier infections tend to be detected. A careful inspection is time consuming and is far from absolute. Under the pressure of production, rapidly moving distribution lines, and undermanned inspection resources, escapes and oversights can be expected, leaving the consumer population at increased risk.

The introduction of live animal and avian imports is a major problem for the quarantine service. While regulations and procedures are in place to detect and reduce the incidence of non-indigenous parasites and disease, it is seldom possible to assure absolute detection and safety. The rapidly increasing cost for achieving near absolute safety usually leads to a compromise between the level of safety and the bearable economic costs. While the margin of risk may be small, undetectable nonindigenous parasitic nematode burdens at low levels can serve as potential reservoirs for parasite dispersion. Generally, suitable vectors or intermediate hosts (the same or related species) are present to disseminate the reservoir of infection. In this situation the cliche "an ounce of prevention is worth a pound of cure" is relevant and signifies the need for a vigilant public health and quarantine service.

While an individual can exercise little personal control over events in commerce and industry, there are several other areas of human endeavor in which the individual has major discretion over factors and activities affecting his future health and well being. Worldwide travel is commonplace in modern society. Travelers, in growing numbers, are frequenting all regions of the planet, for cultural or business purposes. Though the major industrialized nations seldom pose nematode parasite risks to visitors, the experienced traveler to other regions, particularly the tropics, normally takes precautions. Major modern cities may not be worry-free; a newspaper recently reported that Rio de Janiero administrators were contemplating replacement of all the sand at the city's famous artificial beaches, Ipanema and Copacabana, to eliminate the human pinworm nematode infesting the beaches.

Usually nematode parasite infection is a result of ingestion of contaminated food, bites from blood-sucking insect vectors transmitting filarial nematodes, and, to a lesser extent, through skin penetration, e.g., by walking barefoot on infested soil. Crowded public swimming pools pose some risk, as well. In the U.S., newspaper items are not uncommon during the summer season quoting public health reports of high counts of viable *Ascaris* nematode eggs in crowded public swimming pools handicapped by an overwhelmed sanitizing capacity. While it may be impossible to avoid all risk, common sense precautions, e.g., avoiding suspected contaminated foods, unsanitary areas, and contact with publicly handled items, wearing clothing to avoid insect bites, etc., can greatly improve the probability of a pleasant trip. Above all, should a health problem arise upon returning home, the traveler should advise the physician of the travel itinerary in order to help in the diagnosis.

Occasionally unusual problems arise. A patient suffering excruciating headaches was admitted into a west coast hospital for a series of diagnostic tests. While no disorder was detected, the headache attacks worsened. Late one evening, the patient suffered such an acute attack as to become violent. He was restrained and a physician was called; while looking at the patient, they noticed what appeared to be a string on the bridge of his nose. Upon closer examination, a physician picked up the "string" with forceps, only to find it wiggled. It was the parasitic nematode of *Loa loa;* the patient had recently returned from a mission into the African bush.

In another rare incident, a European hospital admitted a patient whose symptoms could not be associated with diseases known in Europe. Fortunately for the patient, a dedicated physician began an in depth case history including old employment and travels. As a result, it was revealed that the patient was an animal handler working with leopards in captivity in an African zoological park and had contracted a nematode parasite common to leopards. With this information, a program of therapy was devised to aid the patient.

Pets that travel are subject to risks similar to those of the owner. Before World War II, dog heartworm was unusual on the Pacific Coast, but prevalent on the Atlantic Coast and in the southern U.S. The human population shift and mingling since the war also involved the movement of pets. As a result of the influx of infected dogs the resident incidence of dog heartworm in the western U.S. is on the rise. It has already invaded the wild coyote population, which now serves as a reservoir for the dispersion of the nematode to domestic canines.

In an extension of the potential risks nematodes pose to the individual traveler, one of the current major public health hazards involves the worldwide human mass migration resulting from catastrophic events on various continents. These grand scale population shifts largely involve migrations from third world countries with high parasite burdens to industrialized nations with relatively low burdens.

While the migrants have been victims of circumstances with respect to parasites, the public health service must confront the problem of containing the infection, controlling the dispersion, and eventually breaking the infection cycle. The complexity of the problem should not be minimized, especially for filarial nematodes that are vector transmitted and others that require an intermediate host for the parasite to complete the life cycle. Even if natural transmitting organisms are not present in the new domicile, there are usually other resident species that can substitute. The potential resident vectors and intermediate hosts may be parasite free, but they can quickly acquire the parasite from the infected host to form a secondary reservoir of infection. As a consequence, the health risk to the resident human population is inversely proportional to the effectiveness of public health practices.

A somewhat different aspect of the health risk equation, in which the individual bears the major discretionary decision, involves the consumption of raw or uncooked foods. The consumption of raw products for nutritional purposes is an ubiquitous natural process with the world's creatures. It is a fundamental event that governs and permits the complexity of interorganismal relations of the living world familiar to all. Man remains the only creature to have developed the use of heat and applied it to the modification of food. Whatever the motivation of ancient man to adopt the notion of cooking food, it remains a common practice in aboriginal and civilized societies. In addition to flavor and texture changes and detoxification of certain products, an inadvertent prime benefit of cooking was the destruction of parasites and other biological disease agents. Whatever the role the benefits of cooking played in the development of man in his society, uncooked food, primarily in the form of fruits and vegetables, continues to provide unquestionable health and nutritional benefits. Excluding occasions of emergency survival, the decision to cook or not to cook is the individual's option, and who, according to nature's prescription, is the one to suffer the consequences. Obviously, a suitable and safe decision, made for one set of circumstances of human habitat can be disastrous elsewhere. An informed judgement is of the essence if the individual is to have a latitude of choice commensurate with reasonable health risks and tranquility. While it is beyond the scope of this chapter to discuss fully all relevant aspects of the issue, several considerations outline factors of importance and that may merit further exploration, depending upon the needs of the reader.

Consider the consumption of raw meat from various animal sources. Over the years it has been this author's pleasure to host dinners or backyard barbecues for nematologists visiting the U.S. from abroad. Invariably these guests request their beef cooked well done, while Americans generally prefer it pink to rare. Everyone usually requests pork, lamb, and fowl cooked well done. The risks of consuming live animal-parasitic nematodes or other parasitic organisms from uncooked infested meats apparently has been inculcated into the world's cultures as a fundamental component, regardless of geographical location. There probably is merit to the view that the dogmatic ban of all meat consumption by some religions, and of pork by others, was empirically inspired in antiquity by these kinds of health risks. Uncooked pork probably remains the most prevalent source of human contraction of the parasitic nematode disease trichinosis, and accounts for upwards of 75% of all reported incidences. Of the many cultures for whom pork is a major protein source, a significant number have devised various curing methods (smoking, salting, drying) to preserve raw pork for future use. Although these practices do protect the product from microorganismal action and provide society with an assortment of magnificent flavors, the nematode in the infected meat remains viable and upon consumption invades the new host. For uncooked processed pork to be free of nematodes, the pig must be reared under conditions where only noninfested feeds are provided and accidental pen invasions by infected rats and other rodents and carnivores, which the pig may catch and consume, are prevented. Alternatively, suspected pork infections must be treated for a period at reduced temperatures. Household freezer temperatures are useless; usually regimes of at least $-35°$F for over a week at the center of the meat parcel are required to kill encysted larvae. Developed nations usually have health regulations in place to protect society from the consumption of uncooked processed meats from commercial sources. While the pig is the most common source of infection, any carnivore, domestic or wild, is suspect. For example, a hunter was recently admitted to a local hospital complaining of headaches, fever, weakness, and general debilitation. The diagnosis indicated parasitism which was confirmed by the case history related by the hunter and subsequent laboratory analysis of the bear meat. The hunter had been successful in a bear hunt, and in the process of skinning and dressing the animal had eaten bits and pieces of lean muscle raw—about a pound. He suffered a massive infection of *Trichinella* and, while he survived, will never fully recover. Other kinds of animal meat sources may have different nematode parasites also transmissible to man upon the consumption of uncooked meat. The incidence, fortunately, is reduced from that of trichinosis. However, the frequency of transmission of non-nematode helminth diseases, e.g., cestodes (tapeworms) and trematodes (flukes), is much greater, as a preference of foreigners for meat "well-done" would confirm. The "avant-garde" consumption of "steak tartare," usually raw beef meat finely minced and flavored with various constituents including a generous proportion of lemon juice, remains a health venture. Advocates are prompt to say the acidic lemon juice "cooks" the meat. The acid does cause the partial denaturation of some of the protein components, but has little effect on any viable parasites. In fact, for any encysted parasites it may initiate the hatching process a little earlier than that normally occurring in the approximately 1/10 molar acid concentration present in the human stomach. For similar reasons the generations old prescribed remedy for anemia, raw liver, has been contraindicated.

Consider an alternate source of raw animal protein, fish. Should opportunistic conditions prevail, fish can become as parasitized by nematodes as can other higher organisms. The kinds of nematodes present are usually different from those of warm blooded animals; however, they seem to survive and cause medical problems to humans often enough. The question of nematodes in fish became apparent to commercial cod fisherman with the introduction of whole body refrigeration of catch at sea to replace the older gutting and "salting down" process for preservation. Apparently, the nematodes in the cod gut became aware of the death of the host and sought escape into the surrounding tissue before freezing. After thawing for market, nematodes could be seen in the fish tissues and if the prior freezing temperature was neither low enough or long enough the nematodes would revive and move.

Today it is not uncommon to find nematodes in the muscle tissue of various species of marine "rock-fish." In fact, as a colleague who abruptly lost his appetite at a fish dinner revealed, they can occur in bunches, as he demonstrated by picking up a bundle of inch-long worms on a fork tine. On another occasion, a market frozen lobster tail allowed to thaw on a kitchen counter revealed an active emerging nematode from the carapace. Fish markets routinely replace the fish, or refund the cost for complaints of this nature. As with uncooked meats processed by various "curing" practices, fish similarly treated are unlikely to be any less risky. The current "yuppie" generation's preference for raw fish as exemplified by the Japanese "shashimi" or "sushi," continues to pose problems to the medical community, as is evident in newspaper reports. Recently a young man was admitted to a hospital emergency ward for excruciating lower abdominal pain. Diagnostic testing excluded appendicitis, but could not pinpoint any cause. Since the agony persisted, exploratory surgery was suggested and accepted. Nothing unusual was found, so the wound was closed, but the pain persisted. As the wound was about to be bandaged, the surgeon noted a piece of "yarn" emerging from the incision; he picked up a nematode, a fish parasite, consumed with the ingestion of raw fish by the patient a few days earlier. In another case, some 30 physicians participated in a private "shashimi" party, from which two-thirds of the party became infected; such judgment by physicians who are expected to be more knowledgeable about such health risks does little for patient confidence in the medical profession. Culinary events of this kind conducted by amateur chefs who may not be sufficiently knowledge-able about the health quality of the starting material are more suspect than those of commercial establishments. Even in Japan, with its tradition of raw fish consumption, the incidence of nematode infection from this source is on the order of 10-15%.

The consumption of raw meat or fish generally is not intrinsically harmful and a practice to be scrupulously avoided; the problem lies in the probability that the consumer will receive a portion unknowingly infested with a nematode, helminth, or other disease agent. In various regions of the world this probability is significantly greater than others. In any event, the degree of risk to be borne is at the discretion of the informed consumer.

Should the consumption of raw plant products be considered a health risk? So far as is known, plant-parasitic nematodes have never caused a disease in humans. Several do transport disease agents (microorganisms) that become established in the aerial portions of plants to cause diseases of livestock feeding on these plants. These observations would suggest that the consumption of uncooked fruits and vegetables would be harmless. This conclusion would be misguided, though, for one of the major sources of human parasites derives from the consumption of contaminated fruits and vegetables, particularly the leafy kinds e.g., spinach, strawberries, etc. that grow near the soil surface. The problem arises from the use of infected human and animal excreta as fertilizer. While such excreta serves as an excellent source of mineral nutrition for plant growth and provides organic matter for amending physical soil properties, associated parasite deposits infest the soil and together with the dust eventually contaminate low growing plants and fruits.

A different but equally important source of infection issues from the invertebrate intermediate hosts of animal parasites which deposit eggs and larval stages on plants. Washing, removes visible soil, but not eggs and larvae; moreover, the dilute household bleach-wash often used to remove many disease agents must be carefully applied to be effective against certain nematode and helminth eggs. While some soil infections may dissipate in several years, others may remain for long periods. For example, in the former U.S.S.R. a study revealed that the eggs of the intestinal roundworm parasite of humans (*Ascaris lumbricoides*) could survive in soil for 30 years. This is a nematode parasite that infects one out of five people on earth. Similar survival properties are found for parasites of intermediate hosts or the normal parasites of livestock which can transfer to man as either an accidental or alternate host. These traits, unfortunately, exist not only in nematodes but other helminth parasites as well.

The current popular craze for organic farming, promoted in industrialized countries, requires a rational measure of judicious consideration. There is no question but that organic farming practices offer many beneficial advantages in terms of mulching, green manuring, soil improvement, cultural options, and reduced use of pesticides; however, the employment of man and animal excreta merits significant circumspection. The mass movements of people and animals is unlikely to diminish, and these shifts augment the potential for dissemination of animal parasites including nematodes at a correspondingly elevated risk to the resident society.

The populations of lesser developed nations are exposed to an additional element of risk from parasitic infections from the use of cattle manure for other domestic purposes. American settlers of the covered wagon migration to the West adopted the use of buffalo chips for fuel on the plains. Asian and African societies (primarily women) have for centuries hand worked wet cattle manure into small pats to dry for fuel, or hand worked manure, soil and water into a kind of plaster to coat a stick and twig frame shelter. Any nematodes or other parasites occurring in the manure have ample opportunity to penetrate the worker's hands, or to be inhaled or ingested.

The importance of animal-parasitic nematodes and helminths as infective agents associated with food and fiber does not merit belittling; the simple fact remains that upwards of three-quarters of the earth's population, that has survived for centuries by using organic farming to the maximum, has carried by far the heaviest parasitic burden. While much has been said about the virtues of organic cultural methods, it is equally important to avoid its flaws. The simple take-home lesson is *caveat emptor;* it is the informed sampler that may enjoy earth's treasures and pleasures with the least risk.

"Nemas are forever."

Viglierchio, 1983

Appendix 1

Some Popular Names Used
to Designate Plant-Parasitic Nematodes

Common Name	Scientific Name
Awl nematode	*Dolichodorus spp.*
Bud & leaf nematode	*Aphelenchoides spp.*
Burrowing nematode	*Radopholus similis*
Cyst nematode	*Heterodera, Punctodera spp.*
Citrus nematode	*Tylenchulus semipenetrans*
Coconut palm nematode	*Rhadinaphelencus cocophilus*
Dagger nematode	*Xiphinema spp.*
Golden nematode	*Globodera rostochiensis*
Lance nematode	*Hopolaimus spp.*
Lesion nematode	*Pratylenchus spp.*
Needle nematode	*Longidorus spp.*
Pin nematode	*Paratylenchus spp.*
Pinewood nematode	*Bursaphelenchus xylophilus*
Potato rot nematode	*Ditylenchus destructor*
Reniform nematode	*Rotylenchulus reniformis*
Rice root nematode	*Hirschmaniella spp.*
Rice stem nematode	*Ditylenchus angustus*
Rice white tip nematode	*Aphelenchoides besseyi*
Ring nematode	*Criconema, Criconemella spp.*
Rootknot nematode	*Meloidogyne spp.*
Seed, stem & leaf gall nematode	*Anguina spp.*
Sheath nematode	*Hemicycliophora spp.*
Spiral nematode	*Rotylenchus, Helicotylenchus spp.*
Stem & bulb nematode	*Ditylenchus dipsaci*
Sting nematode	*Belonolaimus spp.*
Stubby root nematode	*Trichodorus spp.*
Stunt nematode	*Tylenchorhynchus spp.*
Wheat nematode	*Anguina tritici*

APPENDIX 2

Some Common Agricultural Perennials
Subject to Severe Nematode Injury*

Plant Host	Nematodes of Pestiferous Importance
Almond	rootknot, ring, lesion, dagger
Alfalfa	rootknot, stem & bulb
Apple	dagger, lesion, pin, stubby root
Apricot	dagger, lesion
Artichoke	lesion, *Merlinius,* rootknot
Asparagus	lesion, rootknot
Avocado	dagger, lesion, ring, stubby root
Banana	burrowing, lance, lesion, rootknot, spiral
Berries	dagger, lesion, pin, rootknot
Cherry	dagger, lesion, pin
Citrus	citrus, dagger, lesion, (burrowing–Florida)
Clovers	cyst, lesion, rootknot, stem & bulb
Coconut Palm	coconut palm, rootknot, spiral
Coffee	burrowing, dagger, lesion, reniform, rootknot, spiral
Fig	citrus, cyst, dagger, lesion, *Merlinius,* pin
Grape	citrus, dagger, lesion, rootknot
Grass	lance, lesion, rootknot, seed-stem-leaf gall, sting, stunt
Olive	citrus, lesion, rootknot
Peach	lesion, pin, ring, rootknot
Pear	dagger, lesion, *Merlinius,* pin, ring, spiral, stubby root
Persimmon	citrus, lesion
Pineapple	reniform, rootknot, spiral
Plum	dagger, lesion, pin
Strawberry	bud & leaf, dagger, lesion, rootknot, stem & bulb
Sugar Cane	burrowing, lesion, rootknot, spiral, stubby root
Tea	burrowing, lesion, rootknot, sheath, spiral
Walnut	dagger, lesion, ring, rootknot

*The reader is warned that this table is only illustrative & that many different nematodes may reproduce on the same plant.

APPENDIX 3

Some Common Agricultural Annuals
Subject to Severe Nematode Injury*

Plant Hosts	Nematodes of Pestiferous Importance
Bean	awl, cyst, lesion, rootknot, reniform, spiral, sting
Bean, Garbanzo	cyst, lesion, rootknot, sting
Beet, red & sugar	cyst, dagger, lesion, rootknot, stem & bulb, stubby root
Cabbage (various crucifers)	cyst, lesion, rootknot, stem & bulb
Carrot	cyst, lesion, rootknot, stem & bulb
Celery	lesion, pin, rootknot, sting
Chard	cyst, lesion, rootknot
Chive, Leek, Onion, Shallot	lesion, rootknot, stem & bulb
Corn	corn cyst, lance, lesion, rootknot, sting, stubby root
Cotton	lance, rootknot, sting, spiral, stubby root
Cowpeas	lesion, rootknot, sting
Cucumbers	cyst, lesion, rootknot, reniform
Eggplant	lesion, rootknot
Fennel	lesion, rootknot
Garlic	lesion, stem & bulb
Lettuce	lesion, rootknot
Melons	lesion, reniform, rootknot
Oats	cyst, lesion, rootknot, stem & bulb
Peanuts	lesion, rootknot, sting
Peas	cyst, lesion, rootknot
Pepper (capsicum)	awl, lesion, reniform, rootknot
Potato	cyst, lesion, golden, potato rot, reniform, rootknot, stubby root
Radish	cyst, lesion, rootknot, stem & bulb
Rice	cyst, rootknot, rice root, rice stem, rice white-tip
Soybean	dagger, lance, reniform, rootknot, soybean cyst, sting
Sweet Potato	ring, rootknot, stubby root
Tobacco	lesion, rootknot, stunt, stem & bulb, stubby root
Tomato	cyst, lesion, rootknot, spiral, stunt
Wheat	cyst, lesion, rootknot, wheat

*The reader is warned that this table is only illustrative & that many different nematodes may reproduce on the same plant.

Appendix 4

Some Common Ornamentals
Subject to Severe Nematode Injury

Plant Hosts	Nematodes of Pestiferous Importance
African violet	bud & leaf, lesion, rootknot
Anemone	bud & leaf, lesion, rootknot
Anthurium	bud & leaf, lesion, rootknot
Begonia	bud & leaf, lesion, rootknot, stem & bulb
Bottlebrush	Lesion, rootknot, spiral
Boxwood	lesion, rootknot, spiral
Cactacae	cyst, lesion, rootknot, spiral
Camellia	rootknot, sheath, spiral, stunt
Chrysanthemum	bud & leaf, lesion, rootknot
Coleus	bud & leaf, rootknot, stem & bulb, stunt
Columbine	bud & leaf, lesion, rootknot
Cyclamen	bud & leaf, lesion, rootknot, stem & bulb
Daffodil	bud & leaf, lesion, stem & bulb
Dahlia	bud & leaf, dagger, lesion, rootknot, stem & bulb
Dianthus	lesion, pin, ring, rootknot
Dichondra	rootknot, spiral, stunt
Easter Lily	bud & leaf, lesion, rootknot
Fern	bud & leaf, lesion
Fuschia	bud & leaf, lesion, rootknot, spiral
Gardenia	lesion, rootknot, spiral
Geranium	lesion, rootknot
Gladiolus	lesion, rootknot, stem & bulb
Grass	foliar, seed, stem gall, cyst
Hydrangea	lesion, rootknot, spiral, stem & bulb
Iris	lesion, potato rot, rootknot, spiral
Lilac	lesion, rootknot, spiral
Narcissus	bud & leaf, lesion, stem& bulb
Oleander	lesion, rootknot, stunt
Peony	bud & leaf, lesion, rootknot, stubby root
Petunia	lesion, rootknot
Phlox	lesion, rootknot, stem & bulb
Ranunculus	bud & leaf, lesion, rootknot, stem & bulb
Rose	dagger, lesion, ring, rootknot, spiral, stunt
Snapdragon	bud & leaf, lesion, ring, rootknot
Sweet Pea	cyst, lesion, rootknot, stem & bulb
Tulip	lesion, stem & bulb
Wisteria	lesion, rootknot, spiral, stunt
Zinnia	lesion, ring, rootknot

APPENDIX 5
Some Common Forest Trees
Subject to Severe Nematode Injury

Plant Hosts	Nematodes of Pestiferous Importance
Acacia	rootknot
Alder	dagger, needle
Ash	dagger, lesion, needle, ring, spiral, stubby root, stunt
Birch	lesion, rootknot
Cedar	lesion, spiral
Cypress	dagger, *Gracilacus*
Douglas Fir	dagger, lesion, spiral *(Criconemella annulata, Xiphinema californicum, Trichodorus californicus, Filenchus vulgaris, Gracilacus epacris)*
Fir	dagger, lesion, needle [Red fir: *C. annulata, Pratylenchus macrostylus, Merinius conicus, Sphaeronema californicum, Filenchus aguilonius*]
Maple	dagger, needle, rootknot, spiral, stubby root
Oak	needle
Pine	pine wood, dagger, lance, lesion, needle, ring, rootknot, spiral, stunt. [Ponderosa pine: *C. annulata, Meloidogyne spp., Rhizonema sequoiae, T. californicus, X. bakeri, X. californicum.* Jefferey pine: *C. annulata, X. californicum, Meloidogyne spp., Tylenchorhynchus cylindricus, Sphaeronema californicum*]
Redwood	*Bakernema spp., Boleodorus spp., Pratylenchus spp., Rhizonema spp.* [Coast redwood: *Gracilacus epacris, Rhizonema sequoiae, Boleodorus thylactus, Trichodorus californicus, X. californicum*]
Spruce	lance, lesion, spiral, stunt

Brackets indicate the decreasing frequency of occurrence of nematode species from samples about the roots of the target tree in natural timber forests of California.

Some of the Common & Abundant Nematode
Parasites of Animals That Relate to Man*

Disease	Nematode	Common Host
Ancylostomiasis	Hook worm [old world] *(Ancylostoma duodenale)* *(Ancylostoma canium)*	man dog
Anisakosis	Stomachworm *(Anisakis* spp.*)*	seals, walruses, herring, man (eating raw fish)
	Codworm *(Phocanema decipians)*	seals, dolphins & fish (larva migrans in man from eating raw fish)
Ascariasis	Intestinal roundworm *(Ascaris lumbricoides)* *(Ascaris suum)* *(Toxocara canis)* *(Toxocara mystax)*	man pig dog, dog family cat, cat family
Capillariasis	Capillus worm *(Capillario* spp. 100+ spp.*)*	man, rodents & other animals
Contracaecumosis	*Contracaecum* spp. 140+ spp.	birds & fish
Dirofilariasis	Heartworm *(Dirofilaria immitis)*	dog & cat families and other animals
Dracunculosis	Guinea worm *(Dracunculus medinensis)*	man
Elephantiasis	Filarial worms *(Wuchereria bancrofti)*	man
Enterobiasis	Human pinworm *(Enterobius vermicularis)*	man, other animals
Haemonchosis	Sheep wireworm *(Haemonchus contortus)*	sheep & other herbivores
Loaiasis	Eye worm *(Loa loa)*	man
Necatoriasis	Hookworm [American] *(Necator americanus)* *(Necator braziliensis)*	man man

Table continued on next page.

Appendix 6

(Continued)

Disease	Nematode	Common Host
Porcine pneumonitis	Pig lungworm *(Metastrongylus elongatus)*	porcine species
Renaliasis	Giant kidney worm *(Dioctophyma renale)*	man
River blindmess	Filarial worms *(Onchocerca volvulus)*	man
Strongyloidiasis	Strongyles *(Strongyloidea spp.)*	ruminant, horse, pig, man
Thelaziasis	Oriental eyeworm *(Thelazia collipaeda)*	dog, rabbit, man
Trichinosis	Trichina *(Trichinella spiralis)*	man & other carnivores
Trichostrongyloses	*Trichostrongylus* spp.	herbivores
Trichuriasis	Whipworm *(Trichuris* spp.)	man & other animals

*The reader should be aware that this table is merely illustrative and by no means complete. There are thousands of nematode species infecting animals including fish, amphibia, reptiles, birds, mammals, insects, mollusks and other invertebrates. A nematode species often infects a variety of host animals, e.g., upwards of fifteen nematode species are able to infect man and dog.

Supplementary Reading

Ayoub, S.M. 1977. *Plant Nematology, An Agricultural Training Aid.* State of California, Department of Food & Agriculture, Sacramento, California. 157pp.

Chitwood, B. G., & M.B. Chitwood. 1950. *Introduction to Nematology.* University Park Press, Baltimore, Maryland. 334 pp.

Christie, J.R. 1959. *Plant Nematodes.* H.W.B. Drew Company, Jacksonville, Florida. 256 pp.

Craig, C.F., & E.C. Faust. 1943. *Clinical Parasitology.* Lea & Febiger, Philadelphia. 809 pp.

Crofton, H.D. 1966. *Nematodes.* Hutchison & Company, London. 160 pp.

Decker, H. 1972. *Plant Nematodes & Their Control.* Kolos Publishing Company, Moscow. Translated in 1981, Amerind Publishing Company, New Delhi. 527 pp.

Dropkin, V.H. 1980. *Introduction to Plant Nematology.* John Wiley & Sons, NY. 293 pp.

Jenkins, W.R., & D.P. Taylor. 1967. *Plant Nematology.* Reinhold Publishing Company, NY. 270 pp.

Kirjanova, E.S., & E.L. Kall. 1980. Translated from Russian, *Plant-Parasitic Nematodes & Their Control.* Amerind Publishing Company, New Delhi. 748 pp.

Levine, N.D. 1980. *Nematode Parasites of Domestic Animals & Man.* Second edition. Burgess Publishing Company, Minneapolis, Minnesota. 477 pp.

Maggenti, A.R. 1981. *General Nematology.* Springer-Verlag, NY. 372 pp.

Nickle, W.R. 1984. *Plant & Insect Nematodes.* Marcel Dekker Inc., NY. 925 pp.

Poinar, G.O., Jr. 1983. *The Natural History of Nematodes.* Prentice-Hall, New Jersey. 323 pp.

Scognamiglio, A. 1978. *Nematologia Agraria, Edagricole, Bologna.* 541 pp.

Soonin, M.D. 1985. "Filariata of animals and man and diseases caused by them." In: *Fundamentals of Nematology,* Oxonian Press, New Delhi, India.

Soulsby, E.J.L. 1982. *Helminths, Arthropods and Protozoa of domesticated Animals.* Lea & Febiger, Philadelphia. 809 pp.

Thorne, G. 1961. *Principles of Nematology.* McGraw-Hill Book Company, NY. 553 pp.

Yorke, W., & R.A. Maplestone, 1962. *The Nematode Parasites of Vertebrates.* Hafner Publishing Company, NY. 536 pp.

Glossary

AB Cell: The first cell from which embryogenesis derives is referred to as P_O, the parental germinal cell. The first division results in two cells S_1, the first somatic cell and P_1, the stem cell from which other tissues derive. The S_1 cell (AB cell) divides again into what is referred to as A and B cells.

Acetylcholine Esterase: The enzyme which hydrolyzes the nerve transmitter, acetylcholine, of the synaptic gap in the process of restoring the system to transmit the next nerve impulse.

Adenophorea: One of the two classes of the phylum Nemata.

Adventitious: Secondary growing, meristematic points other then the primary point of stem or root.

Alimentary System: The organ system of animals responsible for ingestion, digestion and excretion.

Alternate Hosts: A term often used interchangeably with intermediate host, hosts necessary for the development of preadult stages.

Amoeboid: Relating to characteristics expressed by amoebae.

Amphids: Paired structures of the nematode head that are believed to be sensory in function.

Amphimictic: Refers to a type of reproduction that requires males to fertilize females.

Amphimixis: Reproduction in which the embryo derives from the union of egg and sperm from different individuals.

Amygdalin: A cyanide containing polysaccharide, a sugar polymer, found in some plants, e.g. prunus species.

Anion: A negatively charged ion that migrates to the anode of an electric field.

Annelids: Representatives of the phylum, *Annelida,* including earthworms, marine worms, leeches among other segmented worms.

Anterior: Towards the head end of a nematode.

Anthelmintic: A drug used for therapy on an animal host suffering from parasite burdens.

Apices: The points, as the growing point of a plant or the points of a triangle.

Ascariasis: The host disease caused by ascarid parasitic nematodes.

Asexual Reproduction: A type of reproduction not involving an exchange between male and female sexes.

Autosomes: Those chromosomes not involving sex determination.

Auxins: A type of indole containing plant growth hormones.

Bioelectric: Biological processes involving electrical fields and currents.

Biological Agents: Organisms, or substances that affect other organisms or their processes.

Biotypes: In Nematology it is one of the terms used to designate morphologically indistinguishable populations with different physiological characteristics, e.g. host ranges.

Blastula: An early embryo stage in the form of a sphere, fluid filled, but bounded by a single cell layer.

Body Alae: Longitudinal cuticle thickenings extending away from the nematode body in the form of stubby wings or flaps.

Brackish Water: Water with mineral and organic substance content intermediate between fresh and sea water.

Buccal Cavity: This is the mouth cavity interior to the oral opening of nematodes.

Caudal Alae: Cuticle thickenings that resemble short wings or flaps at the tail end of a nematode.

Cation: A positively charged ion that is attracted to the cathode of an electric field.

Cephalic Setae: Sensory structures protruding form the head region of a nematode.

Chemical Potentials: A measure of the driving forces or energy of ions to undergo a process or reaction.

Chemoreceptors: Sensory receptors that detect chemical substances present in the nematode environment.

Chitin: An Amino-containing polysaccharide common in the cuticle of insects and crustaceans.

Chlorosis: The plant physiological disorder in which chlorophyll is deficient and photosynthesis is limited.

Chords: In nematodes these are longitudinal bundles of hypodermal tissue (usually containing nuclei) extending along the body top, bottom and sides.

Chromatin: The protein-nucleic acid material of the nucleus carrying the genetic information.

Chyme: The digesting mixture filling the lumen of the intestine.

Ciliates: Cilia carrying unicellular organisms.

Circadian Rhythm: Diurnal changes.

Cloaca: The chamber into which the intestine and reproductive systems empty in the male nematode.

Collagen: The protein making up the bulk of connective tissue.

Collagenous: Containing collagen or collagen-like material.

Conformation: The spatial arrangement of a molecule (in three dimensions).

Conidia: Reproductive structures formed by some fungi.

Conifers: Cone producing trees or shrubs, e.g. pine, redwood, fir, etc.

Connector Neurons: Nerve cells that connect nerve bundles.

Copepods: Small fresh water or marine crustacea.

Cortex: The outer tissues of a stem or root between the epidermis and the central pericycle.

Cross-Fertilization: The union of gametes from an individual male and individual female as distinct from self-fertilization in hermaphroditic individuals.

Cunnicular Regions: Regions of a drainage network where smaller tubes connect larger ones.

Cuticle: The non-cellular external component covering the cellular component of the nematode body wall.

Cyclotron: Atomic subparticle accelerating machine.

Cyst: The dried female body wall of certain nematodes in which eggs remained. In animal tissue it is a walled off structure containing a dormant viable nematode.

Cytology: The study of structure and function of cells.

Cytoplasm: Cell contents exclusive of body wall and nucleus.

Dauer Larvae: A quiescent, sometimes dormant, stage of a nematode often serving to withstand unfavorable conditions.

Definitive Host: The host which supports and harbors the adult nematode parasites.

Dentate: Nematode stoma types containing multiple teeth.

Denticulate: Nematode stoma types containing large numbers of very tiny teeth.

Deoxyribonucleic Acid (DNA): A nucleic acid present in the nuclei of cells consisting of a 5-carbon sugar, phosphoric acid and organic bases that carries the genetic information specific for the reproduction and growth of plants and animals.

Deportment: Conduct or behavior.

Detoxification: To render toxins or poisons harmless.

Diatoms: Microscopic unicellular algae.

Dimorphism: The state in which two members of a species occur in distinct forms, e.g. males and females.

Dioecious: Distinctly different forms as in dimorphism.

Disease Symptomatology: A term used to summarize the characteristics by which a host exhibits the diseased condition.

Distinctive Interactions: Relationships between two or more pathogenic agents, the results of which lead to a disease of the host not occurring in the absence of the other, which may be more than additive for the two pathogens or an entirely new disease.

Dorsal: The back side of the animal.

Dracontiasis: The disease resulting from infection by the guinea worm..

Eclosion: The process by which the immature stage of a nematode emerges from the egg casing (hatching).

Ectoderm: The outer layer of cells of an embryo that in a nematode gives rise to the cuticle and other tissues.

Ectomycorrhizae: The resultant root forms from the interaction of certain fungi that cover the root as a mantle to effect a beneficial relationship for both the plant and the fungus.

Ectoparasites: Parasitic nematodes that feed upon plant tissue by use of a stylet or spear while the nematode itself remains outside of the tissue.

Egg and Cyst Parasitic Fungi: Fungi that parasitize free eggs and eggs within cysts.

Electric field: A condition whereby a specific space or region is subjected to a difference in electric potential (voltage) and through which passes little or no current.

Electrode: This is a junction device through which given potential is applied to create an electric field.

Electrolyte: A substance dissolved in a solvent which transmits an electric current.

Endocrine: Internal animal gland secretions that control physiological reactions.

Endocuticle: The internal portion of the non-living cuticle.

Endodermis: That embryological component of cells that give rise to certain internal organ systems such as the intestine.

Endomycorrhizae: The resultant root forms resulting when certain fungi penetrate between root cells to provide a beneficial relationship for both fungus and plant.

Endoparasites: Parasitic nematodes that penetrate into the host tissues.

Endoparasitic Fungi: Fungi that grow within a host.

Entomogenous Nematodes: Nematodes intimately associated with insects including parasites of insects.

Epicuticle: The outer components of the non-living nematode cuticle.

Epidemiology: The science dealing with explosive or rampant dispersion of diseases.

Esophageal-Intestinal Valve: A control device between the esophagus and the intestine to prevent intestinal contents from moving back into the esophagus.

Esophagus: The forward muscular portion of the gastrointestinal system that serves as a pump to ingest nutrients and move them through the gut.

Exocuticle: A composite layer of the cuticle internal to the outer epicuticle.

Exoskeleton: A rigid skeleton external of the body proper as occurs with insects and crustacea.

Ex-Osmosis: The process by which water is withdrawn from an organism by use of hyperosmotic solution.

Exteroceptors: Sensory receptors that detect changes in the environment.

Ferromagnetic Organelle: A cell structure containing iron particles that are magnetizable.

Filariasis: Diseases caused by filarial nematodes.

Filarid: Refers to nematodes which exhibit a microfilaria stage.

Filiform: Having the shape of a thread or filament.

Flatworms: Platyhelminthes, e.g. planarions; flukes.

Foliar: Relating to leaves.

Foregut (Stomodeum): The intake region of the alimentary system and includes the "mouth" portion and the esophagus.

Frass: Feces of wood boring insects.

Free Energy: A measure of the order of a system and the resultant equilibrium.

Free Radicals: Highly reactive unstable particles as a consequence of the presence of an odd electron.

Fumigant Nematicides: Chemical agents applied for the control of nematodes whose activity is based in part on volatility for dispersion.

Fungal Hyphae: Filaments of growth that make up the mycelium of growing fungi.

Fusiform: Spindle shaped, a quasi cylindrical particle tapering at each end.

Gamete: The male or female reproductive cell.

Ganglion: A mass of nerve cell bodies, a nerve center.

Gastrula: An early embryo state consisting of a sack-like body made up of a double layer of cells.

Geotaxes: Movements towards or away from gravitational forces.

Germinal Primordium: The initial cell or cells from which arises the reproductive system.

Giant Cells: Huge special plant root cells induced by certain sedentary parasitic nematodes and from which they feed.

Glucoside: A molecule complexed or intimately tied to glucose sugar.

Gonad: A germ gland or sex gland, e.g. ovary or testis.

Gonochorism: Reproduction that requires cross fertilization of females by males.

Gravid: Refers to an egg containing female.

Habitat: The particular natural environment which is favored by an organism.

Haemocoel (Hemocele): The space making up the body cavity of arthropods.

Haploid: That condition in which a cell possesses half the normal cell chromosome complement as in a sperm or unfertilized egg of bisexual species.

Haemolymph: The natural fluids filling the haemocoel.

Hermaphroditic: Relating to hermaphroditism.

Hermaphroditism: A mode of reproduction wherein the same individual possesses both male and female reproductive organs.

Hindgut: The rectum, the section of the alimentary canal preceding the anus.

Homothermic: A constant temperature, warm blooded animal.

Hyperplasia: Increased cell division in plant tissue.

Hypertonic: High concentrations of solutes in a solution that enable the extraction of water through a semipermeable membrane.

Hypertrophy: Swelling of cells, cell enlargement.

Hypodermal Layer: Hypodermal cells arranged in a layer as in the hypodermis.

Hypodermis: The thin layer of hypodermal cells underneath the cuticle.

Hypotonic: Low concentrations of solutes in a solution that loses water through a semipermeable membrane.

Hyproxyproline: A hydroxylated proline, a cyclic amino acid.

Incidences of Parasitism: Occurrence, the presence of a parasitic species in an animal host.

Incisures: Groves in the cuticle of nematodes.

Indigenous Regions: Geographic regions in which the organism is found naturally and usually whose presence has been of long duration.

Infection Court: The site about the point of host penetration by a disease agent and which renders that region susceptible to invasion by other pathogenic agents.

Inositol: A cyclic alcohol that is a necessary nutrient.

Integument: A term often used interchangeably with cuticle but also sometimes body wall.

Intermediate Host: A temporary host for some animal parasitic nematode that is required for completion of part of its life cycle before in can infect the definitive host.

Interoceptors: Sensory receptors that detect internal events taking place within the organism.

Interspecific Crosses: Sexual reproduction between what are believed to be different species.

Intertidal Zones: That strip of shoreline that is described by the difference between high and low tides.

Intestinal Mucosal Plug: A small mass of mucosa lining the intestine that a nematode mouths and from which it extracts nutrients.

Intestinal-Rectal Valve: A valve between the intestine and rectum that controls the passage of intestinal contents.

Ionic Regulation: The capacity of an organism to adjust and adapt its ionic contents to be in equilibrium with the environment.

Isotonic: The kind of solution whose solute concentration is such that there is no net flow of water in either direction through a semipermeable membrane.

Lachrymatory Fluid: The fluid comprised by tears.

Lateral: Side.

Lipids: Fatty substances, fatty acids, esters, glycerides.

Lip Region: The most anterior annulation in which the lips are found.

Lips: Cuticular structures of various shapes about the nematode oral opening that are lip-like.

Lumen: The cavity or space within a tube.

Macerate: To soften or break apart.

Malpighian tubules: Excretory structures of beetles and other insects.

Mechanoreceptors: Sensory receptors that detect touch or tactile stimulation.

Meiotic: Cell division that is a reduction division process, i.e. halving the number of chromosomes present in the original cell.

Melanin: A polyphenolic naturally occurring pigment that may be reddish brown to black.

Meristem: Undifferentiated plant tissue which is capable of continuous cell division, e.g. a growing point.

Mesenteron: The intestine.

Mesocuticle: The composite layer of the cuticle between the exocuticle and the endocuticle.

Metamorphosis: A change from one state of a life cycle to another requiring a reorganization of body tissues.

Metanephridia: Excretory structures of earthworms.

Micrometazoan: Those groups of metazoans (multicellular animals) that are small or microscopic in size.

Microbivorous: Those organisms ingesting live microorganisms as a food source.

Microfilaria: Motile embryos in arrested development between fertilized egg and first stage larva and found floating in the blood stream and lymphatic fluids.

Microplasma: Sub-viral size infectious particles.

Microtrophic: Feeding upon microorganisms.

Microtubules: A class of structurally similar organelles resembling tubules that are important elements facilitating motility and morphogenesis.

Microvilli: Minute finger-like projections that increase surface area for absorption of nutrients.

Mid-Gut: The intestine between esophagus and rectum.

Millimolar: A dimensional value indicating solute concentration, i.e. 0.001 Molar, or 0.001 molecular weight of substance dissolved in one liter of solution.

Mitotic: Normal cell division in which chromosome number is unchanged.

Mitochondria: Complex convoluted organelles of the cytoplasm responsible for the generation of energy for the cell.

Modulating Agent: A substance which can adjust, change or modify a response process of nematodes.

Molting: The casting off of a cuticle at periodic intervals to facilitate the growth and development of the individual.

Morula: The globular mass of cells in early embryogenesis.

Motor Nerves: Those nerves which activate muscles.

Mutagenic treatments: Kinds of treatments, chemical, radiational, etc. that modify genes to give rise to mutants.

Mutants: Those individuals whose genes have become modified to give rise to new or different properties not possessed by the ancestors.

Mycophagous: Fungal feeding organisms.

Mycorrhizal Association: Organisms relating or interacting with mycorrhizae that is the root form when beneficial fungi colonize certain plant roots.

Natural Pesticides: Substances which inhibit the infection or growth of a pest but that are naturally produced by the host plant.

Necrotic Tissue: Dead and dying tissue.

Negative Taxes: Movements away from a stimulant source.

Nematode trapping Fungi: Certain fungi that develop sticky knobs, constricting loops or other trapping devices to snare and infect nematodes.

Nematophagous: Organisms which utilize nematodes as a food source.

Nepoviruses: Polyhedral (globular-like) shaped virus particles transmitted by *Longidorus* or *Xiphinema* species of plant parasitic nematodes.

Nerve Ring: A concentration of nerve cells partially banding about the nematode body in the head region that connects or joins nerve trunks going forward and backward along the body. Also called the circum-esophageal commisure.

Neuron: A nerve cell body including dendrites and axon.

Neurosecretions: Secretions believed to originate from a nerve cell.

Nictating: A kind of waving motion exhibited by some microscopic animal parasitic nematodes that climb to the top of a blade of grass and, while attached to the blade tip by the tail, wave the body in the air to facilitate attachment to or infection of a passing host.

Non-Fumigant Nematicides: Water soluble or dispersible chemical agents applied for the control of parasitic nematodes.

Nucleoside: An organic base-pentose sugar molecule that combines with phosphorus acid to make nucleic acids.

Occam's Razor Philosophy: An ancient philosophy which advocates the use of the fewest and simplest assumptions to explain an observation.

Ocelli: Paired lens-like structures surrounded by pigmentation present in some nematodes.

Oligochaetes: Annelid representatives related to earthworms.

Onchocerciasis: The disease caused by the filarid nematode *Onchocerca volvulus*. Also called "River Blindness" disease.

Oral Opening: The mouth opening of the nematode.

Oocyte: The female reproductive unit before maturation.

Organelles: Sub-cellular units or structures, usually in the cytoplasm with specific individual functions in support of cellular life processes.

Orphan Drug: Drugs that are useful for the cure or treatment of diseases so rare that their preparation is a commercial loss unless government subsidies cover most of the costs of synthesis.

Oviparity: Reproduction whereby eggs are expelled from the female body before embryogenesis takes place.

Ovoviviparity: Reproduction whereby eggs may begin to embryonate before being expelled from the female.

P_0 Cell: The first cell division occurring in the egg gives rise to two cells, a S_1 or AB cell that eventually produces primary ectodermal tissue and a P_1 cell that is precursor to all other tissues.

Papillae: Projections from the nematode body shorter than setae but are believed to be sensory in nature.

Parasite Burden: The number of nematode individuals present in an animal is referred to as the parasite burden.

Paratenic Host: A temporary host in which no development occurs but in which the parasite is maintained live and infective of the definitive host that ingests the paratenic host.

Parthenogenesis: a form of asexual reproduction requiring no fertilization by males.

Pathogens: Disease agents.

Pathotypes: A population of a nematode species that exhibits a host range other than that typical of the species. Sometimes used interchangeably with biotype, mutant, line, race.

Pentose: The general term for a five carbon sugar.

Perineal Pattern: The characteristic pattern of swirls and ridges exhibited by rootknot (*Meloidogyne* spp.) about the anus and vulva that are used for identification of the species.

Peri-Parturient: The period preceding and following birth.

Peristaltic: A wave like motion of the intestine or hollow muscular structure that forces the tube contents onward.

Pesticide Resistance: The capacity of pests to cope with or nullify the effect of pesticides.

Pestiferous Nematodes: Those nematodes that are pests to man directly or to his endeavors.

Phenol: Carbolic acid, often used to refer to a class of related compounds.

Pheromones: Volatile or water soluble substances released by an individual of a species that conveys a message usually to another individual of the same species.

Phoretic Dispersal: Incidental transportation of a disease agent by an animal.

Phospholipids: A class of fatty substances containing a phosphoric acid in combination, commonly occurring in membranes.

Photoperiod: A period of exposure to light, usually sunlight.

Photosynthates: Various products of photosynthesis.

Phototaxes: Directional movements in response to a light source.

Phylogeny: The scheme of organismal relationships deriving from evolution.

Phylum: A broad taxonomic category above class and below kingdom.

Phytotoxic: Substances which are harmful or lethal to plants.

Plasmolysis: A process by which the internal pressure of a cell decreases by loss of water or fluids to result in a flaccid cell.

Plerocercoids: Tapeworm larvae from an intermediate host.

Poikilothermic: Animals whose body temperatures are largely governed by ambient temperature.

Polar Bodies: The nuclei resulting from reduction division to produce the vital haploid eggs that are normally destined to death and elimination.

Polar Groups: Substituents of molecules which exhibit differentiated charges from the remaining part of the molecule.

Polyhedral: Many sided globular-like structure.

Polyphenols: Macromolecules of polymerized phenols.

Polyploidy: Chromosome numbers in nuclei that are multiples of normal (2n).

Polysaccharides: Macromolecules of sugar polymers, e.g. starch, cellulose.

Posterior: Refers to a direction towards the tail.

Positive Taxes: Movements towards a stimulating source.

Pre-Plant Treatments: Usually refers to soil treatments conducted before planting.

Primary Hosts: The primary host is the principal host and a definitive one.

Probolae: Moveable cuticular appendages of ornamentation at nematode's anterior tip about the oral opening. May be sensory.

Proboscis: Feeding structure of the mosquito.

Proctodeum: Rectum or posterior ectodermal part of the alimentary canal.

Proline: A cyclic amino acid.

Prophase: The early period of cell division during which the chromatin threads of the nucleus condense into chromosomes in later stages.

Proteolytic Enzymes: Enzymes that are able to hydrolyze, degrade, digest proteins and peptides.

Pseudogamy: A type of reproduction which requires copulation for the sperm to induce embryonation; however, the sperm never fuses with the ovum but degenerates.

Races: A population of a species morphologically indistinguishable from other populations of the species but with different characteristics usually expressed in host ranges. A term often used interchangeably with pathotype, biotype or mutant line.

Rain Water: Usually refers to cloud derived water with very low concentration of dissolved materials.

Rectum: The terminal section of the alimentary canal.

Registration: The process through which a drug or pesticide is evaluated for safety and efficacy and approved by government agencies for commercial use.

Reticulum: Network.

Rhabditid: Any representative from the group *Rhabditis*.

Rhizosphere: The soil region in close proximity of a root system and in which there is a wealth of flora and fauna.

Salinity: The degree of dissolved mineral salts that occur in soil water: often expressed in terms of concentration or conductivity.

Saprophyte: Any organism that lives on dead organic matter, as some fungi and bacteria

Saprozoon: An animal that obtains its nourishment from dead organic matter.

Sarcoplasm: The protoplasm, i.e. cellular contents of the muscle cell exclusive of muscle fiber.

Scanning Electron Microscopy (SEM): A research instrument that utilizes an electron beam to reveal the surface characteristics of a specimen.

Secernentea: One of the two classes in the phylum Nemata.

Seminal vesicle: Pouch-like structures in the male used to store sperm.

Semi-Permeable Membrane: A membrane that permits the passage of certain molecules, usually very small, but prevents the passage of large molecules like sugars, proteins, etc.

Sensilla: Sensory devices of nematodes that provide information about the environment.

Sensing: The ability to detect events or changes in the environment.

Septicemic: Refers to contamination or infection of animal tissue by microorganisms usually by bacteria or fungi.

Serpentine: Snake-like movement.

Sex Attraction: The capacity of one sex of a species to attract the other.

Sex Ratios: Refers to the proportion of males to females in a given population of nematodes.

Sinusoidal: Bending in and out, a serpentine-like wave form.

Somatic Cells: Cells of body tissue as distinct from germ cells of the reproductive system.

Somatic Chromosome: A chromosome of a body cell with the normal diploid number.

Somatic Musculature: Body musculature as distinct from esophageal, vulva, spicular or anal musculature.

Spear: The solid protrusible devise used by some nematodes to puncture cells to feed. Also termed odontostyle.

Spermatheca: The storage receptacle of females for sperm acquired in copulation.

Spermatocyte: Cells which arise from spermatogonia during the process of sperm generation.

Spicules: The nematode male copulatory organ.

Stem Cell: That cell which arises from parental germinal cells in the scheme of cell lineage during embryogenesis usually indicated as P_1, P_2, etc.

Stoma: The mouth or buccal cavity.

Sulfhydryl Groups: A sulfur-hydrogen containing radical found in several amino acids and as such is a component of proteins that is easily oxidized.

Surface Tension: The resultant character of a liquid surface or interface generated by the attractive molecular forces of the liquid which tends to maintain the liquid mass in the form providing the least surface area.

Sustainable Nematode Control: A nematode management strategy whereby nematode crop injury can be reduced to tolerable levels essentially indefinitely with minimal environmental repercussions.

Swarming: The process by which certain nematodes actively flock together as intimate masses.

Symbiosis: An intimate relationship between organisms that is mutually beneficial.

Syngamy: Bisexual reproduction.

Tactile Responses: Responses of a nematode to touch stimulation.

Tetrad: In the meiotic division process the chromatin condenses into strands doubling to provide four chromatids held together by a centromere. One tetrad for each original pair of chromosomes.

Therapeutic Intervention: Most commonly represented by medication but can be any disease curing activity.

Thermotaxes: Directional movement in response to heat stimulation.

Tobraviruses: Rod-shaped viruses transmitted by trichodorid nematodes.

Torque: An action resulting in a rotation, twisting or torsion motion. A moment of force about a pivotal point.

Transmission Electron Microscopy (TEM): A research microscope that utilizes an electron beam to reveal certain structural components of a very thin slice of tissue.

Triradiate: That which describes having three radiating arms or branches.

Tryptophane: An indole containing amino acid.

Tubiform Setae: Long cuticular tubular extensions (setae), some useful in locomotion.

Turgor pressure: Internal pressure of protoplasm or fluids usually osmotically generated whose function is to keep the cell or body walls distended.

Vas Deferens: The tube connecting the testes to the ejaculatory duct.

Vector: An organism which actively transmits a disease agent to a host.

Vermiform: Worm shaped.

Vesicle: A small sack-like container or bladder.

Vestigial: Rudimentary, relating to a trace of something more complex.

Viruliferous plants: Virus containing plants.

Viviparity: The production and release of live, active progeny from the mother as distinct from producing eggs.

Vipary: Production of individuals.

Zoospores: Motile asexual reproductive units produced by certain algae or fungi.

Subject Index